Leading Systemic School Improvement Series

...helping change leaders transform entire school systems

This Rowman & Littlefield Education series provides change leaders in school districts with a collection of books written by prominent authors with an interest in creating and sustaining whole-district school improvement. It features young, relatively unpublished authors with brilliant ideas, as well as authors who are cross-disciplinary thinkers.

Whether an author is prominent or relatively unpublished, the key criterion for a book's inclusion in this series is that it must address an aspect of creating and sustaining systemic school improvement. For example, books from members of the business world, developmental psychology, and organizational development are good candidates as long as they focus on creating and sustaining whole-system change in school district settings; books about building-level curriculum reform, instructional methodologies, and team communication, although interesting and helpful, are not appropriate for the series unless they discuss how these ideas can be used to create whole-district improvement.

Since the series is for practitioners, highly theoretical or research-reporting books aren't included. Instead, the series provides an artful blend of theory and practice—in other words, books based on theory and research but written in plain, easy-to-read language. Ideally, theory and research are artfully woven into practical descriptions of how to create and sustain systemic school improvement. The series is subdivided into three categories:

Why Systemic School Improvement Is Needed and Why It's Important. This is the *why*. Possible topics within this category include the history of systemic school improvement; the underlying philosophy of systemic school improvement; how systemic school improvement is different from school-based improvement; and the driving forces of standards, assessments, and accountability and why systemic improvement can respond effectively to these forces.

The Desirable Outcomes of Systemic School Improvement. This is the *what*. Possible topics within this category include comprehensive school reform models scaled up to create whole-district improvement; strategic alignment; creating a high-performance school system; redesigning a school system as a learning organization; unlearning and learning mental models; and creating an organization design flexible and agile enough to respond quickly to unanticipated events in the outside world.

How to Create and Sustain Systemic School Improvement. This is the *how*. Possible topics within this category include methods for redesigning entire school systems; tools for navigating complex change; ideas from the "new sciences" for creating systemic change; leadership methods for creating systemic change; evaluating the process and outcomes of systemic school improvement; and financing systemic school improvement.

The series editor, Dr. Francis M. Duffy, can be reached at 301-854-9800 or fmduffy@earthlink.net.

Leading Systemic School Improvement Series
Edited by Francis M. Duffy

The Future of Schools

How Communities and Staff Can Transform Their School Districts

Merrelyn Emery

Leading Systemic School Improvement,
No. 6

ROWMAN & LITTLEFIELD EDUCATION
Lanham, Maryland · Toronto · Oxford
2006

Published in the United States of America
by Rowman & Littlefield Education
A Division of Rowman & Littlefield Publishers, Inc.
A wholly owned subsidary of The Rowman & Littlefield Publishing Group, Inc.
4501 Forbes Boulevard, Suite 200, Lanham, Maryland 20706
www.rowmaneducation.com

PO Box 317
Oxford
OX2 9RU, UK

British Library Cataloguing in Publication Information Available

Library of Congress Cataloging-in-Publication Data

Emery, Merrelyn.
  The future of schools : how communities and staff can transform
their school districts / Merrelyn Emery.
    p. cm. — (Leading systemic school improvement series ; no. 6)
  Includes bibliographical references.
  ISBN-13: 978-1-57886-377-8 (hardcover : alk. paper)
  ISBN-13: 978-1-57886-378-3 (pbk. : alk. paper)
  ISBN-10: 1-57886-377-5 (hardcover : alk. paper)
  ISBN-10: 1-57886-378-2 (pbk. : alk. paper)
  1. School districts—United States—Administration. 2. Educational
change—United States—Citizen participation. I. Title. II. Series:
Leading systemic school improvement ; no. 6.
  LB2817.3.E44 2006
  371.200973—dc22   2005031155

∞^TM The paper used in this publication meets the minimum requirements of
American National Standard for Information Sciences—Permanence of Paper
for Printed Library Materials, ANSI/NISO Z39.48-1992.
Manufactured in the United States of America.

Contents

Acknowledgments

$\mathcal{T}$his book has lurked in my mind for a long time. So many times over the last 40 years, the conversations around a group of colleagues gravitated to schools and universities. We realized that what we had learned from our work with changing organizations eventually had to be applied to the education system, just about the last great bulwark of change. Learning and education were among our major preoccupations, as conscious learning is one of the most distinctive characteristics of the human being.

We worked at various times with different parts of the education system, and this book articulates the learning from these diverse experiences. There was never an opportunity to engage with a whole system, because the time was not yet right. I believe that time has now come. The interest and energy now being devoted to educational reform in the United States at a time of international uncertainty signals a turning point in cultural appreciations. My thanks go to all these colleagues whose contributions are woven into these chapters.

There are others I must thank. My parents, Jack and Melva Burchett, were school teachers who dedicated their lives to helping children learn in the outback, the Aboriginal camps, the country towns, and the cities. How many lessons they taught me, I will never know. I am also deeply indebted to the many other teachers who expressed their ideals through their dedication to their charges. I hope this book is worthy of them all.

Fred Emery cared immensely about the education system and never missed an opportunity to engage with it, despite some less-than-happy experiences in it. He helped me look clearly at education as a system-in-environment while working within it. Schools and learning were never far from his mind, and I have drawn on many of his insights.

Although this book was always an idea, it is doubtful that it would have been written without the direct stimulus of Frank Duffy. His invitation to expand on how my ideas about open systems, the organizational design principles, and the methods derived from them could be used to redesign entire school systems for improved student, teacher, and system learning was exactly what I needed to begin organizing those ideas.

Tim Butterfield and Annie Kentwell served as my readers and gave me honest, direct, and constructive criticism of the drafts. The readability of this final copy owes much to them both.

Finally, thanks go to my children, whose own struggles with schools and learning sharpened my views of the strengths and weaknesses of the system and motivated me to seek better answers.

Introduction

𝒯he education of our children is one of the most important issues for the citizens of any country (Phillips, 2001). Education's special status is indicated by the fact that it rivals the weather in the extent of its discussion (Gardner, 1991). Gardner has spent his life researching schools and learning in the United States, where he believes that educational problems have become a virtual obsession among policymakers but not necessarily the public.

Every developed country in the world engages in lively public discussion of education, and although the history and appearance of education in each country has its unique features, the schools and the debates have a prevailing similarity (Bruner, 1996). Schools the world over are recognizably schools. The same problems and the same failings are documented in every country that shares a Western education system. Gardner (1991) asserted, "The same kind of misconceptualizations and lack of understanding that emerge in an American setting appear to recur in scholastic settings all over the world" (p. 4).

This discussion is not a new phenomenon. The cultural revolution of the 1960s and 1970s witnessed fervent intellectual activity about the future of our societies and the role of education within them. This period saw the rapid development of ideas about the nature of learning and knowledge and what to do about them. One movement in educational thinking advocated so-called progressive ideas. Rigid regimentation of classrooms was to be replaced by a child-centered education, discovery learning, and open-plan schools (British Psychological Society, 1986).

This feverish activity spawned a multitude of experiments. Advocates of change believed that students needed participation to express their purposes, a belief that learning is best achieved when people pursue goals that matter to them and when they can seek the help of those whose expertise they respect.

The changes were beginning to happen in one state or another, and none of them necessarily cost a dollar (Schoenheimer, 1972). However, the most striking feature of the evolution of the debate about education in Western industrialized nations—in particular, the debate about educational inequality in all its forms—has been the rapidity with which ideas have been disseminated, rejected, and/or modified (Tyler, 1977).

Indeed, educational practice has persisted, remarkably unchanged and continuous for the last hundred years or more of mass education. Educational institutions have shown an astonishing ability to shrug off repeated demonstrations of more effective practices. When such demonstrations and repeated criticism of the established ways cannot be ignored, they have been discredited by any available means. Fred Emery (1980a) stated, "The standard defence is that there is nothing wrong with the practices that could not be cured by better text books, better trained teachers, more highly rewarded and hence more highly motivated teachers, better classrooms, better teaching aids. . . . We have learned that the established paradigm is, for all practical purposes, unchallengeable at the level of practical evidence" (p. 42). This sentiment was echoed in the United States with only slightly different words: "Better prepared teachers, more dedicated administrators" (Gardner, 1991, p. 185).

In 2000, the *Harvard Educational Review* republished Ray Rist's 1970 classic on the importance of social class in schools and included an author update—namely, that Rist saw little change. So much of the reality of the education of Black youth is no different today from 30 years ago, particularly in urban schools:

> Schools are still facing many of the same issues now as they did then. It would not be misleading . . . to say that the more time passes, the more things stay the same. . . .
>
> The sobering reality is that when it comes to both color and class, U.S. schools tend to conform much more to the contours of American society than they transform it. And this appears to be a lesson that we are not wanting to learn. . . .
>
> While the rhetoric is that of opportunity . . . the reality for those in the lowest 20 percent quintile of economic resources is quite different. Indeed, those in this bottom 20 percent have in the last thirty years actually lost ground to the rest of the society. The schism is real. The stratification of the American underclass is now more permanent and pervasive than thirty years ago. Add to this the isolation from the centers of economic growth of those who are both poor and minority and the picture is not a pretty one. . . .
>
> Our strategies for urban schools and the teachers within them seem caught in a *cul de sac*. We go round and round with the same remedies and the situation does not improve. (Rist, 2000a, pp. 258–264)

Today this "continuity of practice" has flowed from mass primary school to mass secondary school to mass tertiary school and has now flowed onto industrial training and management education. Reform has not done much to change schools, as schools are amazing, robust institutions. Educational policy has often overstated what is wrong with schools, and it has understated how hard it is to get from here to there (Harvard Graduate School of Education, 2004).

We may agree that it is hard to change entrenched systems, but nevertheless change is happening all over the world. Slowly but surely, people are learning to transform their school districts toward the ideals that they hold for their children and their communities. In the following chapters, I distill these lessons from history and around the world into a systemic project covering the central components of a school district in a logical but free-flowing set of steps.

As seen in chapter 1, a growing chorus claims that change efforts must be systemic to be effective, although a lack of knowledge exists on how to make open systemic change. Duffy and Dale (2001a) find that "in the literature on school improvement there are many reasons *why* schools must be improved. In the same literature, there are many authors telling you *what* the outcomes of school improvement should be. . . . Very few of them, however, talk about *how* to redesign entire school systems for high performance" (p. 275). This book is an attempt to do just that—talk about how to redesign a whole school system. It is a sequel to *Knowledge Work Supervision* (Duffy, Rogerson, & Blick, 2000), which is a new strategic, comprehensive, and systemic approach to transform school systems in fundamental ways, producing continual learning and improvement throughout the entire system. *Knowledge Work Supervision* is similarly informed by Blick and Bradshaw's work (2001) on participative strategic planning and participative democracy in school districts. It also incorporates many of the insights of contributors for *Creating Successful School Systems* (Duffy & Dale, 2001b).

This book goes further, however, by introducing new variations of previous work, using examples from many different fields of endeavor. I explain the historical rationale for these concepts and processes so that readers can understand their relevance and the ways in which they increase the reliability of the overall change proposal.

Changing a school district can be a large project, but large projects for the reform of schools are not unknown in the United States. One project consisting of 17 school districts, coordinated by the Northwest Tri-Country Intermediate Unit, an educational agency responsible for the support and enhancement of its participating districts, has been proceeding since 1987 (Leuenberger, 1994). Although size may not be an obstacle, the remarkable ability of school systems to shrug off change tells us that such projects will certainly be challenging. Drucker (1982) forecast that attention would shift back to schools and education as the central capital investment and infrastructure of a "knowledge society." He also thought that reforming them would require "something far scarcer than money—thinking and risk taking" (p. 138).

• 1 •

Overview

$\mathcal{T}$he introduction of this book documents the outstanding feature of the global education system: its inertia. It has survived numerous challenges—theoretical, practical, and legislative. Although some changes have taken root and many lessons have been learned about how to achieve these successes, the characteristics that make schools so recognizable around the world remain. The system has displayed its robustness by accommodating these changes to continue virtually unchanged in its fundamental shape.

THE NEED FOR SYSTEMIC CHANGE

"Why do good ideas about teaching and learning have so little impact on U.S. educational practice?" (Elmore, 1996, p. 1). How do teachers understand the nature of knowledge and the student's role in learning, and how do these ideas about knowledge and learning get manifested in teaching and classwork? Core educational practice includes structural arrangements as well as assessment procedures. Elmore has argued that the failure to develop, incorporate, and extend new ideas about teaching and learning in anything but a small fraction of schools and classrooms indicates a central problem in U.S. education, one that points to a deep systemic incapacity of U.S. schools and their practitioners.

Another reason for the lack of change is that, historically, "sociologists, educators and politicians have been wildly unscientific." Their models of change and their subsequent policies and changes were all based on single factors, whereas the problems they hoped to address were multicausal. These changes also failed because they ignored the "over-arching structures and the

1

great institutions of society" (Tyler, 1977, p. 115). Social science, at least since World War II, has been expected to provide evidence and expertise to guide educational reform, but it may not have been up to the task. Even today, basic questions about education and its role in our societies remain unanswered, and most policies and reforms fail to deliver their promised goods. Many people are still ignoring the powerful forces generated by structure and institutions, hence the need to use systemic and comprehensive conceptual frameworks and methods that guide structural change, particularly those that have established their reliability and effectiveness over long periods.

Incremental change fails because education is a system, not a collection of parts. Even the recent major, more systemic strategies for restructuring—site-based management and schools of choice—have encountered multiple problems, as have efforts to introduce total quality management into schools (Duffy, Rogerson, & Blick, 2000). Many, other seemingly well-designed and well-intentioned efforts first engender enthusiasm and energy that fade away, only to be displaced by apathy or growing cynicism about change (Blick & Bradshaw, 2001).

Although these changes may have been more systemic than those changing the curriculum, these examples indicate that something fundamental is still missing. Today around the world you can hear agonized shrieks by administrators and legislators to the effect that they have tried everything. It is true that they have tried many things, but it is also true that they have made few radical breaks from the past.

As early as 1974, Russell Ackoff saw that "education needs an extensive redesign, one that will bring it into the Systems Age" (p. 74). Patching up will not solve the problems. The 1980s saw a movement toward "stressing the significance of systems thinking as a means of understanding the interactions taking place in schools" (Thomas, 1985, p. 322). Since then, a rapidly growing global consensus has taken form regarding the future of our schools. The extent of this consensus is impressive, as it spans interest groups often viewed as being disparate or even conflicting in their traditional perspectives and objectives. The expression of the consensus may involve terms such as *restructuring*, *whole system redesign*, or *systemic school improvement or reform*, but in essence it revolves around an open, systemic approach to educational change. It is an open-systems approach because it encompasses the relationships of the school district, with its external environments as well as its internal relationships.

This growing consensus springs in part from the accumulating knowledge that the myriad of single-factor changes has not resulted in the changes desired by their initiators and supporters. Changing textbooks, altering student ability groups from homogeneous to heterogeneous and back again, adopting a new reading program, and implementing cooperative learning is the equivalent of "rearranging furniture" (Roy & Piperato, 2001, p. 201) or "rearranging the deck chairs on the *Titanic*" (Blick & Bradshaw, 2001, p. 196). "Piecemeal, incremental, and reactive reforms in public education that fail to empower educators and parents are not what the system needs and certainly not what children and communities deserve" (Duffy, 2001, p. 274). America has excellent innovations, but a system of care lies just beyond reach (Washington, 2004).

Genuine and fundamental change in schools that incorporates technology requires change in all aspects of a school and its environment, "including developing community support, parental involvement and relationships with businesses and organizations" (NFIE, 2000, p. 19). Nothing less than whole communities organizing systemic change is needed to meet the challenges of the 21st century (Aigner, Raymond, & Smidt, 2002). This proposal envisages the community organizing systemic change, followed by structural change within the school district, followed by change of classroom practices. It covers multiple causes, is multidimensional in practice, and therefore addresses Tyler's criticisms (1977).

THE UNIQUENESS OF SCHOOLS

Changing school districts represents a major challenge, not least because they are unique. Anybody contemplating change in this system will feel the need to explore its exact nature before embarking on the change process. Schools and school districts have four major characteristics that taken together mark them as distinct. The first is that although public school districts may superficially look like organizations, they are also community entities, for many reasons:

- Schools physically exist within, and are often a central focus of, a community. The future of students is intimately intertwined with the future of their community, and communities will frequently fight and struggle to improve their schools because they recognize the importance of their children's education for their economic and social future.
- Schools are publicly funded, and local communities invest their own money, sometimes heavily, into procuring additional resources for their schools and children.
- Schools reflect and transmit the culture of their communities across the generations, preserving its unique features. Children "are respecters, even venerators, of custom; and in their self-contained

community their basic lore and language seems scarcely to alter from generation to generation" (Opie & Opie, 1959, p. 2). But schools not only preserve; they also create, as education "fuels the sense of possibility." Students who emerge with a sense of a desirable future have an understanding of the world and a confidence that they can create a evermore desirable future. Any student who fails to emerge with such a sense puts the broader culture at risk. Alienation, defiance, and practical incompetence undermine the viability of a culture (Bruner, 1996). How people think about schools is a function of how they think about their culture and its goals. What they intend to do in school makes sense only when they consider it a part of what their culture or society intends to accomplish through its investment in children.

- Parents and teachers are usually members of the community and are richly networked with a range of other community organizations, businesses, and interest groups.
- A child's home is the most powerful influence on a child's life and learning (Coleman, 1966), and "continued parental involvement throughout a child's years of schooling has a strong positive impact on learning" (NFIE, 2000, p. 151). A school can also be a principal instrument for progress toward a more egalitarian society (Garforth, 1980). Chapter 9 looks at some of the forces in American schools that act for and against these purposes and examines ways in which schools can exert more force toward the egalitarian ideal.

Many communities are beginning to see and change themselves as whole systems. They realize that shared learning can have a profound impact on the quality of life and standard of living for citizens (Schwinn & Schwinn, 1996). An energized community is a solid foundation that can truly address the future of the educational process (Bruner, 1996), and, once energized, receiving an invitation to help plan and implement change in their school district can rapidly generate confidence and trust. In these circumstances, a community will throw its multiple resources into constructive change with gusto.

Involving everybody in the process from the beginning will produce a widespread sense of ownership in the process and its outcomes. People will therefore be more motivated to carry the desired outcomes through to full implementation. However, given the history of change in the educational system, we should expect some resistance (Williams, 1975, 1982). Such opposition provides a strong reason to thoroughly prepare the ground for change by involving all parties in planning for the school district. Resistance is better prevented than cured. It largely flows from imposition and lack of understanding (Coch & French, 1947). When people in the community and school district have planned their futures, why would they resist their own desired change? (M. Emery, 1999)

The move to school-based management has strengthened the view that schools belong within and to their communities. In fact schools cannot be extracted from communities without damaging the essential nature of either the schools or the communities. As community entities, schools require variations on methods appropriate for changing communities rather than organizations. Because organizations and communities have different characteristics, methods such as the search conference (discussed later) have adopted different procedures to accommodate these characteristics. Procedures such as selecting participants vary between communities and organizations, and search conferences for organizations are often more complex and demanding than those for communities.

The second characteristic that makes schools and school districts unique systems is that they are people-to-people systems. As opposed to people who work with technology (people-to-technical system), as found in a factory or an office, people in school systems work with people around purposes concerning other people. The best-known examples are those of hospitals and schools. In hospitals the primary purpose is to improve the health of patients. School staff are primarily concerned with the learning and growth of students. Although they may work with a technical system, such as a computer or the library, this work is merely a part of what is required to fulfill the primary purpose. The reason for redesigning these systems is to get the best possible match between the most desirable characteristics of both the people and the system they are working with.

Systems also exist where the focus is the social environment. People work with this environment to do strategic planning or to gain an appreciation of the external forces impinging on an issue. The search conference is one such example. In the search, people work to get the best match between their ideals and the most powerful value shifts taking place in the global social environment.

Many complex projects require all three types of systems (Trist & Murray, 1990a). Changing a whole school district involves people-to-environment and people-to-people, as both strategic planning and organizational design work are required to meet the complexity of the task. In some large school offices, specialized administrative staff may see themselves working primarily with technical systems.

The third characteristic of schools flows from the second. When a people-to-technical system needs redesign, the task falls to the people because, obviously, machines or books cannot design systems. In other words, the people and technical systems are different and incommensurate. In a school we have people working with people, and, as all people are purposeful, they must make their own plans and do their own designs. It is unethical to treat people as being anything other than purposeful. It is also ineffective because those being planned for may not like the plan or may wish to get revenge for not being involved. Being purposeful, they may decide to ignore the plan or actively sabotage it. If this happens, no matter how good the plan, it will fail. Students frequently ignore teachers' instructions. For this reason, communities need to plan their futures and resist having designs imposed upon them.

Many hospital staff have not been patients and do not have an intimate knowledge of being a patient. Staff have no idea how it feels to be subjected to a particular treatment and cannot therefore adequately plan on behalf of patients. Oliver Sacks (1984), a neurologist who became hospitalized for the first time, provided some insights into just how different the worlds of patients and medical staff are: "I was stunned. All the agonised, agonising uncertainties and fears, all the torment I had suffered since I discovered my condition, all the hopes and expectations I had pinned on this meeting—and now this! I thought: what sort of a doctor, what sort of person is this?" (p. 73). Sacks was also forced to realize and endure the "profoundest passivity" of patienthood and realize that it was "the only proper attitude at the time" (p. 80). (Profound passivity is not a proper attitude for students, however.)

Without adequate knowledge of what one's designing for, the design will be inadequate. In people-to-people systems, both sets of people must be involved in the design. In other words, schools are much more complex than many other systems. They share with other systems the need for long-term strategic goals and effective organizational designs for the staff. However students must also do designs for effective learning. These two designs, for staff and students, must fit together to get the best for both systems, which means that students must be involved in the design process wherever possible. Qualified staff can adjust the processes to take account of age and legal constraints to this involvement and still be responsible for ensuring that standards of teaching and learning are maintained and that the curriculum is followed. They can give young children their choice of project through which to practice learning. Staff can just as easily teach arithmetic through the medium of gardening as through abstract exercises in a classroom. This level of involvement satisfies the children's interests and meets the legalities. Making decisions about your own learning is a powerful determinant of intrinsic motivation. I discuss student participation in chapter 3.

One additional complication is peculiar to the major purpose of schools, and it arises from the way that people learn. American schools have been widely criticized for turning out young adults who appear not to have learned even the basics, but the same failings of misconceptualization and lack of understanding are found the world over. Gardner (1991) has attributed much of this failure to the fact that every student has a 5-year-old mind inside, struggling to get out and express its theories about how the world works. Children arrive in school with powerful theories about the world (F. Emery, 1980a; Gardner, 1991) and about people (M. Emery, 1999). Furthermore, the child's schooling rarely challenges these theories, a fact that accounts for many of the misunderstandings mentioned earlier.

Children are not born as blank slates waiting for teachers to write upon them. That belief underlies the predominant preoccupation with teaching, but the theory behind it is out of date (F. Emery, 1980a). New evidence shows that people learn directly from their perceptions and experience from the earliest ages. This is called *ecological learning*. It is from this learning that people build theories about how the world works.

Today students view much of the material as being alien, "if not pointless" (Gardner, 1991, p. 149). Students simply do not see the useful deployment of basic skills at home or in school. The real world is in the media, in the shopping malls, and in the streets, but no solid connections are made between that world and life in the school. If skill acquisition was embedded in the context of a real-life project, it would constitute a challenge. In apprenticeships, for example, the reasons for learning a specific knowledge or skill to a certain level of quality are evident in the purpose to which the product or service is put, and the money earned from practicing the trade (Gardner, 1991).

One of the major points of reform is to ensure that the inquiry methods, the ways of employing students' minds, are those that are central to a democratic culture (Bruner, 1996): "Education does not only occur in classrooms, but around the dinner table" (p. xi). Chapter 8 explores ways in which learning from the dinner table and the classroom can be merged to bridge the gaps between the world in which the students live and the abstract knowledge they are required to understand. Chapter 9 elaborates on the importance of the dinner table, as the social class and educational climate of the family continue to be the most important influence on students' achievement.

These four characteristics define schools as unique and complex systems composed of purposeful people who learn as much, if not more, from their perceptions and experiences outside the school as they do within it. Schools therefore demand a unique and systemic approach to reform. Only when educators act on the totality and uniqueness of the school district in its environment can they contemplate a vibrant, healthy community of learners.

THREE COMPONENTS OF CHANGE

All of the critical elements required to change a school district can be incorporated within a systemic process based on three interlocking components: the involvement of the community as an owner of and contributor to school districts; the reorganization of staff and students from a bureaucratic hierarchy to a participative democracy; and the achievement of a balance of learning and teaching using the power of ecological learning.

These three components of change cover the major problems of the school system previously identified by analysts. The components also cover the key factors that mark an open, systemic approach to change. Reformers can truly affect the system only by aligning classroom and school district strategies (Anderson & Cascarino, 2001). Approaching these tasks in the following order—community first, school district structure second, and educational practice third—yields a flowing, holistic process. The flow is from the broadest level of community planning, through school district planning, through redesign of school district structures, to the educational processes in classrooms. This process is a logical sequence of building foundations, momentum, and increased confidence.

Community development needs to precede change within the school district to build a reserve of social capital or trust in the community in regard to its school district. Americans have gone from seeing education as the panacea for social ills to blaming it as part of the problem. When goals are not achieved, trust diminishes (Harvard Graduate School of Education, 2004). Yet it is easy to accumulate trust between a school and its community, as it builds every time people recognize a positive connection between the two. A thousand experiences, programs, connections, and trust-building opportunities are happening every day that can build or destroy a school district's social capital (Smith, 2004).

The power of a change from bureaucratic to democratic structure is incalculable, as it affects so many other factors. As I explain in the overview of the organizational design principles, many of the presenting symptoms of educational ill health will simply fade away as staff and students enjoy working and learning in democratized structures. One of the major effects will be the increasing intrinsic motivation of staff and students. It is critical, however, that the change of design principle must be based in the industrial realities of school life. If it consists of only cosmetic changes, such as change of label, its success will be short-lived (M. Emery, 1992b).

Many reforms have failed because they have not taken account of how people learn. The two current theories of human perception, learning and development, are vitally important to the future of the school system, as they go to the heart of the teaching–learning debate. The core of the traditional educational paradigm lies in assumptions and theories of learning, not in educational practice. The assumptions and theories define the practices (F. Emery, 1980a).

For sustainable change, schools need to integrate ecological learning into their practices. Teachers can elicit students' existing, extracted concrete knowledge and use it as a foundation for further learning through projects close to students' hearts. Teachers can inject complementary abstract knowledge, as groups of students immersed in fascinating projects willingly accept helpful hints (Lippitt & White, 1947). Such change will make children's experience in school truly exciting and motivating.

Taken together, these three changes amount to major inclusive reform that uses multiple strategies on multiple sites (Slee, 2000). The changes proposed here increase active engagement with the school system across a broad front for consequent rises in learning, creativity, and productivity. "It is time to wholeheartedly begin to genuinely re-embed all our schools within community and environment and redesign them for both the second Design Principle and ecological learning, the education of perception" (M. Emery, 1999, p. 240).

METHODS

The methods that I describe in this book are tried and true. They flow from the established framework of open systems theory and are based on a view that "adults can take responsibility for their own learning if the necessary time and resources are available to them" (Davies, 1993b, p. 272). The necessary resources include the conscious conceptual knowledge behind everyday phenomena and the opportunity to practice this knowledge in relevant, meaningful settings.

The current state of learning about search conferences and the two-stage model comes from literally hundreds of examples from around the world. Many of them have involved schools, colleges, and universities and their communities, together with policies and strategies for children, family, and youth (Baburoglu & Garr, 1992; Brokhaug, 1992; Haugen, 1992; Kloth, 1992; Morley & Trist, 1992; Rehm, Schweitz, & Granata, 1992).

School district change needs to be systemic to be effective in practice; therefore, it needs to be based on a systemic theoretical framework. Open systems theory provides such a base for the planning, the design work, and the action that follows. The modern developmental era of open systems began about 50 years ago and its concepts, principles, and flexible methods have been developed from collaborative work with real organizations and communities (Trist & Murray, 1990a, 1993). The methods have proven reliable through years of testing in many countries and cultures.

The Open System

The fundamental idea in open systems theory is that all entities have boundaries that are permeable to the environment. People are also open to their environments. All elements within the open system's framework, and the relations between those elements, are governed by laws that people can learn and use (F. Emery, 1977; M. Emery, 1999; Emery & Trist, 1965).

As an open system, a school district consists of purposeful people within two relevant levels of community and a global social environment (Figure 1.1). These levels of system and environment relate to and within one another. Each additional system or environment magnifies the number of relationships. I could have added schools (between the people and the school district), state education departments (between the community and the social environment), and the federal government (between the state and the social environment) to the figure to more accurately convey the complexity of the system. In an un-

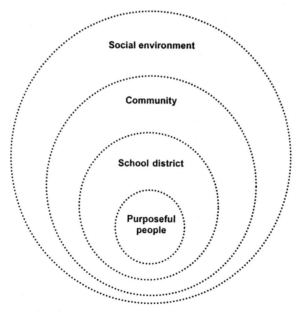

Figure 1.1.   The School District as an Open System: Purposeful People Within the School District, Within the Community, Within the Social Environment.

certain environment, what matters is the dynamic nature of these relationships that hold a school system together (Snyder, 2001).

The global social environment consists of all the changing values, ideals, and expectations that people carry with them. People, communities, organizations and the social environment mutually determine one another. As people continue to change their minds about what they value, they create high levels of relevant uncertainty for those trying to plan change. Today's high relevant uncertainty tolls the death knell for planning processes that assume a stable environment. The path from the present to the future is not a straight line (Duffy, 2004).

The appropriate form of planning for today's world is called *active adaptive planning* (F. Emery, 1977), which means that people actively make their own future, merging their ideals with powerful value movements in the environment. The message is "Don't adapt to change; change to be adaptive." The most important product of active adaptive planning is a learning planning community determined to bring into being its most desirable future. As a system, a school district is more than the sum of its parts (Buckminster Fuller, 1970) and has unique relationships with its schools, its local community, and its other levels of environment (Angyal, 1941; Jordan, 1973).

The Open System's View of People

Four characteristics fully account for human behavior. The first is that people are purposeful: they can behave the same or differently in the same or different environments. They can change their goals in the same environment or decide to change their environment. They could have always acted differently (de Guerre, 2005). They display will (Ackoff & Emery, 1972).

Although people spend most of their time being purposeful, they can also be ideal seeking (chapter 2). This second characteristic emerges in democratic structures such as a search conference or a self-managing group when people must choose between important purposes. In the ideal-seeking mode, people choose outcomes that are endlessly approachable but unattainable (F. Emery, 1977). They rise above self-interest to act for the good of the whole. The ideal-seeking mode is accompanied by feelings of energy, excitement, and joy, and, once experienced, the ideals act as motivators. Ideal seeking is produced at the beginning of the search conference.

The third characteristic is that people need a balance between autonomy and a sense of belonging (Angyal, 1965; Fromm, 1963). Western culture has encouraged autonomy at the expense of belonging, but doing so inhibits personal growth (M. Emery, 1989) and leads people to retreat into private worlds (chapter 2).

The fourth characteristic is consciousness, defined as an ability to have "an awareness accompanied by an awareness of it" (Chein, 1972, p. 95). We have the ability to see ourselves acting in our environment. The experience may be only momentary, but this ability confers special responsibilities because, when we see ourselves deliberately making change to our world, we become conscious of the results of our action.

These characteristics need to be respected in any change process. When they are ignored, the chance of a successful outcome is diminished.

The Organizational Design Principles

More and more people are aware that schools and school districts everywhere have a bureaucratic structure (Gardner, 1991) and that "everywhere its hidden curriculum has the same effect" (Illich, 1971, p. 74). Schools today are expected to change direction quickly in order to adapt to their rapidly changing environment but are bound by their "arthritic bureaucratic" structures (Duffy, 2004).

These arthritic structures, including that of the classroom, produce a major paradox in the education system. The system is autocratic when the right answers are required to pass achievement tests, yet the system aims to inculcate learning, creativity, and responsible citizenship. To learn, students need to ask questions, but "questions are inimical to authority" (Zuboff, 1988, p. 290). People who question are trying to understand; they do not value tradition over change. Obedience does not lead to understanding, yet obedience—to elders and betters and to the right answers—is often the path to success at school.

Many of the problems encountered in schools are caused by the first organizational design principle that produces bureaucratic structures. In the first design principle (DP1), responsibility for coordination and control—the basic dimensions of organizations—is located at least one level above the people who are doing the work, the learning, or the planning. This produces a supervisory hierarchy or a hierarchy of dominance where superiors have the right and responsibility to tell subordinates what to do and how to do it. In the second design principle (DP2), this responsibility is located with the people who are doing the work, the learning, or the planning. This produces a flat organization or a hierarchy of function composed of self-managing groups where all change is negotiated between groups working as equals, regardless of position in the organization. This organization has been called many names, such as *high performing* and *intelligent* (Pinchot & Pinchot, 1993).

Responsibility sets this kind of collaborative approach off from others: "Once the parties themselves get the idea that they are responsible for coming up with the answer, rather than simply turning it over to a third party, they are very likely to begin to think and behave differently" (Kemmis, 1990, p. 113). They begin to reclaim that competency upon which democratic citizenship depends.

The design principles operate at all levels and sectors of society. Three examples should suffice. First, most of our governments are representative democracies—DP1 structures. Voters go to the polls and elect a government to which they pass responsibility for coordination and control for their futures. DP2 alternatives or participative democracies have existed and currently exist (F. Emery, 1976a, 1998). Second, committees are DP1 structures where the chairperson holds responsibility for coordination and control of the work of the committee and its members. Their dynamics fully justify the joke about committees designing camels. Groups with a set of agreed goals can be substituted. Third, a conference is a temporary organizational structure and, as such, can be structured on the first or second design principle. DP1 gives the conventional "talking heads" variety where responsibility for coordination and control of the conference rests not with the audience, the learners, but with the sponsors, organizers, chairs, and speakers. The purest form of DP2 conference is the search conference (M. Emery, 1999). Most American organizations have DP1 structures.

A third form of organization is called *laissez-faire*, which is the absence of a design principle and a coherent structure. Its behavioral effects are primarily negative, similar to those of DP1 but more intense (Lippitt & White, 1943). Unfortunately today, many laissez-faire organizations exist where the structure is DP1 on paper but is generally ignored (de Guerre, 2000, pp. 657–658). Some schools are effectively laissez-faire, as they have no concrete curricula to guide teachers. Responsibility for curricula falls through the cracks between the local, supervisory union and state levels (Shattuck, 2005).

Over time, DP1 actively de-skills and de-motivates, whereas DP2 skills and motivates (Emery & Emery, 1974). If an organization wants high levels of intrinsic motivation, it has no choice but to use DP2. Many organizational problems, such as failure to implement the strategic plan, are failures of motivation. Usually, only those who produced the plan bother with it. Psychological ownership produces intrinsic motivation.

Basic organizational statistics—such as error or accident rates, productivity, machine downtime, or customer complaints—are indirect measures of intrinsic motivation, but such motivation can be measured directly by using six psychological requirements that people have when engaging in productive work (Emery & Thorsrud, 1969). These requirements are tied to the design principles such that low and high scores are found in DP1 and DP2 structures, respectively. DP1 structures in school districts impose limits on what can be done to increase motivation. It is not surprising that when asked what they have done in school that day, children frequently answer, "Nothing." This response communicates a deep truth, as well as a flip reaction, because school is typically "done to students" (Gardner, 1991, p. 243). Yet motivation is all-important in schools: "once students are involved, interested and committed, learning usually follows" (Holman, 1986, p. 46).

Because DP1 entails relationships of dominance and inequality and en-courages competition, it distorts communication. It also amplifies errors (F. Emery, 1977) and inhibits learning (Emery & Emery, 1974). Not only are people unable to set their own goals and challenges, but the structure militates against their getting accurate and timely feedback on performance. These structures cannot provide appropriate environments for learning. DP2 struc-tures provide for basic psychological needs, including being able to learn and go on learning. A DP2 structure attenuates errors over time and produces a "learning organization," one "structured in such a way that its members can learn and continue to learn within it" (M. Emery, 1993d, p. 2). Note that or-ganizations cannot learn because they don't have nervous systems. Only the people learn. I discuss these design principles and their consequences in de-tail in chapter 5.

School district problems caused by DP1 are not intractable, because peo-ple can transform their bureaucratic structures through the participative de-sign workshop described in the following. Staff and students can both work and learn in self-managing groups (chapter 7).

The Two-Stage Model

Until 1991, search conferences and participative design workshops were re-garded as separate methods, the first for participative strategic planning and the second for organizational redesign. Although practitioners had learned to design and manage searches that successfully produced learning, plan-ning communities motivated to implement their plans, implementation had long been problematic (M. Emery, 1999). It experienced an unacceptable failure rate. What finally became obvious was that communities were miss-ing a conscious conceptual knowledge of the design principles. Without this knowledge, search communities muddled through implementation, trying to make committees and other forms of meeting work the way that the search had worked.

The search conference has a DP2 structure that encourages excitement, energy, and joy. It is essential that implementation be carried by a DP2 or-ganization so that it can continue to generate these positive feelings and en-ergy. Without them, implementation falters. When this penny dropped, I stopped conducting a search and hoping for the best and instead began testing a two-stage model (M. Emery, 1999).

In the two-stage model (Figure 1.2), a modified participative design workshop (PDW) is hung onto the end of the search conference. In this workshop people design an effective DP2 organization to carry the implementation. Once search participants have conscious conceptual knowledge of the design principles and know how to apply them, they can continue to enjoy positive emotions, generate energy as the process spreads through the community, and accelerate progress toward their strategic goals. The two-stage model is now used instead of the old method (de Guerre & Hornstein, 2004).

Real search conferences often have more steps than those shown in Figure 1.2 (adapted from M. Emery, 1999, p. 172), as each is custom-designed for each unique community, organization, and issue. The first phase of the search explores the social environment as it did in the first search conference (in 1959; see Trist & Emery, 1960), the reason being that open systems theory has rejected linear planning in favor of active adaptive planning for our unpredictable social environment (F. Emery, 1977; M. Emery, 1999). The second phase explores the system, and the third integrates the learning from the previous phases.

In the first phase, people pool their perceptions of change in the social environment and extract meaning from them to produce a picture of the

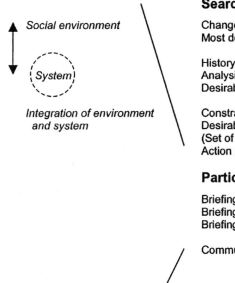

Search conference

Social environment

Changes in the world around us
Most desirable and probable worlds

System

History-significant events and changes
Analysis of our community today
Desirable future of our community

Integration of environment and system

Constraints and dealing with them
Desirable and achievable community
(Set of strategic goals)
Action plans

Participative design workshop

Briefing 1, followed by analysis
Briefing 2, followed by design
Briefing 3, design practicalities

Community implements and spreads

Figure 1.2.   Minimum Design of Two-Stage Model.

most probable future. They also blend their ideals with the most powerful forces in the social environment in order to produce a picture of the most desirable future. In the second phase, the participants learn about the unique character or personality of their system by collectively compiling its history, analyzing its current state, and determining its most desirable future. The most desirable future of their system consists of a set of strategic goals. In the third phase, participants return to their previous work to extract further guidance on dealing with constraints and doing action planning. Learning how to maneuver using the strategy of the indirect approach (chapter 4) ensures that a school district will stay actively adapted to its changing community, staff, and students.

The search conference maintains a strict division of labor between participants and the process managers. Participants work on the content, produce the outcomes, and implement them. They take responsibility for these tasks. Process managers take responsibility for the process and stay out of the work. Their concern is to produce a responsible, learning planning community that knows how to, and wants to, bring about a more desirable and adaptive state of affairs than currently exists. The process of the search is "to will into being a world that the community must experience in common: it is to create a common future" (Kemmis, 1990, p. 119). To achieve this common future, the managers ensure that the process stays task oriented.

Much of participants' learning in the search is through puzzle learning, which is unlike problem solving in that, until each piece is individually located and placed, it is not possible to determine which piece must be found next. The process is not linear, and participants may return to previous work at any stage if the task requires it. Puzzle learning is learning to be creative (Ackoff & Emery, 1972).

Throughout the search, participants use their knowledge extracted from their perceptions and experience—from their ecological learning. People do perceive the extended social environment, but because our culture provides few opportunities to use this knowledge, it remains tacit or unconscious (Polanyi, 1958, 1969). By using this knowledge in the search, people become confident of their abilities to create a desirable future. The energy generated sustains the intensity of meaningful work and motivates further efforts toward task and community cohesion. This dynamic cycle produces a self-generative, confident community.

When the community has a set of agreed action plans, it reconvenes for the PDW (Figure 1.2). The form of PDW required here is a modified form of the original, which was invented in 1971 to redesign existing organizations (Emery & Emery, 1974).

The two forms of PDW do not differ significantly in the first phase, which applies the design principle to analyze the effects of structure on people. They differ slightly on the second phase because designing an organization from scratch is much simpler than redesigning an existing one. The main difference is in phase three, where much more work is involved in ensuring that all details of a redesign will work in practice. The form used in the two-stage model (chapters 5 and 6) is therefore much shorter and less complex than that for redesign (chapter 7).

The briefings in both forms of PDW are critical because they deliver the conceptual knowledge that enables participants to understand their organizations and to change them. In both forms, there is a rule that no designs may be imposed. This means that only those who are going to implement the action plans design the organization and that those who work in a section of an existing organization redesign it. This principle fulfills an urgent need in the next phase of school reform, "a deep commitment to make teachers (all staff) partners in renewal at all levels" (Bruner, 1996, p. 85).

When staff, and students on occasion, redesign their own schools and offices, they will undoubtedly identify the "effective organizational structures" that represent a crucial step toward the improvement of schools (Gardner, 1991, p. 261). Gardner identified "valued national understandings" about schools and learning as another crucial step in reform. Obtaining these understandings in the community and school district would appear to be a first, realistic step.

Throughout the two-stage model, people learn to participate by participating (Pateman, 1970). Both the search and the PDW have been explicitly designed for this purpose, and together they promote the mutual learning that creates self-transforming networks (Schon, 1971), communities that nurture and develop their members (F. Emery, 1978c).

THREE SCHOOL DISTRICTS

Throughout the book I illustrate various options for improving a school district by way of three school districts, chosen to be as diverse as possible. They vary in geography, size, and demography. Commerce City in Georgia is the smallest, whereas Tucson Unified School District in Arizona is one of the hundred largest districts in the United States. Huntingdon Area School District in Pennsylvania lies in the middle of the range. Size is an important variable in project design, and the three communities demonstrate the flexibility of the principles and methods.

AN EIGHT-STEP PROCESS

As discussed, the school system is not only unique but also more complex than most other systems. Eight steps are required for holistic transformation. Steps 1–5 cover the first component of community involvement; steps 6 and 7 cover the second component of reorganizing staff and student structures; and step 8 covers the third, balancing teaching and learning. Chapter 9 introduces a possible step 9, which holds promise for raising educational achievement into the future. The chapters provide brief historical overviews of evidence relevant to their subjects and elaborate the major concepts, principles, and methods introduced here.

Step 1: Preparing for the Total Process and the Community Search Conference

Preparation is a crucial first step in the success of any venture, as any event is only as effective as its preparation. In chapter 3, I explore the preparation required for such a major project as improving a school district, which involves learning about the processes required and the negotiations needed between senior school system managers and unions (the industrial issues involved in changing a school district are discussed in chapter 7). I also discuss the preparation for a community search conference.

Step 2: Revitalizing the Community

Active, cohesive communities create a sense of belonging and form a positive, energetic context for the work of improving the school district. Their goals for learning guide the school district through its planning. In chapter 2, I discuss the power of communities to make change, and I explain that the consistency of direction between the future of the community and its school district flows from human ideals. In chapter 4, I describe the process of a search conference designed to mobilize and revitalize the community of a school district, and I offer possible options for the Georgia, Pennsylvania, and Arizona communities.

Step 3: Ensuring Implementation of the Community Plan

Once the community has a set of action plans, the crucial phase of implementation begins. Adding the PDW to the search has substantially raised the probability of successful implementation. In chapter 5, I begin with a historical review of the effects of the design principles, and I explain why the change to DP2 generates and sustains the energy required for implementation. I also elaborate on the PDW to design organizations and illustrate the various options in the three diverse communities.

Steps 4 and 5: Planning and Organizing to Improve the School District

Steps 4 and 5 involves a second round of two-stage events in which staff and students from the school district work on the future of their district with members of the community. In chapter 6, I describe the processes and highlight some significant differences between the first and second rounds of planning events.

Steps 6 and 7: Effectively and Democratically Organizing Staff and Students

Step 6 involves using the original form of PDW for redesigning existing organization structures. Because a change of design principle has consequences for most of the supporting administrative systems, it raises industrial issues. In chapter 7, I detail both the preparatory work required for a change of existing structure and the processes in the workshops. I also discuss the flexible ways in which workshops may be grouped to most efficiently involve all staff in the district. When the staff have finalized their design, they perform step 7, creating a democratic structure for students.

Step 8: Balancing Teaching and Learning

Step 8 involves changing practices so that the school district places equal emphasis on teaching and learning. Achieving a balance between teaching and learning involves using our capacity for extracting meaningful knowledge from the world around us. In chapter 8, I document the theories of perception and learning that lie behind the emphases on teaching and learning, the different types of knowledge involved, and the ways in which they can be used appropriately in today's schools. The chapter contains examples of how teachers achieve this balance in different areas of study.

Step 9: Icing the Cake for the Future

Step 9 is not a natural part of this sequence of activities; it is, however, a way to enhance the learning of adults and, in the process, begin to close the achievement gap between the social classes. In chapter 9, I document the evidence that social class is the most powerful influence on the educational and life success of children. The more that parents engage with learning and the more books that they have in a home, the higher their children's motivation to learn and the higher their children's academic achievement. Schools can do much to encourage, if not provide opportunities for, the further learning of parents. In chapter 9, I provide examples of school districts increasing community learning and laying a better foundation for generations of children to come.

The Power of Community

𝓛iving in an active, cohesive community is a delight. People know and trust each other, as they have been working together on agreed community purposes. Trust, also known as social or human capital, is the glue that welds people into a genuine community. Cohesive communities display feelings of well-being and high energy levels. Hard work is easily accomplished and difficult decisions are made with little conflict. Discussion and negotiation replace conflict and negativity, and once a decision has been made, the community swings into action to implement it. This collective action increases the levels of positive feelings and energy within the community, building an even stronger foundation for future community achievements. Active communities are powerful contexts for school districts, infecting them with enthusiasm for change.

THE IMPORTANCE OF COMMUNITY FOR DEMOCRACY

The educative nature and benefits of participation have long been seen as being important to a democratic society. The American philosopher John Dewey (1922) promoted learning for democracy and democracy in learning. He recognized that these two dimensions were inseparable to make progress in the functioning of our democracies. In planning for their desirable future within a participative democratic structure, communities learn and grow together. This form of community development is powerful because it promotes freedom (Freire, 1972). Individualism and community enhance each other when people are working in democratic structures. It is only on the basis of equality and shared understanding that mutual tolerance of individualities can be maintained.

Democracy is not primarily a form of government nor even a way of making decisions; it is a way of living. People strive to increase their quality of life in communities by using processes to preserve their uniqueness and desirable characteristics (Megill, 1970). The search conference and PDW use structures based on the second design principle so that from the very beginning of the processes, democratic community is created, experienced, and learned through the activity of planning. These methods go straight to the heart of a democratic community by putting the participants in control over the content and outcome of the planning. Participants become more and more creative as the process unfolds and reach a point where work and creative play are indistinguishable. Active adaptive planning develops community through participation.

Successful community development is holistic and empowering, as it allows mutual needs to be met with shared emotional ties and support. A sense of community and community competence go hand in hand as individual and community capabilities are facilitated. Citizen influence in decision making is fostered with the acceptance of joint responsibility between community organizations and municipal governments (Florin & Wandersman, 1990). Community development also includes initiating partnerships or networks between business and other enterprises with benefits for all parties. Networks are often seen as the structure through which many forms of interorganizational cooperation are channeled and trust is built (Bachmann & Witteloostuijn, 2003). Since the early 1980s, organizations have increasingly developed sets of alliances with other organizations with different sets of competencies. Externally and internally, they have taken on the characteristics of networks (Limerick & Cunningham, 1993). Communities, networks, and participative democracies share the important properties of equality and cooperation.

Social capital is a fashionable term at the moment, but it is merely new language for an old debate in American intellectual circles going back to 1916 (Putnam, 2000). The original idea included "good will, fellowship, sympathy and social intercourse among the individuals and families that make up a social unit. . . . The community as a whole will benefit by the cooperation of all of its parts" (Hanifan, 1916, cited in Putnam, 2000, p. 19). Perhaps part of the popularity of the term today lies in its economic connotations, those that were deliberately invoked by Hanifan "to encourage hard-nosed businessmen and economists to recognize the productive importance of social assets" (Putnam, 2000, p. 445).

As making a profit adds to economic capital, so does volunteering beget more volunteering. Social capital and community development are intimately related as activists were once urged to build social capital to improve their rural communities (Putnam, 2000). However, recent uses of social capital (Baum et al., 1999; Duenas, 2000; Onyx & Bullen, 2000) have become fuzzy, and "there is as yet no internationally agreed framework of what constitutes social capital" (Edwards, 2004, p. vii).

Community development is clearer and easier to understand than social capital, and more is known about what makes it successful. Successful processes involve voluntary cooperation and self-help/mutual-aid efforts to improve the quality of community life (Chavis & Wandersman, 1990; Florin & Wandersman, 1990; McKnight, 1995). When people participate in voluntary organizations to produce collective and individual goods and services, they develop a sense of community. Democratic societies depend on strong, cohesive communities.

The Need for Healthy Communities

Until the 1980s, communities received less attention than did work organizations, as researchers believed that most progress would be made by working collaboratively with work organizations and the larger those organizations, the better (F. Emery, 1975). The major reason for this belief was that most people worked for a living in an organization of paid employment. The second reason was that employing organizations with their ethos of competing for increasing profitability would be most motivated to initiate change toward higher productivity, lower costs, and therefore increased profitability.

This strategy was reassessed by the 1980s as unemployment rose in most of the Western industrial democracies. Working hours increased, as did the number of part-time and casual positions. The unemployed and the underemployed today in most industrialized countries have come under increasingly stringent regimes of unemployment benefits and the means for obtaining them. Communities began to notice that they were reaping the whirlwind. Increasingly, the unemployed moped around their community hangouts and homes, and the employed came home only to rest. Rather than continue to involve themselves in the lives of their communities—that is, to volunteer—many could find the energy only to flop in front of the television and escape from the demands of their bureaucratized workplaces. Communities were losing their community spirit (Putnam, 2000).

When communities begin to lose their community spirit, individuals retreat into increasingly private lives. Retreating has significant health consequences, as the cohesion and social support flowing from community are necessary to good health (Marmot, Siegrist, Theorell, & Feeney, 1999; Wilkinson, 1996). People in communities with high levels of social cohesion enjoy better health than do those in communities with low levels. Mutual trust and respect between different sections of society, high levels of participation in communal activities and public affairs, and high levels of membership of community groups all make significant contributions to health (Stansfeld, 1999).

Health is also associated with an egalitarian ethos. Empowering change is central to community health, and the supportive processes used are particularly beneficial for health issues such as the prevention of cancer (Baillie et al., 2004). An accumulated body of research indicates that the engagement of youth with their communities reduces the likelihood of violence and delinquency and promotes competencies and emotional well-being (Zeldin, 2004).

Local communities are the bedrock of our societies, and we need them to be healthy and vital so that they can better provide the support that their members need to stay healthy and vital. Investing in a local community brings many rewards and benefits (Putnam, 2000), and the most powerful learning goes from community to organization rather than the other way around (Brown, 1996; Schwinn & Schwinn, 1996). Unfortunately today, many communities have lost their way and become victim to alienation and isolation (Putnam, 2000). In *The Private Future* (1973), Pawley described the dangers and angst for people and communities who lost their sense of togetherness and reverted to individualism and a lack of trust and cooperation.

Cooperation is one of the foundations of an active, motivated community that knows how to plan and make change together. Cooperation has been described as "the law of life," the most deeply rooted theme running through human success (Gorney, 1968, p. x). It is also a necessity for all species who engage in coordinated and communicative teamwork, from people all the way through to bacteria (Buchanan, 2004).

Spoken language is another powerful dimension of community. It functions as "social cement" (Farb, 1973). Spoken words are powerful communicators of meaning, allowing people to immediately relate themselves to the mesh of relationships within which they are embedded (Ong, 1967). Humanity is learned, and what and how we learn determines who we become. The major mechanism for this learning is spoken language, particularly conversation. Spoken language is the most powerful and active learning medium. It cannot be separated from the whole of behavior (Farb, 1973).

As people withdraw from community and lose the cementing power of spoken language, the trend to withdraw accelerates, leaving a vacuum. The scenario that results from this withdrawal is called *dissociation*, which occurs when people seek to reduce the complexity of their lives by withdrawing from common goals and public space. By withdrawing, they are essentially denying that by cooperating with others, they have a better chance of achieving a more meaningful future. As people withdraw from the public realm, they gradually degrade the web of mutual obligations that characterize a rich and meaningful social life (F. Emery, 1977).

The scenario of dissociation is alive and well in most Western industrialized cultures and amounts to a silent world where people simply do not hear or acknowledge each other (Ong, 1967). Its symptoms include more spectators and fewer players, as in *Bowling Alone* (Putnam, 2000); high levels of television viewing (Emery & Emery, 1976); more random violence with reduced sensitivity to it; and increased apathy (Emery & Emery, 1979). It is a crisis of responsibility (Pawley, 1973).

The United States has witnessed an erosion of solidarity over time (Bhattacharyya, 2004), and trust in others is declining. Trust in others was high for those born up until the mid-1940s, but people have become increasingly less trustful over time. The more cohesive and closely linked a group or community, the higher the trust and the longer they stay together. "A spread of mistrust, although not yet far advanced, may have serious consequences for U.S. society," as declines in trust weaken democracy (Robinson & Jackson, 2001, p. 141). Declining trust may be self-reinforcing and become a spiral that could be difficult to reverse.

"The social conditions in cities compared to the nation as a whole had deteriorated greatly" between 1979 and 1990, causing increased urban distress (Nelson & Schwirian, 1998, p. 419). Because distressing environments reduce the chance of successful actions, people become trapped in a type of closed system—and there have been further signs of decline since 1990. Neighborhood violence is linked to low levels of social power (Duncan, Duncan, Okut, Strycker, & Hix-Small, 2003), and it affects student achievement. "With the accelerating disintegration of family life and the loss of many social supports in the community, children arrive at school far less prepared to deal with the unfamiliar demands that will be made on them. At the same time, the community looks to the school as the institution that is most likely to be able to compensate for its own lacks" (Gardner, 1991, p. 256).

For African Americans, the impact of neighborhood socioeconomic distress on dropout rates has increased markedly over the last quarter century and remains consistently high for white adolescents (Crowder & South, 2003). However, engaging in neighborly behavior increases sense of community and enhances academic performance in the same way that close family ties do (Farrell, Aubry, & Coulombe, 2004). Achievement suffers in nontraditional and mobile communities, but if residents become involved in community-based activities, their children will encounter fewer academic disadvantages. "It is crucial for parents and students in such communities to overcome these structural barriers and increase their participation in community-based activities in order to compensate for the negative consequences of living in such communities" (Sun, 1999, p. 423–424).

Engagement with community is the key to democracy as well as educational achievement. Democracy requires a strong citizenry, one sure of itself. Kemmis (1995) has reflected on his efforts to turn taxpayers into citizens in

Montana and the city of Missoula within it. Citizenship involves intimate connections between the individual and the city or place in general. Only citizenship can save politics from the epidemic dysfunctions in the body politic, the alienation, despair, and cynicism that are destroying democracy. The dysfunctions can be healed by nurturing "the deeply human aspiration toward health and wholeness." "Whole people are capable of reclaiming the human meaning of citizenship from the rubble of a political culture inhabited largely by sullen 'taxpayers'" (p. 14). Kemmis believes that a powerful healing is occurring in the body politic in the United States, and although the process is slow and incremental, it is also evermore self-sustaining.

Individual and Community

One of the major contributors to dissociation is a misunderstanding in our Western industrialized cultures about the dominance of personal autonomy over community in our lives (also see chapter 5). Riger (1993) questioned the relationship: "Does empowerment . . . simultaneously bring about a greater sense of community and strengthen the ties that hold our society together, or does it promote certain individuals or groups at the expense of others, increasing competitiveness and lack of cohesion?" (p. 290; see also, Riger, 1994).

The development of individuality and that of community are not mutually exclusive. Autonomy means being governed from the inside, but for group or social animals, needs for autonomy must be balanced by our needs for belonging. Life is not lived within one's skin but is an autonomous dynamic event that takes place between the person and the environment (Angyal, 1965). Autonomy without a corresponding sense of belonging actually restricts and inhibits personal growth. A balance of autonomy and belongingness results in an ever-increasing expansion of self through participation and relatedness to the wholes of which people are a part (Fromm, 1963). One reinforces the other (Berkowitz, 1996).

We are so accustomed to seeking personal wholeness through various forms of individual self-development that we have forgotten that citizenship, participating in community, is a path to greater individual wholeness (Kemmis, 1995). The good citizen understands that personal welfare depends on general welfare and acts accordingly. The United States has a great tradition of acknowledging community welfare, and people can learn to recapture community by practice (Kemmis, 1990). In practicing community and citizenship, people experience the coincidence of personal and common welfare.

The idea of social capital is similarly associated with positive outcomes for both individuals and societies (Edwards, 2004). It is not wealth that determines social capital: it is the density of the interconnections between all members of the unit that confers the wide-ranging psychological, physical, and economic benefits. When social capital is high, we all win in one way or another (Putnam, 2000).

Communities form an enveloping context for the many organizations, partnerships, and networks within them. In general, people need a community context to fully understand individual phenomena such as youth affairs (White & Wyn, 1998). A long tradition in community education holds that the individual and the community are interdependent and that neither has meaning independent of the other (Willie, 2000). Public education is a community affair, and as discussed in chapter 1, communities and other systems (such as school districts) exist one within another. Although these communities and systems have different purposes that may be linked, one is not subordinate to another. Both are valid entities in their own right (Willie, 2000). To focus on students as individuals without consideration of their group affiliations is unlikely to solve our current problems in teaching and learning.

Although *A Nation at Risk*, the 1983 report of the National Commission on Excellence in Education, served as the stimulus to the contemporary school reform movement, it effectively advocated the achievement of excellence but ignored equity. Community education research has revealed that a good education system needs both excellence and equity (Willie, 2000). As detailed in chapter 9, a student's background is the most powerful contributor to achievement, and acting on the background rather than the individual student is likely to prove more effective in raising achievement.

Excessive emphasis on individualism rather than the individual-in-community has distorted views on the necessity and power of community. Dissociation has grown as responsibility for the public realm has reduced, but putting responsibility back into the hands of citizens can reverse it. The good news for communities suffering from excessive individualism and dissociation is that this reversal is relatively easy to do. Cooperation and trust can be regenerated.

Empowerment and Participative Democracy

People are empowered when they are living, working, or learning in an organization structured on DP2, introduced in chapter 1. They have power when they hold responsibility for the coordination and control of their own affairs, when they work with others to make their own decisions, and when they take responsibility for their collective outcomes and future. These forms of empowering organization are also expressed as teamwork, collaboration, and community responsibility for and control of its own destiny (Kenyon & Black, 2001). More hierarchical and rigid arrangements are less likely to empower (Zimmerman & Rappaport, 1988).

DP2 accounts for the many observations that link empowerment to democratic participation in the life of the community and in people's gaining control over their lives (Chavis & Wandersman, 1990; Zimmerman, Israel, Schulz, & Checkoway, 1992). It also accounts for the perception that empowered people are more likely to have "a concern for the common good and a sense of connectedness to others" (Zimmerman & Rappaport, 1988, p. 747). People in DP2 structures are deeply connected around a set of common goals and need to care for each other and the community in general in order to meet those goals. The consequences of the design principle include a sense of community and, with participation, empowerment, and valuing the involvement of others, form important factors in determining whether a community will successfully make change (Kenyon & Black, 2001; Moore, 2002).

Studies of communities over time show that the higher the level of participation, the better the neighborhood relations and the greater the sense of community. A better sense of community leads to more personal and group power, increased satisfaction with the neighborhood, and internal control. Once community members see that problems are under their control, they see them as being less difficult. They also need to see their communities and their problems in context, as "communities are open systems influenced by their environment as well as by their internal structures" (Chavis & Wandersman, 1990, p. 76). Learning to understand and use environmental change for community benefit is a major component of the search conference.

The Ideals

These participative democratic (DP2) forms of organization produce cooperative behavior and positive emotions (M. Emery, 1986). They also encourage people to function openly and purposefully and to move into the ideal-seeking mode (Ackoff & Emery, 1972). Ideal seeking is an intrinsically attractive and motivating form of behavior that draws people together as they try to improve their lives and communities (M. Emery, 1999).

Ideals emerge as a set of four when people in participative democratic structures choose between purposes (F. Emery, 1977). Ideals show that when people come together to purposefully plan their futures, they make their most desirable future rather than merely adjust to what exists. Ideals are unattainable but can be endlessly pursued. Therefore, they are motivators. Without these motivators, it is hard to maintain a high level of commitment to a desirable future, and without this commitment, energy for action fades away.

The first ideal is a sense of belonging (which was originally identified by Angyal, 1965, who called it *homonomy*). People need to belong to something and value their autonomy. A sense of belonging is the opposite of selfishness. A sense of community or community spirit expresses this ideal, and it is closely tied to volunteering and feeling positive about the community (Department of Transport and Regional Services [DTRS], 2001).

The second ideal is nurturance or cultivation of those things that contribute to the health of the community and its environment. It includes all aspects of helping others to grow, including learning, and it is frequently expressed as social support. Caring for others is the opposite of exploiting them. This second ideal is, of course, central to the purpose of schools. It is sometimes expressed as developing a community's problem-solving capacity, increasing individual skills, and cultivating leadership. Today, communities still have an urgent need for social and emotional support, particularly for those who have suffered from adverse life experiences (Mickelson & Kubzansky, 2003).

The third ideal is humanity or producing good outcomes for all people and not just their physical well-being. This ideal puts people before bureaucratic and material notions of progress. Humanity is the opposite of inhumanity or behaving inhumanely. Successful communities expand the diversity of involvement, develop businesses, enhance services, prevent crime, and improve social conditions (Chavis & Wandersman, 1990).

The fourth ideal is beauty, appreciating situations or arrangements that are intrinsically attractive, such as the beauty of the wilderness or the desert. It includes ideas of leisure as *recreation* for a full and balanced life or seeking spirituality. It is the opposite of ugliness (Chavis & Wandersman, 1990).

Desirable community futures usually contain all four of the ideals, as they collectively express active, not passive, adaptation. For example, as well as finding a sense of belonging, Kenyon and Black (2001) found a "learning exchange" developing problem solving and other skills and cultivating leadership (nurturance). They also found high quality in business and community life, safety, and expanding diversity of involvement (humanity) as well as improving recreational facilities and ecosystems (beauty).

People come together around this set of ideals regardless of the different value systems they may have. For this reason, large groups of diverse people can be found working together around common goals, often to the amazement of observers who may have predicted conflict between them. "I was surprised that this group of disparate individuals reached any agreement on our core environmental issues" (Alan Best, a participant quoted by Schweitz, 1996, p. 38). Because they are so fundamental, so immediately attractive, and so universal, the ideals are immensely powerful. The sooner they are elicited after a group comes together, the more effective the group will be in pursuing its task.

Communities that have become empowered show many and varied results. Atlanta, Georgia, now enjoys a comprehensive program of care for the homeless, a shared management information system of over 70 service agencies, a community court that emphasizes restorative sentencing rather than simply punishment, and the implementation of seven community redevelopment plans. These plans, made by residents and then produced by professional planners resulted in an increased sense of community and new life for the communities themselves (Starnes, 2004).

In 1993, a series of searches was held with the small and remote island communities of Saint Pauls, Kubin, and Mabuiag in the Torres Strait. Three years later, Saint Pauls had made great strides in implementing their housing plans and had restarted their traditional gardens to supply fresh healthy food for themselves and neighboring communities. Their youth were being trained in trades and gardening, with the elders involved in teaching the old culture and skills. They were much closer to self-sufficiency and were delighted with their progress. "We did it!" (Paton & Emery, 1996, p. 29).

The other two communities made less progress, but Kubin had put in family gardens, providing learning opportunities and making the islanders more self-sufficient. The village was much cleaner, with an improvement in the water supply. Mabuiag introduced new sports and recreational activities for young people, built gardens, and organized health workshops with subsequent increased testing for diabetes. These communities were once again taking responsibility for their own destinies, overturning years of dependency and loss of their cultures (Paton & Emery, 1996), and this development continues (personal communication from John Paton, 2004). As these examples from Atlanta and Torres Strait show, it does not matter if communities are rich or poor or if they are used to taking action or not, they will make ideal-based community change to enhance community stability and prevent threats to their quality of life (Carmin, 2003).

The Inseparability of Education and Community

Because the ideals are so powerful and pervasive, it is inevitable that nurturance or cultivation will pop up in some form. I have never seen a report from a community search that did not contain a goal about improving its learning, schools, or education system, regardless of the nature of the community or its main purpose in meeting. People know that education, not ability, is a major factor in increasing participation and the strength of community that participation generates (Hauser, 2000).

Examples abound. The town of Vail, Colorado, made action plans for "strong public education and involvement" (Schweitz, 1996, p. 38). The community of Greenwood, South Carolina, aimed for "a community that cares about learning; where everyone accepts a responsibility for encouraging and enabling all our people to reach their full potential and become positive contributors to our economic well-being and quality of life" (Bundy & McAbee, 1996, p. 23). Michigan created a Service Management Learning Academy to transform its travel and tourism ventures into learning organizations. New courses were introduced into the education system so that quality principles and tools were available for use in classrooms. The three secondary school districts joined with the technical college, university, and chamber's CEO Industry Roundtable to address educational issues from kindergarten through to adult education (La Lopa & Holecek, 1996). Sometimes nurturance is expressed as lifelong learning, which acknowledges that everyone needs to have learning opportunities throughout their lives (Bundy & McAbee, 1996; Heckman, 1995). For example, a search conference for regional planning in the Macatawa area (the cities of Holland, Zeeland, and five adjoining Michigan townships; Heckman, 1995) included "lifelong learning" in its strategic goals. A year later, the conference participants reconvened to celebrate their accomplishments as an open adaptive system learning about and practicing direct participative democracy (Heckman, 1998).

When searches are convened around the specific task of planning the future of their school or school district, the ideal of nurturance may be expressed in many different words for the circumstances individual to that district. Blick (1998) provided three examples: the Marysville Middle School (Washington), the Tulalip Tribes and Marysville School District (Washington), and Madison County (Idaho). In Marysville the main goal was to create a meaningful learning environment that has the capacity for continuous improvement. For the Tulalip Tribes and Marysville School District, the question was how they could best work together to address education in conjunction with the social and cultural concerns that were affecting student learning. In Madison County, the purpose was to get youth and adults to work together for a better future. Each initial event had a mixture of people from all the various communities involved, from the school and central office staff and students (where appropriate).

Competence, Leadership, Voluntarism, and Creativity

Several clusters of factors are associated with empowerment, as shown by three very different community-based organizations. People acquired personal competence as they gain access to a number of different roles at different levels within the organization. A peer-based support system contributed to this competence, simultaneously generating a psychological sense of community. The support system (nurturance) helped people deal with problems and with the challenges involved in increasing control over one's life. The sense of community they created contributed to openness to change and persistence in the pursuit of goals, leading to a greater sense of well-being (Maton & Salem, 1995).

The three organizations all enjoyed inspirational, talented, shared, and committed leadership (humanity). The leadership involved clear pictures of what was to be accomplished, the encouragement of participation in decision making, the generation of resources, the maintenance of stability, and effective responses to changing environmental conditions (Maton & Salem, 1995). Leaders like this who listen more than they talk and share leadership have been found to be important in a variety of studies (Kenyon & Black, 2001). They recognize the inevitability of some changes (Gibson et al., 1999) and get on and deal with them.

Community members often used the terms *volunteers* and *leaders* synonymously (DTRS, 2001) because, frequently, it is volunteers who provide the conditions for the pursuit of ideals. Topsham, Maine, with a population of 10,000, reinvigorated its community through the use of volunteers. This brought people together and saved the community much money (Hitchcock, 1994). Volunteers have initiated programs and moved communities toward ideal seeking in the process of connecting schools and parents. The changes meant that school expectations were better met and that both parties benefited. The learning environment of the children improved, particularly that of disadvantaged groups (Foreman, Gresham, & James, 1997).

People who are actively involved in community and social networks are more likely to volunteer in the first place and to stick with volunteering. Volunteering produces more volunteering, as people who have received help are more likely to help others (Putnam, 2000). Leadership in community development involves sharing and nurturing as much as it involves initiating and doing, and differences between men and women have as much to do with organizational differences as with gender (Pringle & Collins, 1998).

Leaders are frequently seen as those with bright ideas who initiate innovation in a community (Gibson et al., 1999; Kenyon & Black, 2001; Maton & Salem, 1995; McKnight, 1995). Creativity is released in participative democratic structures (F. Emery, 1999), and the resulting innovations are brought to fruition as people learn and support each other in these structures. Note that in none of the above observations was there any mention of leadership being at the top of an organization. In DP2 structures, leadership moves around the organization, as various forms of expertise are required.

Not only do strong, cohesive communities have advantages for the adults, but they also contribute to a child's informal learning and competence by providing a range of resources, knowledge, and opportunities for learning. They offer a range of social experiences and interactions with a variety of people. All these experiences influence the child's attitudes and values. Communities are now recognized as the repository of rich resources of knowledge and know-how applied with ingenuity and flexibility (Marsden, 1991).

A whole community can become a learning society using the resources available as community members harness their creative abilities and create their own learning systems. But to make their dreams for learning come true, community people need design skills so that they can learn how to best employ the resources they have (Montuori & Conti, 1993, quoting Banathy, 1987). These design skills are introduced through the PDW (chapter 5). A community can also be used as a "school without walls," where learning takes place in the environment rather than in a school building. This was part of Dewey's original idea of progressive education, but today it is most frequently embedded in project work based around students' real-life knowledge (chapter 8).

School–home–community relationships can be built into goals and processes (NFIE, 2000). People involved in school–home–community partnerships contribute their expertise by giving talks about their jobs or hobbies or by leading field trips. All sectors of a community have something special to give and receive. Volunteer organizations show students something of the lives of those less advantaged than themselves and how volunteers glue these different sectors of a society together. Business organizations enlighten students about real workplaces and how the production of goods and services depends on the abstract, sometimes seemingly useless knowledge they must absorb in school. Everybody benefits from raising the awareness of young people about today's complex world. Myths are replaced by firsthand knowledge, and the more hands-on the process of acquiring that knowledge, the greater the understanding of the unique character of the community and its relationship to the environment. Recognizing their own people rather than bringing in out-of-town "experts" increases the community's cohesion and confidence in its future.

Trust

Trust, and similar ideas such as solidarity, is an essential component in the development of social capital (Chatfield, 1999; Falk & Kilpatrick, 2000; Flora, 1998; Prestby, Wandersman, Florin, Rich, & Chavis, 1990; Putnam, 2000; Svendsen & Svendsen, 2000). Paternalism or autocracy destroys social capital and trust (DTRS, 2001; Schulman & Anderson, 1999).

Trust is one of the most powerful forces operating in community, and many have captured its essential features. These include the expectation that members of a community will behave honestly and cooperatively (Fukuyama, 1995). Trust is the by-product of community members' honoring agreements about how they are going to work and make decisions together (Lyons, 1998). With trust, people act "without expecting anything immediately in return and perhaps without even knowing you, confident that down the road you or someone else will return the favor" (Putnam, 2000, p. 134). Trust helps community members plan cooperatively and balance risks (Salamon, Farnsworth, & Rendziak, 1998).

Trust is also one of the four necessary conditions for effective or influential communication (Asch, 1952; Heider, 1946; Newcomb, 1953). These four conditions—openness, recognition that we are all human, recognition that we all live in the same world, and trust (Asch, 1952)—are forces that are "universal, tacit and compelling" (Emery & Emery, 1976, p. 20).

Openness means open to the inspection of all. We have to know that we are in a situation that we can investigate and find that things are "what they appear to be" (M. Emery, 1999, p. 112). We also need to experience openness from others. We assume that others will have differences of opinion, and it is healthy to acknowledge such differences. If others are not open about their views and we cannot test whether differences do or do not exist, then we have less of a chance of establishing mutual support and respect. Openness is a necessary precondition for the rationalization of conflict and the establishment of common ground.

The second condition is a recognition that we are all human, that we all share the same human concerns. This recognition is better conveyed by behavior than by words. When we see behaviors and motives similar to our own, we are more likely to want to learn something from the other. When people act as "experts," talking down or behaving arrogantly, we are less likely to attempt to communicate effectively, and learning is diminished. Recognizing that we are all human enables us to agree on purposes and work together toward them.

The third condition is a recognition that we all live in the same world. To achieve it, we must perceive and acknowledge common features of the world around us. Once we identify these common features, we can use the environment as a shared context for planning and action. We can then use this environment to devise courses of action that move us toward common goals and overcome problems.

Trust is a joint function of the preceding three conditions over a period of time. It accumulates as we come to experience the openness of the world we share with others. It also accumulates from the mutual respect and consideration that comes from initiating communication with others. Therefore, trust involves learning to be open and communicative. As it accumulates, so do interpersonal relations strengthen and deepen, increasing the probability of mutual learning. The emergence of trust in others involves our trust in our perceptions and learning and in the confidence of the group as a whole to assume responsibility for their future.

Trust develops through collaboration. When we collaborate, we work together as equals rather than superiors and subordinates. We come to experience trust only in situations where the conditions for effective two-way communication are present and where there are no externally imposed restrictions on expression.

When we agree to enter into a relation of trust, we encounter a paradox. It is the fact that the more we share or give away, the more we have (Asch, 1952; Chein, 1972; Tomkins, 1962). Collaboration increases the extent to which we spontaneously share ourselves with others. Trust accumulates as we take opportunities to work on shared concerns, a process that releases further energy and enhances interpersonal engagement around the task at hand. This in turn leads to mutually supportive action. Without this spiral of trust, learning, energy, and commitment, implementation and diffusion of community plans would be impossible (adapted from M. Emery, 1999).

Positive Emotions and Attitude

It has long been known that positive emotions are powerful drivers of change. The ancient cultures of the world were oral cultures, celebratory and joyful. Work was (and is) accompanied by music and dance, and ceremonies were designed to celebrate the harvest (Caudwell, 1937). People find pleasure in participating in the activity of a group or community (Havelock, 1978), as activity and movement appear to trigger the human responses of energy and joy. Joy is a contagious emotion, and energy is its most visible sign.

The power of the energy of joy has been found in many different situations—from community change to the synchronicity of behavior in human interaction. Hall (1976) filmed children in a playground moving together in a coordinated rhythm. One little girl was moving more than the rest and covered the entire playground. The whole group was moving in synchrony to a definite rhythm, that set by the most active girl. Like an orchestra, the group was responding to the joyful energy of the conductor. "People in interaction move together in a kind of dance," but they are not conscious of this (p. 60). They communicate emotion and bond through participation, not through sending and receiving messages in any mechanical sense. Humans are tied to each other by hierarchies of rhythms.

Excitement and joy are the energizers and motivators and, being highly contagious, create interest in others to become involved (M. Emery, 1986).

These effects are found across cultures (Emery & Bartel, 2000) because the emotional system is the most important source of motivation for people everywhere. The flexibility of the emotional system makes it possible for people to move toward an ideal state (Tomkins, 1962). Excitement and joy enhance personal freedom because they bolster self-confidence (Shand, 1926).

A positive attitude or belief was a key theme in 14 "vibrant small communities" as they worked on their futures (Kenyon & Black, 2001). Not only does being positive help successful communities function day to day, but it also plays a significant role in how they respond to and recover from a disaster. If the community sees itself as being capable, strong, and resilient, rather than as victims whose ability to respond is diminished, they are more able to respond to the challenge and manage the effects of change themselves. The vibrancy of the social environment is a direct and positive influence on the economic viability of the formal economy (Gibson et al., 1999). If community development is to be self-sustaining, it must continue to generate excitement and joy so that it can spread within communities and from one community to another.

The power of joy to infect others with energy and hope has been recently confirmed. Exuberance means overflowing joy and energy and an enthusiasm for life. About 10% of the population is exuberant, and that 10% includes such well-known figures as Bill Clinton. "His energy is infectious." Exuberance is a highly valued and integral part of these people's identities and is a delightful characteristic. "Being a great leader is really the capacity to fire infectious enthusiasm." They get others "very motivated and optimistic about what can be done" (Redfield Jamison, cited in Else, 2004, pp. 44–45).

Exuberance is dampened by rigid, hierarchical, and bureaucratic structures. Children whose lives consist of nothing much but structured school work, sport, homework, and leisure activities become much more passive. Their lives are "really joyless" (Else, 2004, p. 47).

Seven Successful Rural Communities

A study of seven rural and diverse communities showed how the aforementioned factors interrelate and lead to change. These communities suffered many severe problems but had started to overcome their multiple disadvantages. An outside group devised a set of criteria for success and judged those seven communities to be successful on those criteria. In each community, a sample of women who had been chosen by their community peers worked in a series of small groups followed by larger workshops. A questionnaire was developed from community responses and administered at the time of the workshops (DTRS, 2001).

The small groups answered two questions: "This seems to be a go-ahead place. How does the community achieve it?" and "What motivates the community to do it?" The workshops convened shortly after the group work and integrated the answers into one community-owned list. The groups then decided on the goals that defined their most desirable community in 5 years time. They went on to list the major barriers they could see they would face in producing that desirable future and did action planning to neutralize or remove these barriers. After the workshop manager introduced each task, groups were self-managing, and the products were fully owned by participants. These communities have not yet been formally followed up, but anecdotal evidence suggests that action from the workshop planning is continuing.

Figure 2.1 shows the pattern that emerged from each of the seven rural communities and from the total database. The arrows show that accepting change and being creative about facing it leads to the conditions for trust. The conditions for trust lead to the central features of the pattern, ideal seeking within a participative, democratic structure. Strong leaders, those who have bright ideas and get things going in the community, also contribute to this central box. These strong leaders were frequent volunteers. Once the community is in ideal-seeking mode, two things happen. The first is that trust develops. The second is that the community develops positive feelings about itself, and it is these positive feelings that lead to community success. This pattern of results is what we would expect from previous studies and ties their findings into a coherent picture of how successful change happens.

This picture confirms the centrality of operating in a participative democratic structure and emphasizes the vital role that emotions play in producing successful communities. Both the workshop and the questionnaire provided

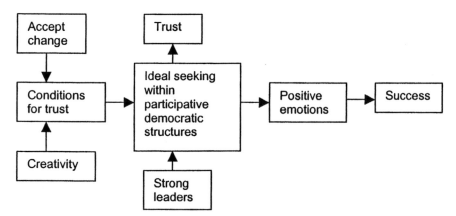

Figure 2.1.   Factors Leading to Positive Emotions and Success.

evidence that when people work together on a desirable future for their communities, they generate excitement and energy. Participants felt more positive at the end of the workshop, after they had planned to overcome their major barriers, than they did at the start. They were more highly motivated to move ahead. People also felt most positive when they were volunteering and had a sense of belonging to their communities. These factors were much more likely to appear when they were working together as equals and could see how to take responsibility and make a difference to their futures.

The study also suggests a simple strategy for rejuvenating communities. The major barrier to success was noticing that others were reluctant to become involved, the problem of dissociation. When young people, in particular, see dissociation as a problem, they are less likely to volunteer. However, once they start talking together about how to overcome this barrier, their mood changes. All that is required is for a few community members to pull others together around a desirable picture of their community, followed up by practical plans to overcome the obstacles they face. Small groups are more effective than public meetings or seminar-type forums with leaders or "experts" up at the front. Once a group has experienced some success with participative processes, others are more likely to become infected with their enthusiasm and volunteer. Volunteering in creative, collective community action is the most powerful way to overcome dissociation (DTRS, 2001).

This review of community development and the characteristics of successful communities has made one thing clear—the features of a successful community are those of a democracy. When communities fall apart, the wider democracy is at risk. Both communities and democracies are dependent on citizens engaging in creative processes to preserve their uniqueness and enhance their quality of life (Megill, 1970). A successful community is a microcosm of a participative democratic state of being.

THE IMPORTANCE OF COMMUNITY
FOR SCHOOL DISTRICTS

As communities are microcosms of democracy, so they are vitally important for the future of schools. According to Washington (2004), it will take a social movement to establish the fundamental connections between national values and education, and while writing specifically of early childhood education, Washington's list of tasks to be accomplished for successful reform are applicable to education more generally. The key task is to build the capacity to engage all age groups and family types through public dialogue and debate, with the purpose of generating shared ownership of the issues. The debates will be rich as a spectrum of people share and collectively make sense of their observations of their lives and of the lives around them.

Debates within the educated elites and the use of the mass media have done a lot to promote debate about reform. Decades of leadership have already created the legacy of opinion leaders being convinced that education is a "social good." The data produced by their efforts have uniformly shown the impacts of parental education on students' life success (chapter 9). Their efforts have produced "a remarkable wave of innovation in social problem solving taking place at the grassroots across the country" (Gardner, 1994). This wave covers just about every aspect of education.

However, as seen in chapter 1, change to the core practices of teaching and learning has been slow. Single-factor efforts to improve school districts have sometimes been successful in improving the single factor focused on, but many of these changes have not met the test of time. While school districts in America have a great deal of autonomy and are therefore subject to heavy pressures from unions, school boards, state legislatures, and the voting public, they have developed strong, protective mechanisms that limit the power of reforms issuing from elsewhere (Gardner, 1991).

In the past, schools have largely found it efficient to operate independently from the rest of society, but this has become extremely problematic. Schools cannot operate in a vacuum today, as many powerful forces for and against learning operate outside of the school context, in the media, in the business sector, and on the streets. Reform must be comprehensive and include all the key factors determining educational practice. To achieve this, it is essential that the community is a partner in change. The community consists of many interests, including respected elders, business people, and officials at all levels but, most important, parents. Only widespread community support for the set of key core reforms can have the momentum to bring these reforms into being (Duffy & Dale, 2001b). If the community fails to support the desires and standards of schools and their staff, the educators are destined to fail (Gardner, 1991).

If Washington's conditions are to be met and schools are to be systemically reformed at their core, people must be able to meet, collectively make sense of their experience, and organize the knowledge into a coherent picture of the desirable future of schools and learning. Only communities contain the diversity of experience required and the power to effectively bring the debates into the open. Once communities have decided for themselves the nature and purpose of their schools, their ownership of the ideas generates the motivation to make the changes. Although some communities have lost the will and the energy to be actively involved in shaping that future, it is not difficult to reengage them.

After insufficient nominations were received for a new board, the Aranda Primary School divided the suburb into 32 neighborhood groups, each of 10 families, and asked one family in each group to host a meeting in their home for no more than 12 to 14 people. A letter was sent to all parents informing them of the project. The board issued guidelines for the host family, who issued a personal invitation. A board member, a member from the Parents and Citizen's Association, and a staff member was allocated to each group. Approximately 70% of families attended a meeting. There was universal support for increased communication between school and parents; parents and teachers continued to meet; and changes were made (Aranda Primary School Board, 1975).

The earlier parents enter a nonthreatening planning process for their school district, the more likely those successes are for both parents and students (Brothers, 2003). Children can make extraordinary progress when they get help from their parents, particularly when working in collaboration with teachers (British Psychological Society, 1986; Thomas, 1985). The participation of mothers in Brazilian schools contributed to personal enhancement, psychological well-being, the acquisition of knowledge and skill, and an expansion of social networks. Poorer and less-educated mothers benefited the most (Dellagnelo, 2000).

Involving a broad cross-section of parents in community and school district planning can overcome some of the misunderstandings and problems encountered in attempts to involve parents in schools. Our traditional views of parental involvement encompass raising money, Parent-Teacher Assocation/ Parent-Teacher Organization, "back to school" nights, volunteering, participating on boards, and attending various activities. As schools have become less hierarchical, less bureaucratic, and less authoritarian, there has been a rash of discussions of participatory governance that call for increased numbers of mechanisms for increased collaboration among parents, schools, and communities. But these activities cannot be done if the family simply does not have the financial resources or literacy to participate (Lopez, 2001). Prior negative experiences in school also often lead parents to avoid these forms of participation. Such parents are therefore seen as not being involved.

However, migrants see involvement differently from the way mainstream United States sees it. "Marginalized groups from immigrant backgrounds are *already* involved in the lives of their children, though they may not be 'involved' in traditionally sanctioned ways" (Lopez, 2001, p. 420). These parents see involvement as teaching their children to appreciate the value of their education through the medium of hard work, which they see as the foundation for success. Schools need to capitalize on these other forms of involvement and take into account those barriers of money and literacy.

The processes outlined in this book do not require literacy and need not involve financial contributions from participants. They include methods such as the community reference system, which is designed specifically to involve all those sections of a community that have been previously marginalized by the unconscious setting of barriers. Parents who feel unable to contribute directly to school affairs because of language or other constraints can set further examples of hard work by working on action plans to improve the infrastructure of their community. In these ways, all sectors of a community can come together around various forms of involvement with the school district. When schools develop an educational vision in concert with the community and when they create a climate of debate about teaching and learning, they can create a "socially just curriculum," even when official policy has given up on the idea (McInerney, 2003, p. 261).

When schools are integrated into their communities, all the boundaries become blurred. For example, students often have the greatest expertise with new technology and can become teachers in the community. "Every community has a wealth of individuals with knowledge, skills, experience, enthusiasm, and other resources to contribute to children's learning" (NFIE, 2000, p. 157). When community members are discovered to have vital skills and knowledge that either the community or the students need, they will almost certainly respond to invitations from their peers or children to contribute, even though they would not ordinarily visit a school or contemplate further formal learning.

These sorts of participative processes operate elsewhere. Freire in South America, for example, worked with those labeled "illiterate" or "ignorant," helping him understand how education and social change affected the poor, who make up the majority of learners. "The failures of our educational system to reach the majority that are not White, upper or middle class can be partly overcome by broadening our understanding of education and learning" (Soler-Gallart, 2000, p. 111). As seen in chapter 9, broadening ideas of schools and learning and involving parents in them has spin-offs for future as well as present generations.

An example of what can be achieved when communities come together around schools is the La Verneda–Sant Marti, a school set up in Barcelona in 1978. It is known as the school where dreams come true. The community came together around the local residents' association and planned a school catering to adult education. They rejected the normal model, which is designed to compensate for what people had missed out on before in their youth. The community explicitly designed a school for its belief that "education is a basic right throughout life" (Aroca, 1999, p. 323). This led them to a school composed of the young and the old where everybody is devoted to the community and its improvement. The school is managed collaboratively by educators and participants who work together within an organizational structure that allows everyone to express their needs, interests, and ideas. Everybody shares in decision making, and learning and creating are the responsibility of all for the benefit of the entire school community. "There is no hierarchy in the school's structure" (p. 320).

Different organizations and communities working together on shared purposes with joint ownership of the change process has proven powerful at producing shared learning in Ireland and the United Kingdom for over 10 years (Lyons, 1998). In South Africa part of the strategies against apartheid was to set up "People's Education for People's Power." One of the principles underlying this strategy was the need to democratize knowledge so that education was accessible to all and relevant to the activities of the people. Education institutions came together with communities to plan and organize. There were democratic discussions with as wide a spectrum of people as possible. One of the programs set up was People's Mathematics (Bopape, n.d.), demonstrating that virtually any subject can be fruitfully worked on by community–education partnerships.

Although examples are abundant throughout the world, the United States has its own outstanding examples of what can be accomplished when communities come together around schools and learning. The Chugach School District (CSD) in Anchorage, Alaska, is an example of whole system change. It is a small rural district with 214 students that went through a process of change that earned it one of the first Baldridge Awards ever given to a public school system. CSD uses a standards-based system and has devised a set of nine goals that cover all aspects of students' learning and community lives.

CSD covers education from preschool up to age 21 in a comprehensive system that occurs 24 hours a day, 7 days a week. Education happens in the workplace, in the community, and in the home as well as in the schools. In addition, CSD runs a Youth Area Watch program for 8th to 12th graders funded by the Exxon Valdez Oil Spill Trustee Council. The program's goals include providing hands-on experiences that enable students to make meaningful contributions to community-based research. This helps increase communication between scientists and the communities affected by the oil spill. Students also undertake long-term monitoring within communities affected by the oil spill. This increases awareness about a variety of ecosystems. CSD has already discovered the importance of integrating ecological and abstract knowledge (discussed in more detail in chapter 8). At regular intervals there are teleconference-based meetings of superintendent and community leaders throughout the district who monitor progress; make changes as required; and promote ethical values, empowerment, innovation, and learning (CSD, 2004). CSD offers a glimpse of the future.

Gardner (1991) saw it as being paradoxical that if there is to be genuine change, it may be necessary not to impose it—but there is no paradox. Imposition always carries a high probability of resistance while homegrown ideas impel people into action. Changes in school districts will come about because those within the district and the community want them to happen, not because of any pressure from outside the system. When community and school district staff share their hopes for and concerns about the future of their children and learning, they will inevitably find common ground. Working together on that common ground can move the school district and its community to a desirable and democratic state for all.

· 3 ·

Preparing for the Total Process and Community Revitalization—Step 1

*I*n this chapter, I look at the preparation required for the overall sequence of events leading to an improved school district and, in particular, to the preparation required for community search conferences and the PDWs to follow. Although school districts are organizations, they belong to their communities, and planning for them involves community events. An initial two-stage process for the future of the community generally means that there will be an active and excited community, anticipating a long process focusing on the future of its children, the school district, and its schools.

It may seem excessive to spend a whole chapter talking about preparation, but an event can be only as good as the preparation that has gone into it. For a long change process, the preparation becomes even more important, as with many diverse parties involved, it is critical that everybody get off to a good and positive start. It is also important because every community is unique, and this uniqueness needs to be captured in the whole design and process. The preparation phase must encompass the normal ways in which the community goes about its business and speaks about itself in its own language while at the same time it is preparing itself to do something that is probably new. The two keys for success here are participation and education.

Every aspect of preparation entails a potential for learning. It is important to remember in this preparation phase that the customer is not always right. Although members of a community know what they want for the future of their community, they may not know the best way to get it. Sometimes what the community asks for may not be the right approach. It may reflect popular myths or the social science fads and fashions of the moment rather than something solid to shape the desirable future the community is hoping for.

As an example, people often complain about communication problems and ask for a method to fix them. Yet communication problems are a secondary phenomenon, a consequence or symptom, not a cause (Emery & Emery, 1976). They spring from the structure of the relationship between people, not from lack of communication skills. The community does not need to address the communication problems, because the participative, democratic structure of the preparation and, later, the search conference will automatically overcome them. Therefore, as many people as possible should be involved in preparatory processes as these help to build a community of learners.

THE TWO-STAGE MODEL AS CONTINUING EDUCATION

Search conferences have been developed for community development (M. Emery, 1974, 1995; Trist & Murray, 1990a, 1990b, 1993; Trist, Emery, & Murray, 1997), and the method has proven appropriate for urban and rural areas and indigenous cultures (Paton & Emery, 1996). They have also been used for community development in many countries, including Canada (de Guerre, 2000), Sweden (Ljungberg van Beinum, 2000), India (De, Goyal, Talbgar, & Paramjit, 1986), and Mexico (Jimenez & Aguirre-Vazquez, 2000).

Although the search conference is specifically designed to make adaptive change, it is also a method for educating about change. Therefore, it serves as a vehicle for adult or continuing education (M. Emery, 1999; Weisbord, 1992; Wright & Morley, 1989). In the search conference, people learn to understand the world in which we live and make choices. The more our choices reflect the ideals, the more we gain insight into and wisdom about those choices (M. Emery, 1999, pp. 99–102). As Schmacher (1973) saw clearly, "more education can help us only if it produces more wisdom" (p. 66).

Participative methods used for organizational restructuring also produce "learning to learn" (Elden, 1983). "New knowledge has to evolve from workers' own definition of the situation and their own way of expressing themselves. This means ordinary people systematically examine their own experience to better understand and control the forces that determine their lives" (p. 226). Everyone needs to participate with a free flow of information throughout the organization (Hamson, 1998). Psychological ownership of any process and its evolving products ensures that there will be decision making based on mutual interests and purposes. The application of "interest-based decision making" to public school labor relations reduced the filing of formal complaints by 70% (Barber, 1998, p. 176). "A work system can become a continuing learning system" (De, 1983, p. 238).

Continuing education is both a set of conditions and a process such that the end product is a person who has learned to learn and hence is able to continue learning. The purpose of this form of continuing education is to identify where radically new learning is required and to create the setting where those who need the new learning are enabled to identify what it is that they need to know. It also helps learners to understand how they can design the conditions for continuing learning to learn into their communities and organizations (F. Emery, 1975).

The process begins with people taking responsibility for their own learning under conditions of mutual support so that a self-sustaining learning community is generated. Then the process of reconstruction or relearning begins. This form of learning makes it quite different from other forms that are more concerned with the transmission of established bodies of knowledge. In the two-stage model, lifelong learning begins to feel familiar and becomes what people do as a matter of course in their lives.

The two-stage model as continuing education emphasizes the importance of the preparation for it, as the preparation introduces many of the concepts participants need later to continue the process. If their plans and designs can later be improved on, the people will redesign them. The children of White Gum Valley who designed their own playground and the many adults who have engaged in this form of planning have demonstrated how the new directions continue to be pursued (Williams & Watkins, 1974). Moreover, "as people identify and begin to pursue directions they find more desirable than the course they are presently on, they can also discover the possibilities for progressively enlarging their aspirations for the future" (Williams, 1982, p. 27).

THE IMPORTANCE OF PREPARATION

The two-stage model comprises three major elements: the preparation, the events, and a long process of implementation to follow. To risk the success of the first round of events in a large and complex process would be to risk the whole process. The major purpose of the preparation is therefore to raise the probability of success of the events and their implementation. It is during the preparation phase that a community or school district begins to generate the interest and excitement about the possibilities of change. The more interest and excitement generated, the more likely it is that the participants in the event will see themselves working on behalf of an enthusiastic community.

COMMUNITY EXPERTISE FOR SUSTAINABILITY

Process managers of the search conference and PDW require some training and experience, and professional expertise will probably be required at other times during the project. The community will be at an advantage if it is at least partly self-sufficient with people who have the concepts and practical know-how to deal with contingencies. School improvement is a never-ending journey, and the district needs to develop future capacity without help from outside (Duffy, 2001). When a community has its own competent trained people who understand how to flexibly apply the relevant concepts and principles, it can face its future with confidence.

Once change is underway, two other types of change will follow. The first is simply that which occurs through evolution as people find ways to improve their arrangements. These gradual, evolutionary changes happen over time. As staff and students move in and out of schools, adjustments will be made on the run. More of a formal process may need to happen at the beginning of the school year, particularly if there is a large intake of new staff who need to be inducted into the principles behind the school's design.

The second type of change consists of puzzles or problems that need to be solved. Once the puzzle or problem has been identified, people with bits and pieces of relevant knowledge need to be identified. Special expertise may be required to design an event so that those identified as having the relevant knowledge can be brought together to solve the puzzle or problem most effectively. Most meetings are not specifically designed to do the job they are expected to do. Merely bringing people together and hoping for the best is not effective.

Each puzzle or problem will be unique and demand something different by way of knowledge and a specially designed event for its solution, even if it is only 2 hours. The concepts and principles discussed in this book allow anybody with basic training to design an effective unique event to meet virtually any contingency (M. Emery, 1999). Although "process manager" is the conventional label for people who do this work, these people also need design skills. Some universities and institutes offer training courses in open systems theory.

THE FIRST SPECIAL MEETING

For a large and complex project such as transforming a school district, the preparation is more important than that for a single search conference and

PDW. It is necessary for the community and all the relevant specific subunits within it, such as the staff of the school district, to understand the whole plan and process and see how the various parts fit together. This is likely to generate significant interest and excitement about the future as people see how the process unfolds to improve the future of their children, school district, and community.

Typically, such an idea springs from a small group of people who talk and involve a few others who collectively help elaborate the original idea until a project begins to take shape. At some point, they approach a possible process manager for a clearer sense of what is involved. Sooner or later, they make a decision to proceed. Many people from different parts of the community and school district are contacted, and tentative plans are firmed up into a viable proposal.

At the point of a definite proposal, it is vital that the project team call a special meeting. The meeting needs to consist of the school and district boards, senior decision makers from the education system and the unions, other interested staff of the school district, and concerned members of the community. "Entire school systems cannot be redesigned unless there is a powerful and productive alliance composed of teacher unions, school district management and school boards" (Duffy & Dale, 2001a, p. 277). These senior members of the school system and unions need to attend this meeting, as only they have the authority to make the decision to change the design principle of their structures. Although all staff and union members will be educated about the change, the decision will be taken at the top (Maccoby, 1976).

At the first meeting of this group, the senior managers and union leaders are joined by concerned community members and staff of the school district. These people should continue to meet as part of this group. They are among the initiators of the project, and their presence reflects the multidimensional, collective and participative nature of it. Their evidence and views about the advantages of a change in design principle, for example (arguably the most consequential decision to be made) are essential to informing that decision. They see issues in the school district from a different perspective, and the project will be the stronger as community views are taken into account. As members of this group, they will learn early on about the ideas and principles behind the project and will be instrumental in educating the community in general, dispelling the rumors than can run like wildfire. They keep the project anchored in the community.

The presentation and content of the proposal to the special meeting needs careful preparation, and the project team and the process managers should jointly run the meeting. The presentation needs to contain an overview of the three components of the change and the steps outlined in chapter 1. It should also introduce the major concepts and principles to be used in the two-stage model and the nature of and steps in the search conference and PDW. This introduction does not need to be long or detailed, just enough to convey the key features so that people understand the essential nature of the process. (They will learn more as the phases of the project unfold, because each phase involves learning.) The project team needs to explain who does the work at each stage and where responsibility is located in the different steps.

This meeting is vital for several reasons. The first is simply that when all major players are involved right from the beginning, there is less likelihood of their mounting active resistance. This project has the potential to touch virtually everybody in the community, so the messages sent out at the start need to reassure people that the changes will be broadly based and participative. When others hear about who attended the meeting, they will realize and become excited about the seriousness of the project and its potential for improvement.

The second reason is that nobody should make a decision to proceed without being totally informed about what the decision entails. It is particularly important for the school district staff. Because changing the design principle has ramifications for pay and conditions within the school district, the decision to proceed with this component of the project should be made after the relevant management and unions have thoroughly examined the proposal and understood its consequences. This meeting is merely to inform these parties that the proposal asks for their consideration.

A third reason is closely related to the second reason—namely, that when a decision is made to proceed, a labor–management agreement needs to be negotiated, often by several parties, if there are multiple unions involved. This can take time as draft changes are circulated and discussed. Chapter 7 deals in detail with the industrial implications of changing the design principle and the necessity of a formal labor–management agreement. If the new arrangements are left informal, without a legal agreement, they will not be sustainable. The process managers will announce at the meeting that they will work with all those involved to ensure that they are completely informed about the change of design principle before a decision to proceed is made. They will also inform the meeting participants that after there is at least an "in principle" agreement, all staff will be briefed about the concepts involved, the likely consequences and outcomes, and the process of doing a PDW. Knowledge of an agreement gives staff some confidence that change will be made.

The fourth reason that the meeting is vital and needs to be held at the proposal stage is to start spreading awareness of the meeting through the community. The community members attending the meeting will carry back understanding of the nature of, and reasons for, the changes taking place in their schools and the community's roles in such changes. As soon as this first meeting is concluded, the project team can embark on preparations for the future of the community.

After the presentation, the meeting should be broken into small groups, each with a mix of the parties present. The task of the groups is to consider the proposal and prepare a set of questions for the project team and process managers. This objective serves two purposes, the first of which is to create relationships between these players. Working together around a task of collective concern is a powerful way to start building trust across the boundaries between subunits within the community. All parties become aware of others' major interests in the proposal and the concerns they may have about them. Building trust involves a shared base of information. If labor relations have been conflicted in the past, it helps management and unions to hear the same things at the same time and to recognize that others have similar or identical concerns. All players gain information about and insight into the project and its possible outcomes, as the project team and process managers answer the questions openly. Openness is a critical factor in success, as seen later in the chapter.

The second reason for using small groups is to illustrate how work is going to be done throughout the process. People find such demonstrations reassuring and convincing.

THE IMPLICATIONS OF THE SPECIAL MEETING

This meeting constitutes a special and powerful group within the school–district–community nexus that forms the foundation of this project. Because some decisions cannot be taken by other than the senior managers and union leaders, it is crucial that they are in touch with developments as they emerge. That means that they meet with other parties at the end of processes such as those for the revitalization of the community and that they also meet at various points within the whole process to make decisions about such matters as changing the design principle underlying the school district's organizational structure.

Normally, this group is given a name such as "strategic leadership team" (SLT; Duffy, Rogerson, & Blick, 2000, p. 6), but it is important to understand what it does and does not take responsibility for. It does not take responsibility for the first phase of the project, covering the revitalization of the community, as that responsibility rests with the community. Neither are the school district–based members of the group involved in that work. At that time, they are engaged in learning about the design principles and their consequences, together with the unions, before considering a decision to change the school district's design principle. Some members of this group may be involved during the planning phase for the school district, as may some of the community members.

The SLT is a major player, however, in the redesign phase. Although some members of the SLT have the power to decide to move to the second design principle, which produces participative democratic structures, neither they nor the SLT determine the detailed shape of those structures. The people who have to live and work with these new structures and their consequences design them just as the community determines its own desirable future.

The original project team that called the meeting can become members of the SLT after the first meeting, when the project is outlined for consideration. Over time the membership of the SLT and that of various subgroups within it will change, and, as its membership can be quite large, it can be used flexibly with different people taking different roles at different stages of the project.

At the end of the meeting, a date needs to be set for a reconvention. Rather than have the project team or organizing group meet separately with all parties, it is more productive to keep them talking and working together. All future meetings of the SLT need to be open and group based so that they mirror the processes used in the project and continue to produce trust. The SLT needs to be dynamic and flexible, which means that it must be a self-managing group in its own right. The more open its processes, the closer its relationships to the broader constituencies and the trust it generates in them. At the end of this first meeting, the project team discusses the community reference system that it is intending to use to involve the community in its future.

THE COMMUNITY REFERENCE SYSTEM

The community reference system (CRS) is the method used in the two-stage model to guarantee that the community selects its own participants.[1] It accelerates community processes that generate interest and knowledge and that build community spirit and cohesion. As the name implies, community members name or refer to other members whom they consider as being appropriate participants according to a set of criteria that the community has decided is desirable.

Using the CRS to select participants has advantages over other methods. When a community has made the commitment to have a search conference, it is seen as a major and formative event in the life and future of that community. Everybody will want to be there. The worst thing that could happen before the event would be the generation of bad feeling in the community if people had to lobby or fight to attend.

If a process of selection is used that is not totally open, the community will be suspicious rather than trustful. This is particularly the case in communities who have experienced bad feelings in the past or where factions within the community are fighting about an issue. It is not at all uncommon as people gather in the first session of the search to be asked how a particular person got there or why a particularly prominent community member isn't attending. The person or group who administered the CRS must be prepared for this questioning and have the records available for perusal.

In 1974, Fred Emery and I designed the CRS for a search conference in Geelong, a community in Victoria, Australia, which was experiencing community conflict because of a controversial proposal for a new road and traffic system. As the proposal stood at the time, a major freeway would split the town, and over 1,000 houses would be lost. Therefore, one of the major reasons for the design of the new method was to make sure that people attended strictly as members of the total community, not as representatives of any interest group or sector of the community. Search conference participants are not representatives; they come simply as themselves (M. Emery, 1999).

Since that time, the CRS has proved its worth, and many have experimented with it, improving its versatility in the process. Some variations on the theme are documented here. The basic steps are as follows:

1. Members of the community collectively draw a rough social map of the community. A simple example is shown in Figure 3.1, which shows

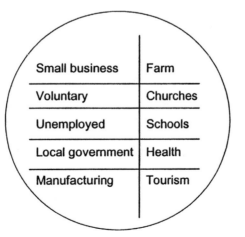

Figure 3.1.   A Simple Social Map.

a community consisting of a range of sectors—fishing or farming, small business, large business, unemployed people, schools, churches, voluntary organizations, or whatever exists within that community.

The map is a guide to the range of knowledge that must end up in the search. Participants are present because of the knowledge they can contribute, not because of who they are. In addition to each of the sectors of the social map, there must also be a full range of the demographic factors that exist within the community. If the community is a multicultural one, there must be knowledge of what it means to be each of the major ethnic groups. Old and young, rich and poor, men and women must be present among the participants. This is easy to accomplish, as people come wearing many hats. An older indigenous man may be a fisherman who also helps guide tourists during the summer.

2. The group must then decide on the relevant criteria against which community members are to be judged. One criterion always applies, namely, that the person has been active and concerned about the community and its future. The others will be those that the organizing group considers most relevant to the task. Some communities decide on 5 years' experience in the community or that the person intends to remain in the community for the next few years. Others will judge people having creative ideas as being more important. There are usually only three or four criteria at the most. However, some communities have been happy just to work with the universal one of being active and concerned.

3. The next task is to choose one person who fits the criteria from each of about 6 to 10 major sectors of the social map. The person chosen is known as the "starting-point person." Examples have included a generous benefactor from the construction industry, a prominent church leader, and a well-known volunteer. It is important to note that these people have not been invited to the search. They simply get the process started. Invitations are issued when the process is complete.

4. Each of the starting-point people is asked for the names of two or three people in the community who fit the criteria. Then each of those named is asked for the names of two or three people who fit the criteria. If, say, there were 10 starting points and each person gave three names, the list of names at this point would number 90, minus repetitions. The list builds up quickly. Even in a large complex community, about three or four iterations of this naming process should be adequate. As the list grows, people note that community members are being recommended from across different sectors of the map. For

example, a church person may have named three people, one each from the small business, farming, and voluntary sectors.

5. When the list is considered adequate, it is scrutinized carefully. Quite a few names are mentioned several times whereas others are mentioned only once or twice. The list takes the shape of a normal curve. Those people who are mentioned many times are automatically put on the invitation list, and others with two or three mentions are added in to make up the numbers required. The list is checked to ensure that all sectors of the map are covered. If a sector is missing, a person from that sector should be substituted for a name from a well-covered sector. The same applies to demographics. All ethnic minorities should be present as well as a mix of rich and poor, young and old, male and female. The list should not be biased. When those working on the list are satisfied with it, they can prepare the invitations.

Please note that we have not mentioned the education or literacy levels of the participants. These factors are not relevant in a community search. Nor in a community search is there a need for "experts" or people with specialized knowledge. All participants are experts in their own right. They collectively know more about their community than any "expert." Similarly, the list does not need to include elected representatives of local government. If it does include them, they also attend just as themselves.

VARIATIONS ON THE CRS

Since the invention of the CRS, it has evolved into a fast and large group method. An initial meeting is held with one or more community members and with the process managers where the CRS is explained; a draft social map is drawn; and some starting point people are named. To a second meeting come the original community members and the named starting-point people. The original community members explain the search and CRS to the new members, show them the draft social map and criteria, and invite more names. This process is continued; the map is improved; and more names are added until there is a sufficient pool of names available for the community to make the selection.

These rolling group-based methods have advantages, because, at the meetings, people have to discuss the whole proposal, its purposes, the major ideas involved, and the draft design of the event. This means that a large group within the community becomes rapidly aware of the idea, understands its foundations, and can explain it to others they meet. This generates interest and excitement quickly because it is so obviously an open, community-owned process. Although the process managers are present, community members manage the meetings while others do the briefings, lending a flavor of the community's uniqueness. This strengthens community ownership and generates trust.

PITFALLS IN USING THE CRS

Using the CRS is fairly simple, and there really are not too many things that can go wrong. The rolling group processes overcome most possible pitfalls, which in the past have been caused by not involving sufficient people. There are one or two examples of mistakes, but perhaps the most important preventative measure is to leave the administration of the CRS in the hands of a group rather than a single person. A single person can have competing demands on his or her time and take shortcuts. These may compromise the integrity of the method and introduce biases. In one example, the person ran out of time to develop the list fully and rang up her friends at the last minute. In another example, the process managers involved in the original meeting with a group within a local government authority forgot to mention that all communications with potential participants must be personal. Therefore, the administrators used their normal process of sending letters through the mail. Most citizens simply throw such letters in the bin and, as was to be expected, the response rate was close to zero.

When people are contacted face-to-face, the response rate is 80% to 90%. For phone contacts, the response rate is 60% to 70%, and for written, it is 30% (Davies, 1983). People are also more influenced by face-to-face contacts and inevitably are drawn into making meaning out of the conversation that takes place.

The pitfalls in using the CRS include the following:

- Having an inadequate social map because not enough people have been involved in the process of drawing it up. For example, a particular social group may be unaware of sectors of a large city.
- Leaving the process in the care of an individual rather than a group. When more than one person is taking responsibility for the overall outcome of the process, many checks and balances must be built in.
- Not leaving sufficient time to administer the process properly. The date should be about the last detail decided.

- Not having community-based criteria to use as a basis for selection.
- Substituting personal contacts for community-selected names.
- Assuming the processes used in a search are the same as those used in normal business.
- Not using personal contact at all times. For example, the telephone is adequate for an introduction but must be followed up face-to-face.

DECIDING ON THE NAME

Deciding on the name of the event is simple: the search conference is about the future of the community, and it is the community that is in the dotted circle (see Figure 1.1). The name of the event is just the "Future of Our Community." If the project is on the future of the school district, then the school district is in the dotted circle, and the name is the "Future of Our School District." Although many issues and concerns about the community are raised in preplanning meetings and are dealt with in the search, this does not mean that the name must express the key issues.

THE COMMUNITY EDUCATES ITSELF

Because the search conference differs from other processes, participants need to understand the basic ideas that lie behind it. Participants may also need to do some research if they find gaps in their knowledge during the preparation. Large communities may also need to train some of their members as designers and process managers to cover the number of events required within a reasonable time.

Learning About Concepts, Method, and Design

Some community members begin their learning about the search and PDW as soon as they become involved in discussion with the process managers. Other participants need to understand the underpinnings of the search conference and PDW and why they will not be doing other things that may be more familiar. They need to understand the design of the event and the ordering of the steps. If they use the rolling CRS process, they may need only a final briefing to ensure common understanding.

In general, more education is better than less. If there is any doubt about whether a piece of the educative material should be included, it is better to include it than to leave it out. Participants need to understand at least the following major concepts and principles:

- *The open system itself and its four components of system, environment, learning, and planning* (chapter 1). Participants then understand the reason for doing the first phase of the search conference, which explores and makes sense of the global social environment. They also see the logic behind the overall design of the search conference as it turns the four components of the open system into a process.

- *The organizational design principles* (chapter 5). When participants grasp these principles, they understand why they take responsibility for the content of the work and its implementation and why the process managers stay out of the content. Use of these principles distinguishes this method from other methods, where participants are chosen from "stakeholders" who may or may not be able to take responsibility for the outcome. Participants also see the logic behind the large- and small-group work and the way in which tasks are set. They see why the search (chapter 4) must be followed by a modified PDW (chapter 5) in which they design an effective organization through which to implement the action plans.

- *The conditions for effective or influential communication* (chapter 2). When these conditions are explained, participants understand the importance of openness in all matters and the reason for not allowing individual writing pads and individual note taking. Participants then also understand the importance of doing a "Most Desirable Future for the World," as this session shows them that they share a common world. This session also reassures them all that they are all equally human, sharing the same concerns as expressed through the four ideals (chapter 2). They come to see that all these conditions are essential for the gradual buildup of trust that occurs throughout the process.

- *Ecological learning* (chapter 8). Participants need to understand that they have all accumulated, from their experience and perceptions, a mass of unconscious knowledge about the way the world works. They begin to realize that they all make the same sort of sense out of it and can have confidence in using it at any time. This concept is even more important for projects for school districts than usual because it is a plank in improving classroom practices.

- *Rationalization of conflict* (chapter 4). This concept must be explained so that the participants are not fearful about conflicts that may develop during the event. They will understand that it is safe to express differences of perception and opinion and to argue strongly for them and that, in fact, it is inevitable with about 30 people that such differences will exist. Both the concept and the process of using the rationalization of conflict should be emphasized, including the fact that it is used from the very beginning of the process. This increases their confidence to participate.

Other concepts may be included here depending on the interest shown by the community. It should go without saying that the educational process will be more effective the more it becomes a participative and practically oriented discussion of the ideas and how they will be used.

The Design and Management of the Event

As mentioned, members of large communities may need to be trained to be process managers, as there will be many events and integration of their results. If community people are interested in getting expertise in design and management, the professionals can train them and take them on as apprentices in the first round of events to gain the necessary experience. This would appear to be the solution for large school districts such as Tucson Unified School District, which has 115 schools. Basing the process on each school means that the process will take over a year if only one or two professional managers run two search conferences and PDWs a week. This creates far too long a gap between the first and the last school. Ideally, as many of these two-stage events as possible will be held at the same time or with a short spread of time so that integration can begin shortly after the last two-stage event happens. Too long a gap results in some schools starting implementation before integration, whereas others may get discouraged waiting around to start the change process. Both these options should be avoided at all cost.

Large communities can be broken into smaller units, and although it is not desirable for community members to manage the process in their small unit, it would be perfectly feasible for them to work in others. The newly trained community members can call on the professionals for help if tricky issues or problems arise. This solution gives the best of all worlds and has the further advantage that the communities are left with a resource of trained and experienced process managers available for future work.

It is important to involve the community in the design of the event. Members have expert knowledge of their unique community, and the process managers engage them in a broad discussion of what is required in the design, the nonnegotiable components and options that need a collective decision.

In general, the design of community searches is relatively simple, but even the most simple of searches can present challenges, and design work should not be rushed. Giving people time to think between meetings of the community and process managers help ensure that the design fits the community's hopes and purposes while remaining as simple, elegant, and manageable as possible.

Research

There may be a need for some research before a community search if people become aware that they have questions they cannot answer. Because every community is different, no exact recipe exists for how to proceed, but some common examples can illustrate options. In many small communities, jobs are being lost and teenagers are leaving town. The community knows that new industries must be brought in if it is to escape becoming a ghost town. What possible industries may be suitable? The answer to this question is finally decided in the search conference, but a task force can be chosen beforehand to research some possibilities that can be put to the broader membership in a special meeting before the search. Other communities have been faced with conflicts between moving toward environmental sustainability and imminent development. Research may need to be done on water quality in the river, the sustainability of local ecosystems, or the economic benefits/costs of the proposed developments. Sometimes a book has been written about the early history of a community. It could be useful for the history session if a few community members read this book before the search.

If all members need to have information for a search, it should be presented and considered before the event. Introducing new information during the process of the search disrupts the flow and momentum of the work and can create dependency. Material sent through the mail is often not read, and if it is, it is often not fully appreciated. It is far more effective to present the material and follow it by group discussion in a meeting held shortly before the search. The meeting need not be long but guarantee that all participants understand the material and start to see its implications for the community.

NUMBER OF PARTICIPANTS

Communities often expect that many people will be reluctant to devote 2 days and 2 nights to a community event. This is rarely the case. By far the most common experience is that everybody wants to be there. However, large numbers are not necessary in any given event, as the search conference is merely a step in a widespread process that eventually involves everybody who wants to be involved. The CRS ensures knowledge about every part of the community is present in the search and even in larger communities; this knowledge is covered when there are about 30 participants.

A good size is about 25 to 35 people. Below 20, the event takes on more of a small-group nature and may lose some of its task orientation. There may also not be a sufficient critical mass of people to generate a range of ideas, together with the enthusiastic discussion of them that produces energy and creativity.

With more than about 35 participants, time becomes a critical dimension. There are trade-offs between the number of people in a small group, the number of groups, and the time available. The more small groups, the more reporting time. There are also logistical problems in trying to integrate the work of many groups. To avoid running out of time or unnecessarily rushing participants, it is both safer and more productive to limit participants to a reasonable number. The quality of the work is higher and more satisfying within the range of 25 to 35 people. Large communities can be split using, preferably, a series of searches followed by an "integration event" (chapter 4).

DECIDING ON A TIME FRAME

Because everything about a search conference is concrete and practical, it is important to have an agreed date for the time horizon of strategic goals. These goals are called strategic because they are long term and imply the need for a strategy, the original meaning of which was the art of maneuvering. This means flexibility of approach while still aiming for the long-term goal. Time frames must be long enough, therefore, to allow this maneuvering in the approach to the goal. Once the time frame is decided, the scenarios at the global and community levels use the same year, so work flows more usefully from one level to another.

One of the major tasks in the first phase of the search conference is to project a most probable future for the global social environment: the world. It is by definition impossible to assign a probability to a trend for an unknown year. So it is just common sense to choose a year in the future that is conceivable by participants and makes sense in terms of the nature of the work to be done.

In the 1970s, normal time frames were about 30 years. Today nobody can conceive of such a time frame, as the rate of social change has been too fast. Nobody is prepared to even guess what the world will look like in 30 years. So as the rate of change has increased, so have time frames shortened. Today, most time frames for communities are about 3 to 5 years. The question needs to be discussed in the community. When it comes to setting a time frame for the school district (chapter 6), other factors may need to be taken into account. In industries, for example, where there is a high rate of technological change (such as in the telecommunications or computer industries), time frames are closer to 2 years than to 10. In school districts that change relatively slow, the time frame may reflect judgments regarding the difficulty of the tasks involved.

DECIDING ON A DATE FOR THE SEARCH

From the discussion here of all the various possible items that need to be taken into account, it becomes clear that the preparation phase can be variable in length. This means that just about the last thing decided on is the date of the search conference. Unfortunately, it is often the first thing that people consider. This carries the danger that they struggle to fit everything into the time available. If they encounter difficulties in the preparation, they may go into the event underprepared. If the CRS has been finalized too quickly without all the necessary checks, the wrong people may be there. Or if participants are not fully briefed and well informed about the nature of the event and the work to be done, they may have serious misunderstandings about what they are there to do.

It is far safer to do all the preparation without rushing and with a sense of adventure and fun so that those involved have a chance to really enjoy the process. Approaching the preparation from this standpoint means that people begin to anticipate the event not only as a turning point in the life of the community but also as a joyful experience for all. When everyone is confident that all the pieces are in place, the date can be safely chosen to suit the maximum number of possible participants.

DECIDING ON A VENUE

By far the best venues are those removed from the everyday concerns of the participants: social islands. The work that people do in a search conference is so different from what they normally do in their offices and homes. Searches are designed for working creatively. For prolonged creative work, busy offices simply have too many distractions with such things as phones or colleagues dropping in. However, the venue need only provide the conditions of space and freedom that support the work to be done and the people doing it. As the search conference participants become welded into a temporary community during the event, being a residential community helps this process along.

However, in today's world of busy people and in communities that are not particularly affluent, compromises will be demanded. The residential requirement can be dropped. It is not at all unusual for the search to be held in the local community hall with participants bringing a dish to share for lunch and dinner. Or, other members of the community may volunteer to organize food. This has the advantage of more members feeling involved in the event as it unfolds, seeing and hearing some of the action as it takes place and keeping the rest of the community up to date with progress.

The disadvantage of dropping the residential requirement is that it becomes difficult to fit in the learning that takes place during the more relaxed, informal, and social time at night as people congregate around the bar for a drink and a chat before bed. Participants have reported that this time provided them with additional insights into the work that fired up creative new ideas for the next day.

Venues do not need to have smaller rooms for breakout groups. A room large enough to accommodate several small groups allows them to communicate easily, sharing information when required. This helps to generate a sense of community. Practitioners learned early in the process of developing the search conference that it is risky to leave small groups together for too long and certainly when they were working in different rooms. The groups took on lives of their own rather than being merely temporary scaffolds for the real work, that of the community as a whole.

One of the major requirements of a venue is that it has plenty of wall space on which to hang the flip charts. Some of the more memorable moments in searches have come as participants realized the room was getting darker and darker as we gradually papered over the huge windows. Similarly, the difficulties of attempting to hang paper from prickle bushes makes one value solid walls. However, successful searches have been held under these conditions and, the whole question of suitable venues is a minor one compared with other more powerful factors, such as the quality of design and management.

Along with venue goes the question of equipment. Keep this simple, too. The requirements are minimal: flip charts, thick felt pens, and masking tape. Make sure there is plenty of everything. Tables are not required. Fancy electronic equipment is not necessary and can detract from the community-building process. Individual writing pads are not allowed. People from oral cultures do not need paper for reporting, as they have retained their excellent memories. Process managers may need it though. This partly explains why it is not necessary for participants to be well educated or literate.

One of the underlying purposes of the search conference is to revive the tradition of the oral culture, which depends on spoken language for its power to bring people together (Ong, 1967). Not everybody in a group needs to be able to write; in fact, there have been searches where participants simply told the process managers what their decisions were, and the managers wrote them up. Similarly, if there are language problems, translators can be used. The critical elements are that people talk and work together using their firsthand knowledge of living in the community. It is this firsthand knowledge that makes the history session so powerful.

THE IMPORTANCE OF OPENNESS DURING PREPARATION

All the essential decisions regarding the design, management, and logistics of the search are made during the preparation phase. It is a vitally important phase for this reason alone. However, it serves another purpose as well, that of building one of the foundations of effective communication: openness.

Everyone must be convinced that he or she in a process that is open in every aspect, that it is what it appears to be (M. Emery, 1999). Openness is one of the four conditions for effective or influential communication first outlined by Asch (1952). The other three are those of acknowledging each other as human, being able to see that everybody lives in the same world, and the gradual generation of trust within the community. The first three contribute to the development of trust (chapter 2). I discuss in the next chapter how these arise during the search. However, openness is distinguished by its necessity from the very beginning of the preparation phase.

Searching is, by its nature, a highly explorative process in which it is inevitable that differences in perception and opinion will be present. People risk exploring only when they are sure that the climate is open and can support their efforts. Should obstacles to openness be discovered during the preparation phase, people back off, reducing the tentative levels of trust they have been developing.

There must be openness in all things. Organizers and managers must be open about their roles, their desires, and their expectations for the event. They must come across as people open to questioning from others. All information about the search, its process and design, must be open. All records kept, such as those about the selection of participants, must be open to inspection. Any records of meetings made at the time should be made on flip charts so that participants know that the records accurately reflect the content of the meeting. Even if they are typed up later, participants must be able to check the typescripts with the originals.

Within the search and PDW, all work done, whether in small groups or the community, is recorded on flip charts. Personal writing pads are not allowed. Making personal notes is a guaranteed way of inducing distrust, as was noticed during the very first search conference in 1959 (Trist & Emery, 1960). Flip charts have the unique characteristic of not being able to be easily changed without somebody noticing. In other words, it is very difficult to "fiddle the data."

Although new technology may appear attractive, it can have damaging consequences. Flip charts are put up on the wall for all to see as their shared community product. The room is gradually decorated by it, taking on the feel of a unique community home. In contrast, computerized white boards reduce a community's work to a small sheet of paper that is then photocopied to become the property of each individual. Rather than small groups standing around a record on the wall, each individual consults their own piece of paper. The sense of sharing and community ownership is lost. In some communities where dissociation is rife and people have lost their sense of community responsibility (Putnam, 2000), the white board compounds the problem rather than helps solve it.

The greater the degree of openness developed through the preparation stage, the greater the trust participants will have during the search and PDW. The more they trust each other, the more prepared they will be to participate fully during the event, thus creating an upward spiral of open communications, trust, and the exciting creative work that flows from these conditions.

NOTE

1. This system is not appropriate as a selection device for people in an organizational search conference. For methods of selection in the case of organizations, consult M. Emery (1999, pp. 188–189).

• 4 •

Revitalizing the Community—Step 2

$\mathcal{I}$n this chapter I look at the sequence of events that bring the community together so that it is active and enthusiastic about change in its school district. The sequence of events includes

- A search conference to the point where a most desirable community is outlined in terms of a set of strategic goals
- An integration event where all the sets of strategic goals are combined into a final list for the community
- A resumption of the searches to deal with constraints and to do action plans
- A PDW where the community organizes to implement the plans effectively (this step is discussed in chapter 5)

The design of the total process covers the events in the process and the steps in the content of the work that participants do within these events. As the purpose of the search is to produce a self-managing learning, planning community, it is important that every aspect of the work that participants do be included in such a way that the learning done flows from the previous steps and builds on them. At the same time, diverse people must come together and cohere into a community that continues to generate its own self-confidence and well-being. The essential personality or culture of the community is grasped as the diverse individuals discuss their views and reach common ground in each of the steps. The search conference revolves around three relationships, and of these, the relationship of participants to the task is central.

The total process design differs depending on the size of the community and the way it is split into areas or neighborhoods. The steps in the process and the ways in which they are managed can be the same for all communities, but in large school districts, the numbers mean a more complex series of events overall. To illustrate the differences, I use the diverse examples of the school districts of Commerce City in Georgia, Huntingdon Area in Pennsylvania, and Tucson Unified in Arizona.

The second major relationship within the search is between participants and process managers, while the third is participant to participant. These relationships are determined by the nature of the process management, how the managers handle each session. While it is fine to talk about producing a democratic and vibrant community, it takes conceptual knowledge of and experience with the management of democratic structures to actually bring one into being. If the necessary conditions for democratic function are not in place, the result is more likely to be laissez-faire and unhappy outcomes rather than true democracy. I discuss the features that the managers must build into the event.

In general, revitalizing a community involves one of three approaches: a single search conference, a multisearch, or a series of searches.

A SINGLE SEARCH

A single search has obvious advantages in terms of ease of organization, time involved, and cost. Although single searches have been successful in communities of about 20,000 to 30,000, they are not ideal, as the ratio of search conference members to community is small. A single search is, however, the perfect answer for Commerce City.

THE MULTISEARCH

The first multisearch was the product of necessity. A "talking heads" conference had been planned as a 5-day event for 120 young "opinion leaders," but 3 days before the conference, the organizers decided it was not going to work. "How does one enlist and direct the energies of 120 combustible prima donnas for five days and live to tell the tale?" (Crombie in Henry & Thompson, 1980, p. 25). The young leaders needed to be energized by a flexible, participative event in which they could plan for and be committed to their own pictures of a desirable future for Australia. A handful of experienced search conference designers and managers flew to Melbourne, and there we designed this last-minute attempt.

As the name implies, a multisearch incorporates several searches working in parallel to the point where they have completed their sets of strategic goals. People from all parallel searches come together to share their strategic goals, integrate them, and organize themselves into action planning groups around the integrated set of goals.

This first multisearch had many problems (M. Emery, 1992a), but "it was a hit. There was intense dialogue across the usual social and political divides . . . and they went away sensing a curious kind of bonding" (Watson, 1991, in M. Emery, 1992a, p. 95). This gave us hope that we could overcome the problems so many other diverse multisearches followed. However, despite our best efforts, the main problems of coordinating search streams and their managers remained, and many multisearches, such as Workplace Australia (Thomson & Nash, 1991), caused more disappointment than joy.

Today, I do not use multisearches. They are like the little girl in the old nursery rhyme who "when she was good, she was very, very good, and when she was bad, she was horrid." Too many things can go wrong with multisearches, and the risks are too great. Avoid them. There is an alternative.

A SERIES OF SEARCHES WITH INTEGRATION

A series of searches with an integration event at the end of the series serves the same purposes and achieves the same ends as the multisearch but has several advantages and fewer disadvantages. The number of individual searches depends on the appropriate number of subunits within the whole. The whole may be a large geographical community as, for example, Tucson.

The critical factor to note when designing a series of searches is that each search takes the whole as its focus, where the whole is the purpose of the search—for example, "The Future of Tucson," not "The Future of Our Neighborhood." Each search follows the same steps.

The searches are run as normal but only to the point of achieving a set of strategic goals. The reason is that it is impossible to integrate action plans. They are by their very nature unique to the people implementing them in their own circumstances. When all subunits have their set of goals, these are taken to the integration event by a selection of the people at each of the single searches. The number to be selected will have been decided at the preparation stage. The purpose of those attending is to integrate the sets of strategic goals into one comprehensive list that includes all, but contains no, redundancies. These are then the goals for the whole community.

At the integration event, the people from each search put their set of goals up on the wall and read them out. Once all sets are up, there will be some questions for clarification and some discussion. The integration process then proceeds as it does within a single search, with the total group participating in putting together items that are the same in meaning or where one item is found to be a subset of another. There is no rationalization of conflict, as all sets of goals are the valid result of the work of the subunit that came up with them.

Another advantage of the series format is that once the integration is complete, all goals can be assigned to the unit that has responsibility for them. Using the example of a school district, most goals will be the responsibility of all schools in the district. Some will be the responsibility of the school district office or board whereas some will be unique to a particular school. That individual school then accepts that responsibility. The richness and diversity of the whole is captured; nothing is lost; and each subunit retains its individuality. Everybody is clear about where responsibility lies for a particular item so that nothing can fall through the cracks, leaving a gap in the overall plan.

Many situations have demanded a series of search conferences, and there has been considerable experimentation with how best to integrate the results. A series of six searches in Fremantle, Western Australia, culminated in the redesign of the city to host the America's Cup. These conferences energized the city with guidelines for redevelopment that included access to the river for all, provision of lower-cost housing, preservation of historic areas, and limitation of the height of buildings to retain their essential character.

About the same time the Chamber of Commerce in Hobart, the capital of the state of Tasmania, Australia, ran a series of 16 searches. This series of searches revitalized these neighborhoods, but the full value of them was not realized by the city council. Neither of these examples used a formal integration process. Neither did a long series of searches with the leisure clubs in New South Wales (M. Emery, 1995). There is no doubt that this was one of the main reasons for the only partial success of the latter two examples. Without integration, no critical mass of energy develops around a central theme, leaving each of the individual subunits to manage on its own.

Davies (1981, 1992) used a series both for a union and for statewide aged services. In the union, he tried a cascading approach where the results of previous events at branch level were progressively fed into the next event, building a richer, cumulative picture over time. This worked well but tends to become awkward over a long series. In the Torres Strait Island, there was a series of five successful island- and community-based searches (Paton & Emery, 1996). The series culminated in a search for the region—that is, Torres Strait Islands—but here, although the accumulated energy generated by the first set of community searches influenced the regional search, the results did not directly feed into it.

The advantages of a formal, planned integration were illustrated by the series of searches for the eastern region of the U.S. Forest Service. At the time there were 14 national forests with a regional office. Searches were held in 13 of the forests, including one for the regional office. Each had an identical design, focusing on the region so that results from each in the series could be easily integrated to form a picture of the region as a whole. The 13 sets of strategic goals, one from each search, were taken to an integration event where they were rigorously discussed and finally integrated into a set of strategic goals for the whole. In addition, the accumulated data were used to obtain a quantitative picture of the reality and meaning of the region for the people who work there (Alvarez & Emery, 2000).

This example from the United States will be used as the model for the community examples described here, without the final step of quantifying the results. I apply the major lessons learned from the design of the series and its integration.

STEPS IN THE SEARCH CONFERENCE

The next step is to think carefully and decide about the tasks that the community needs to do while in the search conference, the learning it must share and build into its plan for the future. In chapter 1, I illustrated the funnel shape of the search conference and the irreducible minimum number of steps in the three phases of the search:

- Learning about the social environment
- Learning about the system
- Integrating those learnings into action plans so that the system remains active and adaptive as its social environment continues to change over time

Community searches are usually quite simple with the minimum number of steps. They consist entirely of volunteers, in contrast to organizational searches whose complications are discussed in chapter 6, where I focus directly on the school district.

The minimum steps in the search conference process then consists of

- Changes in the world around us, compiling the data
- Most probable and most desirable worlds
- Where we have come from, the history session

- Analysis of our community at the moment
- The most desirable future of our community, strategic goals
- Constraints and dealing with them
- Most desirable and achievable strategic goals
- Action plans

The diversity of the three examples has no effect on this aspect of design, so each has the same steps.

A search conference usually starts in the middle to late afternoon for the good reason that people are better prepared for relaxed, creative work later in the day (M. Emery, 1999). This gives time for a welcome to the event, a final prebriefing followed by an "expectations session" as well as some social time over drinks and dinner. The content work starts after dinner.

An expectations session is essential. It serves two major purposes. First, it lets participants get to know each other in a nonthreatening setting. People introducing themselves around a circle is not a satisfactory way of getting to know somebody. Some people find it intimidating and intrusive. It is far more effective and comfortable for people to sit around in small groups, getting to know each other as they discuss and write up their expectations of the event. It is better to have everybody knowing a few people reasonably well than most forgetting names and knowing few. Small groups generate confidence.

The full instructions for the expectations session are for the group members to introduce themselves, discuss their expectations, and write them up on the flip chart. The reporter introduces the members to other groups and reports the expectations. To facilitate this process, people are assigned to groups randomly.

The second reason for the expectations session is that, despite the prebriefings, some people may have misunderstood the nature of the event or what it can be expected to achieve. If these misapprehensions are left unsaid, they are sure to surface some time during the process. In the experience of many search conference managers, they often surface at the most critical parts of the process, when they can be most destructive. This is to be avoided at all costs. If there are such misconceptions, the process managers need to correct them immediately. The expectations session need only last about 45 minutes in all, but it is invaluable.

The expectations session is followed by drinks and dinner so that participants can socialize with new acquaintances. Informal meals such as buffets are preferable, as people can circulate. If the participants are bringing and sharing food and drinks, they will organize the meal in the style normal for their community.

Changes in the World Around Us

Work proper starts after dinner. It is important to maintain the easy, informal atmosphere developed over dinner, as the participants are engaging on a task they have probably never attempted before. It is not commonplace for people to work at the level of the global social environment—the world—so a nonthreatening setting is crucial. Getting to grips with the social environment and working out how to respond to its changes and challenges will determine the survivability of public education (Snyder, 2001). The community needs to understand the social environment not only for its own health but also for that of the school district. In the next stage of this project, the community and school district jointly face the pressures that the social environment is exerting on school districts.

To get to grips with what will be happening in the world in the future, it is necessary to compile a comprehensive database of what has happened over the last few years. Participants are asked to contribute what they have seen happen around the world over the last 5 to 7 years. Because this is not an everyday task, much of this knowledge, which has been directly extracted from perception, is originally unconscious or tacit knowledge (Polanyi, 1969). However, it is easily brought to consciousness.

The ground rule for the first session is that "all perceptions are valid" (M. Emery, 1999, p. 189). Managers simply write up these perceptions of changes in the world as they are said in the total community. The ground rule confirms that all participants are equals, with nobody able to contradict the perceptions of another. If a participant has observed an opposite phenomenon to another, it too is written up. Gradually, even people who may not be particularly self-confident will see that it is safe to join in by contributing their perceptions.

Later, when groups attribute the same sorts of significance to the same changes, grouping them in similar ways and building similar scenarios of where the social environment is headed, participants enjoy confidence in their abilities to know their world and begin to deal with it. The process has the effect of bringing into being a community of peers, learners, confident in their collective ability to make desirable changes.

Managers let this session run until the process slows down. They may prompt in certain areas to make sure the database is comprehensive without big gaps, such as family, workplace, or environmental changes around the world. The session usually takes between 45 minutes and an hour.

Most Desirable and Most Probable Worlds

Depending on numbers, managers divide the community into groups, again at random. Given that these community searches have about 30 to 35 participants, four groups is appropriate. Managers may assign the task of deciding on the most probable future of the world to two groups who work in parallel and the task of deciding on the most desirable future of the world to another two groups. This grouping has the advantage of providing an early opportunity to establish the rationalization of conflict as the normal way of approaching differences. This again reassures the community that the process is safe and that individuality is protected while all can contribute enthusiastically and creatively to the task.

The tasks for the two groups need to be clearly spelled out by the managers. The task for the groups looking at the most probable future of the world is to examine the data and decide what the world will most probably look like in 5 years if nobody does anything differently between now and then. Some changes or trends will appear strong and growing, merging with others to produce large, powerful trends, such as an aging population or the growing gap between the haves and have-nots. These two dimensions taken together are already fueling other major changes—in health care, for example.

The trick for participants is to read through the data and see what is coming through in terms of the human values that are driving the future. In other words, the most probable future is a linear projection of the most powerful value changes in last few years. It is sometimes forgotten that even technological change is a result of people's decisions. This is shown by the fact that many technological innovations fail in the marketplace every year. They are those with uses, outcomes, or consequences that people simply did not value.

Because these scenarios are built on changes that emerge from trends running through the data, participants are warned not to set their headings or categories before carefully examining the data. The parameters that emerge as the most powerful rarely conform to Aristotelian categories, such as social, political, economic, or environmental. They are more likely to cut across two or more of these. If the headings are decided first, the group will be put in the position of trying to force the data into the headings rather than letting the data speak for themselves.

Groups are also encouraged to write their reports in the present rather than future tense, as the points they are making are end points, outcomes. The trick is to describe the year in the future as if the group were taking a snapshot of what they saw as they walked around in that year. This imparts a greater sense of the reality of the future and, once the pattern for doing this is established in the search, makes it easier to distinguish between the end points and the means of achieving them. The groups are to report no more than six discrete items or parameters of that most probable world on only one flip chart sheet.

For the group looking at the most desirable future of the world, the task is to examine the data while being conscious of the fact that many people are out there trying to improve the world at the moment. Given this, the group must decide to what extent the world will have improved in 5 years. Notice that the groups are not asked to map an ideal future, although their most desirable future elicits ideal seeking. The most desirable future differs from an "ideal future" because it has a reality check built into it, the time frame attached to the scenario—2010, for example. This means that their most desirable future must be reasonably realistic given the time available to produce it.

The groups doing the most desirable scenario must also report no more than six discrete items or parameters of that most desirable world on only one flip chart sheet. They are given the same instructions about categories and writing their scenarios in the present tense.

The reasons for these specific instructions about the number of points and pages are, first, that participants must work hard to distill their scenarios from the data and the assumptions they have been given. Endless "shopping lists" are of no use. They indicate that little thought has been put into answering these questions about the future. Dealing with and learning from the external world is vitally important to guaranteeing the effectiveness of a community into the future. This point is explained and discussed in the preparation stage, and the instructions only reinforce it.

The second reason for these instructions is that the two reports on each future scenario must be integrated. If the reports consist of many sheets of paper and endless points, the task of integrating them becomes a logistical nightmare. Six points from two groups give plenty of scope for a comprehensive picture of a future, even when there is significant overlap between the two. And there usually is a significant overlap because not only have people seen the same things happening in the world, but people also take the same meaning from those things. This overlap gives everybody confidence in the validity of their perceptions, their ecological learning, and indicates that the changes taking place in the external world can be used to improve the effectiveness of planning.

The whole community is also informed that, once in their groups, they are free to add items to the database if something important has been left out. The condition attached to doing this is that the group must inform the rest of the community that an additional item has been added. Shared information is central to building a community.

Future Scenarios and Effective Communication

The distilling of these two scenarios for the future of the world serves several purposes. At the practical level, the scenarios act to guide future work. Participants return to them to compile and deal with constraints and to get help with the details of action planning. The scenarios also produce the realization that everyone is human (most desirable future) and share the one world (most probable future)—two of the conditions for effective communication (Asch, 1952; M. Emery, 1999).

Working on the most desirable future elicits the set of four human ideals (chapter 2). These ideals are the key to realizing that all participants share common human concerns. As the two groups work on their most desirable world, it becomes impossible for anyone in those groups to mistake the deep-seated concerns that all share about the future of the world and its people. Regardless of such characteristics as gender, age, or political inclination, these usually unspoken concerns surface in unmistakable ways. This sometimes comes as a shock to people who believe that political, religious, or ethnic affiliations are the most powerful determinants of attitudes and behavior. Expecting significant differences between people, they see them united in their desire to produce a more ideal-based world. This new awareness is strengthened when the community sees the overlap of items between the two group reports.

The four ideals surface in just about every picture of the most desirable future. They may be expressed in slightly different words, but their intrinsic sense—and the fact that they are almost always shared by the two groups—immediately raises confidence in the power of the total community. It also reduces fears of conflict and failure.

No less important is the work done on the most probable world. As it builds directly on the database established immediately beforehand by the total community, it reinforces the notion that, indeed, we all do live in the same world. Participants also learn that the world can be quite objectively observed and understood.

Once these two conditions are in place, they, together with the continuing openness in the content and process, generate more trust within the community. The first phase of the search conference is a powerful one in many ways. Dealing with the world around us is the first work done for these very reasons. The earlier these conditions apply, the sooner the community starts to develop trust in itself and its people.

Integration and Rationalization of Conflict

Once the groups have finalized their scenarios, the reports from the two groups of either most probable or most desirable scenarios are put side by side. Groups are asked to briefly report from the flip charts one after the other. Then the first set of questioning begins so that everyone is clear about the reports. Nobody should be asked to agree with something that he or she does not fully understand.

Once both the reports are fully understood, the second set of questions begins. These questions ask for any disagreement or argument about the scenarios. There can be a substantial amount of discussion at this point, and it is important that the discussion stay focused on the evidence. The purpose is to get the most accurate and realistic pictures of the future world. Again this questioning is essential, as the search has as its major aim the building of a learning, planning community. Communities are built on common ground and trust, and anything but an honest sharing of views inhibits development.

It is at the point of testing possible disagreements that the rationalization of conflict (F. Emery, 1966; M. Emery, 1999) really swings into play. It is an effective method that avoids excessive individualism on the one hand and "group-think," or conformity, on the other. It acknowledges the reality of disagreement, finds the common ground, and separates it from the areas of disagreement. If somebody is not committed to an item, the first step is full discussion in the community. Sometimes the disagreements are merely semantic, or a slight modification of the point will resolve the difference. If it becomes clear that there is substantive disagreement that cannot be resolved through negotiations, then and only then is the item placed on a separate sheet of paper under the heading "Disagreed." The item is then removed from the original report and ceases to be part of the common base from which work proceeds. In this way, differences are acknowledged but are not permitted to tie the community into endless wrangling and the possible generation of bad feeling.

Use of this process from the very beginning of the search reassures those who may be afraid of conflict that they have nothing to fear in voicing their views. If there are major points of disagreement in a search, they are most likely to occur when the group is considering the future of their own community. These disagreements may even be known before the event begins. By starting to use the process with the world around us, the disagreements are already being put into context. This can change perceptions about the conflict.

The major purpose of the rationalization of conflict is to establish exactly where the line is drawn between agreement and disagreement so that the common ground is clearly known. Conflicted groups often exaggerate the extent of a conflict, and the longer it goes on, the greater it is assumed to be. Once the common ground and the disagreements are clearly separated, the community continues to work on the common ground without fear of freedom of expression. People then feel much more free to express their views excitedly and strongly (M. Emery, 1999).

Although consensus is frequently sought in other methods, it is strictly unrealistic to expect 30-plus people from different parts of a diverse community to agree about everything, even for part of the time. Time can be wasted aiming for consensus, and some people will hide their views in the interests of getting on with work. That would defeat the purpose of bringing them together in the first place, to determine an agreed set of strategic goals for community development. Helping groups find common ground to build on is central to doing work in a community setting and building commitment to a shared purpose (Joyner, 1996).

Once the rationalization of conflict is finalized, the integration proceeds. It is a simple process. The two reports are hanging side by side so that the easiest way to begin is to number the points on one of the reports from top to bottom, if it is not numbered already. The community is asked whether an item on the other list has the same meaning as Point 1 or could be put with it as part of the same item. If there is such an item, it is also given the number 1. If there is no such item on the other list, the original number 1 remains as a stand-alone item. Each of the items on the first list is dealt with in turn. When the first report has been dealt with, some items on the second will have been assigned numbers and some will not have. These are then numbered sequentially as further stand-alone items. In this way all the richness of the reports is preserved and nothing gets lost. Just the redundancies are removed.

It is useful to take a break at the end of the integration, as this period can serve as the time during which one or two people from each group take the marked-up reports and write a final integrated version. This is done publicly as others have refreshments and anyone can join in and help. The stand-alone items can be cut and pasted into the final version to save time. The integrators need to understand their job as one of sticking as much as possible to the words used by the original reports or their modifications made during the discussion process. If they integrate statements by abstracting too far from the originals, both groups will be unhappy when the final version is reported and checked. When the community pronounces that it is happy with the final integrated reports, the process is complete. The total search community now owns the agreed pictures of the most probable and most desirable worlds.

Integration is used after every session in which groups work in parallel. It is the cement that binds the community into an evermore coherent entity. Without these processes, work is left at the small-group level. People can see overlaps and disagreements, and if these remain untested, they can create problems down the track. Without the rationalization of conflict and integration, there can be no self-confident community, nor can there be a clear set of conditions for effective communication and trust.

By the end of the first phase, dealing with the world around us, the community is enriched. It has confronted its fears and conquered them. Now enlivened and more trusting, its members are ready to enter the next phase, the exploration of the community itself, always a challenge but one the participants are now ready to meet.

The History Session

The history session in a community search is usually one of the most formative and emotional episodes in the event. Many have been reluctant to acknowledge the important influence of unique character as it emerges from historical continuity over time (Dubos, 1976), but it is important when developing community that the characteristics that set it apart, define its uniqueness, are identified and described (Kemmis, 1990). People care deeply about their communities, where they have come from and what has made them look the way they do today. Their sense of belonging incorporates their tacit knowledge of their community's uniqueness, and the history session is their opportunity to weave a rich fabric of meaningful events that describe the development of that uniqueness from past to present. Because the task is essentially building a shared understanding of the community's development, all the work is done in the community. It is a large-group conversation. The managers do little more than try to keep a roughly chronological sequence of events and their impacts.

The history session is as much a part of the context of the overall task as is learning about the external social environment. People assume that everybody knows the history, but that is untrue. The younger generations may not comprehend the magnitude of the changes that a community has undergone. Even those who have the longest-living memories may not understand that people from the other side of the tracks or from different ethnic backgrounds have placed a different meaning on the events they shared at the time. Therefore, there may be different perceptions or interpretations of the history, and it is important that these are heard and understood by all.

The history starts at the beginning of the community and covers the period to the present. If there was an indigenous history before European settlement, it is imperative that it be included. It is good practice to talk beforehand and ask the oldest people in the room to start telling the history. Others will ask questions. As the time moves closer to the present, more people contribute. The conversation zigzags backward and forward in time as people remember important events and further meanings are uncovered. The history reveals the community's unique personality, enhances the common ground, and leads directly into an analysis of the community at the moment.

The Community Now

This session bridges the gap between the history session and the work of deciding what the community will most desirably look like in the future time frame. It is scaffolding for the hard work to follow. Again, it is conducted with the total community.

The simplest, easiest, and most comprehensive way of analyzing the community is to set up three flip charts headed "Keep," "Drop," and "Create." Because it is a data-gathering session, there is a ground rule that anyone can put any feature of the community on any of the three lists. For example, if a person wants to keep front fences, front fences are put on the Keep list. If somebody else wants to get rid of front fences, it is also put on the Drop list. In this way a range of perceptions of every aspect of the community is canvassed. The group work that follows decides between these views.

Managers may prompt participants if they see a particular aspect of the community being neglected. But the session rarely takes longer than about 30 minutes, as by now the community is cohesive and at ease working together.

The Most Desirable Community

For a community search of about 30 people, three groups can work in parallel to decide on a most desirable community. A random selection yielding heterogeneous groups will work well unless the community has experienced recent conflict. If the community has experienced conflict, I would specifically design the composition of the groups so that each contains a mix of the conflicting parties.

The specific instructions for the three groups are to report back no more than seven points on no more than two sheets of flip chart. The larger and more diverse the community, the more points they are given. Again, groups are asked to keep their points concise, concrete, and written in the present tense. Goal statements must also specify exactly the direction of the changes envisaged. Although "We have a better education system" sounds good, it does not convey much meaning. Is there to be a new curriculum? Are the teachers to team-teach? Or is the system to be more student oriented?

Nobody can predict how difficult a community will find this task, but at least 1 hour should be allowed. As managers walk around the groups, they can ask the groups if they need more time. A group may be hurried up if the other two have finished. Two hours for completion would not be excessive.

The process for reporting, rationalizing conflict, and integrating is exactly the same as that described for the world. The number of goals is usually about 10, and if there are many more, it is possible to ask the community to group closely related goals so that the number remains manageable for the later stages of the search. It is for these strategic goals that action plans are done.

The history, analysis, and most desirable community sessions form the second phase of the search conference, dealing with the system. The participants are now ready to begin the third phase, the task of integrating the work from the first two phases, environment and system, to achieve an active adaptive future.

Constraints and Dealing With Them

The constraints session is the first step in the third phase of the search, where participants integrate their learnings about the environment and their own community. This first task is to identify the major constraints or obstacles that the community can see it will face in pursuing its most desirable future. Constraints can arise from within or without the community. Participants are asked to go around the walls, looking particularly at the changes in the world, the most probable world, and the Drop list. These are the most likely sources of obstacles.

Groups form around each constraint to work out how to deal with it. It helps to give the groups a little informal briefing on the strategy of the indirect approach (Boorman, 1971; Hart, 1943, 1946; Sun Tzu, 1943). This briefing amounts to a few handy hints for the groups to consider as they confront the obstacles. People in Western countries tend to adopt the strategy of the direct approach without thinking of an alternative. This is not a smart thing to do, particularly when dealing with social issues. People who are confronted head-on usually become reluctant to change. Such a course can be self-defeating.

The strategy of the indirect approach involves maximizing progress toward goals while minimizing the wastage of resources. Rather than choose one starting place—one "pilot," or demonstration site—the indirect approach involves working across the whole community or organization. It is a broad-front approach, not putting all your eggs in one basket. The last 40 years have shown that, contrary to expectations that success breeds success and that one can start anywhere and follow to where it spreads (Duffy, 2004; Wheatley, 2001), change in isolated parts of a system does not spread (Davis & Sullivan, 1993; Herbst, 1976; Williams, 1982).

Other lessons from the strategy of the indirect approach are to work first with those who are most likely to join you, leaving the hard ones until last and pulling out if attacked. Sources of resistance can be surrounded or encapsulated: difficult people can often be better approached by their friends who share your goals rather than be approached by you. The strategy of the indirect approach demands constant evaluation of the whole situation so that adjustments to strategy and tactics can be made at any time. This produces the necessary flexibility of a plan (Grasmick, 2001) and is the core of the idea of remaining active and adaptive (M. Emery, 1999).

Working positively and practicing with the strategy of the indirect approach avoids participants becoming depressed as they think about the obstacles in front of them. This possible reversion to negativity is one of the reasons that constraints are left until the end of the search. By the time the community has achieved agreement on its goals, it should be cohesive and confident of its capacity to make its own future.

When the groups report their ideas to neutralize obstacles, there is no need for any rationalization of conflict. Groups may discuss how to take the ideas further and may generate and share some other bright, creative ideas. All ideas then become the property of the search community.

Reviewing Strategic Goals

Having worked on ways around the constraints, the community now has an opportunity to review its strategic goals to see if they still look manageable and realistic. This review is brief, as people discuss their goals in the light of the work done on the constraints. It is rare that the goals are changed. The work done on constraints is usually sufficient to reassure people that they can successfully deal with such obstacles. If it does so happen that a goal needs to be revised because it looks too optimistic, the community discusses how best to do this and finalizes the revised list of goals.

Action Planning

Once a set of most desirable and achievable goals is in place, the action planning can begin. Participants self-select around each of the strategic goals with a minimum of two people working on each one. Once again, the managers can give a set of handy hints on how to approach the task.

The first is for each group to return to the accumulated work around the walls, looking particularly at the changes in the world, the most desirable world, and the Keep and Create lists from the community analysis. Opportunities can be found either externally or internally.

The second handy hint is to augment the usual "what, how, when, and by whom" approach with a list of possible allies. Smart action plans generate resources and involve greater numbers of people over time so that the task of building the future is increasingly shared within the community.

The third handy hint shows the community how to set out a set of subgoals nested in time. As the time frame for the final implementation of the goals is 5 years away, any goal must be broken into a logical set of subgoals. These not only make it easier to approach the action planning task but also serve as built-in progress-monitoring points for the implementation.

The final handy hint is simply, do not attempt to "sell" your goal. Selling, or trying to convince others of the desirability of a goal, is more likely to turn them off than on. A participative democratic approach in which others are free to come up with their own goals is much more successful. Participants can be confident that the same goals will be reached because the others will also be basing their goals on the ideals (chapter 2). When people set their own goals, they are committed to them. When they are asked to swallow somebody else's goals, they may be resistant.

This is the approach followed in this book. As I have never heard of a community search that did not have a goal relating to its school or education system (chapter 2), I am confident that each community search will have at least one. Some aspects of the goal can be immediately worked on by community members. Other aspects of the goal will need to be elaborated in joint work with school district staff, and the group implementing this goal can then start planning for one or a set of searches to be conducted through the school district. These will focus specifically on improvements to schools and the district as a whole (chapter 6). The community group or groups will continue to work with those involved in this second round of searches, functioning as organizers and liaison groups between school district and broader community. This principle applies to any strategic goal so that energy and action spread rapidly throughout the total community.

About one third of the total working time should be left for action planning. This is a long time for a group to be working alone, so it is advisable to build in an interim reporting session. Because all the action plans must be coordinated, these interim reports are simply work-in-progress reports so that the community can get a feel for how the work is hanging together. Sometimes two groups find that they are targeting much the same people and can work together. Some action plans may be somewhat revised. Interim reports ensure that final reports are of high quality and well coordinated.

When a search conference is the first event in a long project, as is the case here, one relevant point revolves around dealing with constraints and making action plans. It is quite likely that some perceived obstacles may arise from within the individual school district. These constraints may involve concerns about such issues as low job satisfaction, low morale, poor communication, or lack of cooperation. It is also likely that some goals will target increasing motivation and student achievement. Both these constraints and goals arise from dysfunctions caused by the current bureaucratic structures. A change in design principle from the first (DP1, for bureaucracy) to the second (DP2, for participative democracy) will do more than anything else to remove the barrier and move the school district toward its goals.

The redesigns that are done in the PDW within the schools and district offices change these structures (chapter 7) and reduce, if not do away with, many of the internal problems of school districts. The process managers can reassure participants that these constraints and associated goals can be safely left to the PDWs by explaining more of the theory or by giving examples to show that these problems are not due to personality differences or problems with communication skills. Strategic goals usually contain more than one discrete point so that participants can plan for other aspects of the goal. A typical strategic goal for education says, "We have a school district working hand in hand with the community for lifelong learning, with excellent, motivated staff, and high-performing students." If the community holds over work on the motivated staff and high-performing students, it still has much work to do on producing a district working toward lifelong learning in cooperation with its community.

PROCESS MANAGEMENT

Process management is concerned to get the task done on time with good quality. It is also concerned with the relationship between the managers and that between managers and participants. When there is more than one manager, and this is desirable, the managers must share responsibility for the whole of the process. At no stage should a manager become associated with a small group or become involved with the content. These things cause a loss of responsibility of the community for its work and outcomes. Managers do not have to live with the consequences of the search. The participants do.

The managers' role is to look after the quality of the learning environment and process. They have to juggle time and tasks. If a particular session has taken much longer than expected, they have to decide how best to use the remaining time. Managers often have to make difficult decisions on the run. It is difficult to be alert to all the nuances of the process while, for example, writing up or negotiating the integration of group reports. One manager can watch and listen while the other talks.

Managers must ensure that the job gets done. Searching is serious work, and although it is fun, it is not done for fun alone or for participants to get to know each other. Both managers and participants implicitly have a contract when entering a search. They are both bound to the task and to each other through this implicit contract. When managers and participants have a good relationship, participants swing into the creative working mode quickly and easily, and managers rejoice with them as they realize their creative potential.

THREE DIVERSE EXAMPLES OF A
COMMUNITY SEARCH PROCESS

- The school district of Commerce City in Georgia has three schools: an elementary, a middle, and a high school. As well as teachers, instructional aides, guidance counselors, and librarians and media specialists, there are five district-level and five school-level administrators (GreatSchools.net, 2005). The total population of the district is 5,205 (National Center for Education Statistics, 2002).
- The Huntingdon Area School District in Pennsylvania includes six schools, four elementary schools, a middle school, and a senior high school. The school district office has a superintendent, an assistant superintendent, and a business manager. There are several Parent-Teacher Organizations (Huntingdon Area School District, 2005). The total population of the district is about 20,000 (National Center for Education Statistics, 2002).
- The Tucson Unified School District is one of the hundred largest districts in the United States, with about 115 schools and a total population of about 444,000 (National Center for Education Statistics, 2002).[1] It has a School Community Partnership Council made up of a district council and four area councils. These are volunteer organizations of parents and Tucson Unified School District staff to facilitate communication between each community and the district (Tucson Unified School District, 2005). The School Community Partnership Council would be a most appropriate body to convene a first meeting to kick off the overall process in Tucson.

The steps within the search and its process management need not vary between communities, but because of the differences in community size, each example requires a quite different overall process.

The Community of Commerce City

With a population of about 5,000, Commerce City can be handled by a single search conference as described here. In general, a single search is appropriate for a population of up to 15,000 to 20,000. A single search has been used with larger numbers than this, but it is definitely advantageous to conduct more than one.[2] Naturally, if the costs of running multiple searches are prohibitive, a single search can still be used.

The Community of Huntingdon Area

With a population of just over 20,000, it would be possible to run a single search in the Huntingdon Area, but my preference would be for two or three searches running in parallel, with an integration event at the end. The advantages of running three rather than two are that more people are involved, and as the areas covered by the searches are less populous, knowledge of and action toward the goals spread through them faster. However, these advantages are balanced by the costs involved. In this design, I err on the side of financial caution and opt to use two searches.

The citizens of the Huntingdon Area can use their local knowledge to draw the line between the communities for the searches. They can then use the CRS (chapter 3) to select participants for each half. Each half proceeds with its preparations as described here. The steps are the same as discussed for a single search, except the two searches stop after they have decided on their set of strategic goals.

The two searches can be held one after the other or on the same days in different parts of the area, depending on the availability of experienced, trained managers. The integration event will proceed soon after the searches.

As there are only two sets of strategic goals to be integrated, each search community can select at least 10 to 15 of its members to attend the integration event. The event starts with brief welcomes and introductions, and then the two sets of goals are put up on the wall. Each search group reports its goals and invites questions for clarification only—that is, there is no rationalization of conflict. I have never heard of a conflict between goals, but if there are search communities that have goals that appear to conflict, these goals can be taken back to their individual searches for implementation. This could simply be a case of unique characteristics, and such diversity of opinion may apply in a large city, for example, as what may apply on the south side may not apply on the north side. The integration process need take no more than a couple of hours.

The groups integrate the goals in exactly the same way as within a search. Responsibilities may be assigned, if this is relevant. There may be one or more goals that are idiosyncratic to a particular part of the area. The two searches then reconvene and do the work in the third phase in the same manner as described for a single search.

The Community of Tucson

The community of Tucson Unified numbers about 444,000 people, organized into four enrollment areas, six wards, and dozens of individual neighborhoods. Although these numbers are big, there is nothing about the task that represents a challenge other than time, resources, and cost. Searching in this community is simply a multiple of smaller versions. The most appropriate areas for subdivision of the community appear to be the four enrollment areas, each of which has its area council for school community partnership.

With local knowledge, these four areas need to be subdivided again, into perhaps four smaller community units. That would yield 16 search conferences across the city. Each would proceed as described here, until the integration event. These numbers suggest a slight modification of the procedure to keep the process clean and orderly.

The much larger numbers in Tucson mean that a two-stage process of integration is necessary. In the first stage, six people from each of the four searches in an enrollment area can meet and integrate their four sets of goals into one—a total of 24 people in all. In the second stage, two people from each search can meet and integrate these four sets into one for the whole of the Tucson community, meaning there would be 32 people working. It is not good practice to leave just one member of a search to report and explain work. Two heads are always better than one, and mutual support should be built in whenever possible.

It would be an advantage to rewrite the goals after the first stage, and the final list certainly needs to be rewritten. It is always advantageous that this be done immediately on site, before people have time to forget. At the end of the second stage, responsibilities are assigned as discussed here, and the process is complete. Search participants then take home the shared goals and any that were idiosyncratic to their particular part of the city. If both stages can be held at the same venue, this two-stage process would probably take half a day or so. The two stages do not need to be done on the same day, however. These processes can be used flexibly.

The remaining task is to ensure that the community has the most effective form of organization through which it will implement its plans, the subject of the next chapter.

NOTES

1. The numbers vary slightly depending on whether you consult the U.S. Department of Education or the National Center for Educational Statistics, as slightly different classifications and databases are used.

2. This refers strictly to geographical community searches. Many successful national and issue searches have been held with about 30 participants. National searches often involve peak organizations.

The Community Organizes
to Implement Its Plans—Step 3

$\mathcal{O}$nce the action planning for the community goals is complete, the question then becomes, how are community members going to work together to implement the plans? Practitioners have learned many hard lessons about what elements to build into the implementation for it to be sustained. The most powerful element is an organizational structure that generates the positive feelings and energy required to sustain implementation over long periods. These qualities also attract others to the work. The results of the event will be awaited eagerly by the community, and many will wish to become involved in the implementation of the plans. This means that the participants do not need to sell their plans, a process that can raise suspicions. Because the community understands the purpose of the event and its most probable outcomes, plans can be put into action without fuss. To continue generating positive feelings, energy, and motivation through implementation, participants must work in a participative, democratic structure.

The best way to bring democratic organizations into being is through the PDW, which has proven its worth since 1971. Studies continue to show that when communities plan but do not follow up with a PDW, they confront local power structures and flounder on organizational dilemmas (Schafft & Greenwood, 2003). In the PDW, participants learn about and apply the two organizational design principles briefly introduced in chapter 1. These principles produce the two fundamentally different forms of organizational structure: bureaucratic and participative democratic. Here I look in more detail at the design principles, their effects, and how to use them for effective, democratic community organizations.

The PDW comes in two forms: one for an existing organization that needs to be redesigned (see chapter 7) and one for an organization that needs to be created. I discuss this second form here, as before the search conference, the community participants had never come together as an entity; therefore, a structure needs to be created. Adding a PDW to the search creates the two-stage model of participation that ensures that the participants leave the process with the most effective form of organization to implement their plans (M. Emery, 1999).

HISTORY OF THE DISCOVERY OF THE DESIGN PRINCIPLES

There are two genotypical design principles, and all organizations are the result of applying one or the other. Before design principles were identified (F. Emery, 1967a), they had a history in other work that facilitated their final identification and corroborated their effects. As research on these principles continues, the more powerful they are seen to be.

Autocracy, Democracy, and Laissez-Faire

The first landmark in the discovery of the design principles consisted of a series of experiments carried out in the United States from 1938 to 1940 to learn more about the phenomena of autocracy and democracy. The participants were boys organized into clubs, each with leaders adopting different leadership styles. Although it began as a study of autocracy and democracy, it rapidly changed into a study of three forms of "social climate" (Lippitt, 1940), or what we today call "structure." The third form, laissez-faire, was discovered by accident, as it arose from a misunderstanding of the nature of democracy. An inexperienced leader, Ralph White, became baffled by the anarchy created by two boys who were "real hell raisers." He let all the boys "do their own thing," which resulted in some very negative effects. His understanding then was that democracy could mean total individual freedom. His approach with this group allowed the distinction between democracy and laissez-faire to be made. Many people practice laissez-faire thinking that they are being democratic just because they are not controlling autocratically (White, 1990). Unfortunately, this confusion of democracy and laissez-faire is still with us.

The second series of studies of the three structures used four 10- and 11-year-old boys' clubs. Each club experienced different rotating patterns of autocracy, democracy, and laissez-faire and different adult leaders, all of whom had been trained in the three roles. The study revealed stark differences between the three leadership modes. Although the autocratic leaders behaved throughout as dictators, the democratic leaders functioned mainly as a friendly resource and help to the groups, whereas the laissez-faire leaders gave individual freedom. In autocracy, the centerpiece and focus of the work was the leader; in democracy, it was the group; and in laissez-faire, there was none.

The autocratic leader made all the rules, dictated the activities, and praised and criticized personally. The democratic leader discussed rules and encouraged group decision making about goals, with technical help from the leader if required. The democratic leader was fact oriented in praise and blame and was a group member in spirit. There were no rules made in laissez-faire; the leader supplied materials and gave information only if asked, did not participate in the group work, did not praise or blame, and did not attempt to regulate work (Lippitt & White, 1943).

The three structures produced very different behaviors in the boys. The autocracy group showed two major clusters of behavior: submissive and aggressive. In the submissive groups, individual boys became dependent on the leader with virtually no capacity to initiate group action. In the aggressive groups, the boys felt frustration directed at the leader (Lippitt & White, 1947) and rebellion (Lippitt & White, 1943). In other words, the authoritarian leader produced either dependency or a reaction called "fight/flight."

When the leader left the room in the laissez-faire condition, one of the boys exerted leadership and "achieved a more coordinated group activity than when the relatively passive adult was present" (Lippitt & White, 1947, p. 323). This phenomenon is called *pairing* (Bion, 1952, 1961; M. Emery, 1999). These three symptoms of group dysfunction—dependency, fight/flight, and pairing—are discussed in more detail later.

Aggression in autocracy and laissez-faire was directed toward other groups and individuals as well as toward the leader. The group experienced interpersonal tension and scapegoating. At a point in one of the sessions, a stranger entered and made remarks critical of the boys' work. The autocratic groups expressed both submission and aggression toward the stranger. The democratic groups rejected the stranger's criticism and resisted taking their frustrations out on other groups (Lippitt & White, 1947).

The boys made more demands for attention in autocracy than in the other two conditions. They were dependent on the leader for task-oriented matters and social status. This meant that competition developed between the boys themselves. In laissez-faire and democracy, the boys sought more attention and approval from each other. However, only the democratic groups showed evidence of stable cooperative structure.

Morale—in the sense of cohesion, using *we* not *I*, working together for group goals, and being friendly rather than hostile—was highest in the democratic groups and lowest in the autocratic groups. The submissive groups suffered the lowest morale. In both autocracy and laissez-faire, the boys experienced a great deal of frustration, of both the need for autonomy and the need for sociability. The researchers were surprised by the extent to which autocracy inhibited the normal, free and easy sociability of the boys. This was particularly so in the submissive groups (Lippitt & White, 1943).

Frustrations in laissez-faire were also high—frustration from the need for worthwhile cooperative achievement and that for clear structure and frustration from the "vicious cycle of frustration-aggression-frustration" (Lippitt & White, 1943, p. 503). The boys wanted to accomplish things, but lacking a structure for cooperation, they were all talk and no action. They became dissatisfied with the chaos, confusion, and uncertainty. Even the boys who tried hardest to use their freedom to get work done found it impossible, as they experienced constant interference from other boys.

The amount of productive work varied significantly between the autocratic, democratic, and laissez-faire conditions. When the leaders arrived late in the authoritarian groups, the boys had made no initiative to start new work or to continue with work already under way. In the democratic condition, the groups were already productive. The groups in laissez-faire were active but not productive (Lippitt & White, 1947). When the leader left the room in the groups showing a submissive reaction, the percentage of time spent in serious work dropped from 74% to 29%. In the groups showing an aggressive reaction, the drop was from 52% to 16%. The motivation to work was leader induced, not intrinsic to the boys. In contrast, the democratic group remained stable, with a negligible drop from 50% to 46%. A similar negligible drop was seen in laissez-faire (Lippitt & White, 1943), but as little work was done anyway, this remained unsatisfactory.

The democratic groups had by far the highest quality of work and made far more suggestions about how work could be done. They had internalized the group goals. Pride in work also differed significantly. The democratic groups presented their work or took it home, whereas in one authoritarian group, the boys actually tried to destroy what they had made.

The democratic leaders stimulated eight times as much independence as the authoritarian leaders and twice as much as the laissez-faire leaders (Lippitt & White, 1947). Democracy, not laissez-faire, resulted in the greatest individual differences. Although fewer expressions of individuality in autocracy should surprise no one, many will be surprised by the fact that there was less individuality in laissez-faire (Lippitt & White, 1947). Contrary to what many believe, freedom to do whatever one pleases actually results in a reduced opportunity to express individuality. Autonomy without a balancing degree of belongingness with peers restricts and inhibits personal growth (M. Emery, 1999).

As each club experienced a different sequence of social climates, it was possible to see effects arising from the sequences. Groups that passively accepted an autocratic leader at the beginning of the sequence were much more frustrated and resistant to another autocratic leader if they had experienced a democratic leader in the meantime. If a group had not had the democratic experience, there was little effect.

When translated into the context of schools, it means that schools that lack a specific policy about the way to organize classrooms and students will be subject to a changing array of teacher styles and preferences over time. Should students at any stage encounter a democratic teacher, their approach to their next teacher will be colored by their experience with that democratic teacher.

Overall, the three social climates had dramatically different effects, and climate proved to be the most powerful factor of any measured. The democratic form showed its superiority on every measure. This result has been found many times over in just about every form of human endeavor, although there has been an updating of the language since the design principles were discovered. *Climate* is now referred to as *structure*. Laissez-faire is now known as the absence of a design principle because there are no structural relationships between the people (M. Emery, 1999). Because laissez-faire is qualitatively different from both autocracy and democracy and its effects are so negative, it cannot be a half-way house between bureaucracy and democracy (Fiorelli, 1988; F. Emery, 1988). Unfortunately today, many laissez-faire organizations exist where the structure is DP1 on paper but generally ignored (de Guerre, 2000). They tend to fail (Trist & Dwyer, 1993).

Democratic Workplaces

These experiments were creating excitement around the world when a change in technology in an English mine caused some unexpected results. The miners had worked in small cohesive, multiskilled, self-managing groups, as this was the safest way to work in a dangerous environment. The new technology destroyed the old team structure, changing the form of organization to "one man, one job."

Rather than increase productivity and profit, the change brought the opposite. There was an increase in accidents and four interrelated "defense mechanisms" against the new work structure: *informal organization*, or forming cliques; *individualism* or competition, playing politics; *scapegoating*, or passing the buck; and *withdrawal*, or absenteeism and "psychosomatic" illness (Trist & Bamforth, 1951). These defense mechanisms were the same reactions as those observed in autocracy. They showed that these effects held regardless of whether the setting was experimental or in a real workplace. The social scientists then worked with the miners to reconstruct the old team structure around the new technology. They matched the best features of the technology with the best features of democratic social structure. This matching is the key point of what came to be known as *sociotechnical systems* (STS). It is the "people to technical system" discussed in chapter 1.

Research was then conducted into designing and analyzing STS around the world, including those in Third World countries such as India (Rice, 1993). The main characteristics of STS were extracted (F. Emery, 1978a), and this groundwork led to the success of the Norwegian Industrial Democracy Project. By 1960 Norway had still not fully recovered from the devastation of World War II and needed revitalization. Representative democracy did not work (Emery & Thorsrud, 1969). It still doesn't (Palmer & McGraw, 1996).

The Norwegian government decided on a national experiment, redesigning four nationally significant industrial sites into "sociotechnical," or participative democratic, systems. The experiments were successful, with increased productivity and lowered costs across all sites (Emery & Thorsrud, 1976). It was during the Norwegian work that Fred Emery (1967a) was able to extract and define the two basic design principles that underlie organizational structures. Even organizations that fly by night on the margins of mainstream society embody one of the two design principles in understandings that exist between employer and the employed. Normally, the design principle is embodied in a collective bargaining agreement, an individual contract, a duty statement, or in job criteria.

The Norwegian project showed that successful demonstration or pilot sites are not copied in the surrounding areas. This finding has been replicated many times since. Success does not necessarily breed success. The industrial democracy program was revived later in Norway with the democratization of shipping, in partnership with the school system (Thorsrud, 1983; Herbst, 1993). But the nine-step method (F. Emery, 1967b) of STS used in the Norwegian experiments became widely known, and Davis (1971) became a leading proponent in the United States.

The Invention of the PDW

Large companies wanted Fred Emery to begin STS projects after he returned to Australia in 1969. He explained that this was not the way to proceed. Emery and Thorsrud knew by the end of the Norwegian project that the workers in the plants already had sufficient knowledge of the work to do the analysis themselves with the help of only a few social science principles. Emery and Thorsrud set about designing new methods, and neither used STS again.

Emery called his new method the PDW. Those in a workplace use it to redesign their own organization. The only expert knowledge required is understanding the design principles and the six psychological factors that people need to be able to engage in productive work. They are given at the beginning of the PDW, in the form of a simple briefing. Emery tried his new method at a RAAF factory in 1971 and in 1972 used it in all six plants at the ICI chemical production site in Sydney. There is now a form of PDW for existing organizations and one for designing organizations from scratch (M. Emery, 1999, 2000c). I discuss the latter later in the chapter.

Such was the success of sociotechnical organizations and new methods that by the 1980s democratization had ceased to be the exclusive concern of academics and was becoming an everyday reality for many organizations (Kolodny & van Beinum, 1983).

APPROPRIATE ORGANIZATIONS FOR PEOPLE AND PRODUCTIVITY

Emery and Thorsrud (1969) built on previous work to confirm that people have six psychological requirements if they are to engage in productive work. These requirements are called the "six criteria" for short.

The Six Criteria

The six criteria consist of the following:

1. *Elbow room*, which means adequate autonomy for people to make decisions about their work or activity. To a reasonable extent people must be their own bosses, not have others constantly telling them what to do. On the other hand, they must not have so much elbow room that they do not know what to do next.
2. *Continual learning*, for which there must be
   a. *Adequate room for people to set goals for their activities that present challenges for them.* Only the individual knows what constitutes a reasonable challenge for him or her at that time. The organization must have an adequate set of guidelines so that people do not get confused by having too much room to set goals for themselves.
   b. *Accurate and timely feedback so that people can correct their mistakes or set higher challenges for themselves.* There is nothing wrong with making mistakes, but if feedback is not useful or not delivered when required, a person's learning will be inhibited.

3. *Variety of tasks and functions*, adequate so that people can avoid boredom and fatigue. But they must not have so much variety that they cannot settle into a satisfying rhythm of work.

4. *Mutual support and respect*—people need conditions in which they can help others and be helped by others without having to ask. People must also be respected for the contribution they make rather than for their qualifications, for example. The most important support and respect come from peers.

5. *Meaningfulness*—people must know that they are contributing to their society. Meaningfulness has two parts:

   a. *Doing something with social value, which is in part a judgment made by the wider society.* Professions such as teaching and nursing are accorded high social value, even if this is not reflected in compensation.

   b. *Seeing the whole product or service to which the individual contributes.* Many people are condemned to work on parts of projects or services without knowing the final outcome.

6. *A desirable future*, not having a dead-end job. People have to see that the organization is contributing to their career path as they see it, by providing opportunities or further skills and knowledge.

The six criteria are the intrinsic motivators, the things that make people want to leap out of bed and do a great day's work. They are closely related to the genotypical organizational design principles (F. Emery, 1967a; Emery & Emery, 1974). It is difficult to get high scores on the six criteria from autocratic structures. This applies even when management has gone out of its way to attend to all external motivators, such as money or good conditions (Herzberg, 1987).

The first three criteria pertain to the individual who can have too little or too much of them, and these are measured using a scale from −5 to 5, where 0 is optimal. The second three pertain to the climate of the organization, and of these, one can never have too much. They are measured on a scale from 1 to 10. A completed matrix for the six criteria is shown as Table 5.1. They have been routinely measured in countless PDWs since 1971 (M. Emery, 1993a), and when, for example, surveys about job satisfaction are conducted, they come back with a number of factors that boil down to these six. They have been found to work equally well in many countries.

The Genotypical Organizational Design Principles

Because people are purposeful, they need appropriate organizations so that they become and stay motivated while they work, learn, or plan. Appropriate

Table 5.1.   Completed Matrix for the Six Criteria

	ME	DS	TP	KN	FR
1. Elbow room	1	−2	−3	−1	−5
2. Continual learning					
a. Setting goals	2	−3	−3	−2	−5
b. Getting feedback	−3	−4	−2	−2	−3
3. Variety	4	2	−3	−2	1
4. Mutual support and respect	8	7	8	9	8
5. Meaningfulness					
a. Social value	7	8	8	7	9
b. See whole product	8	7	8	7	8
6. Desirable future	6	8	7	7	5

Note: Initials represent the names of the participants filling out the matrix.

organizations are built on the second of the genotypical design principles, that which produces participative, democratic organizations.

Genotypical implies coming from the DNA (Winby, 1998), as in one's natural hair color. When people dye their hair, it takes on a different, phenotypical appearance. After the dye washes out, the hair returns to its genotypical, natural color. Although all organizations look different in superficial ways, they share one or the other of the genotypical design principles. Most organizations in the United States today share the first genotypical design principle (see Figure 5.1).

Figure 5.1 shows the basic structures produced by the two genotypical design principles. The basic module flowing from the first design principle (DP1) is a section of an organization with a first-line supervisor (S_1). The

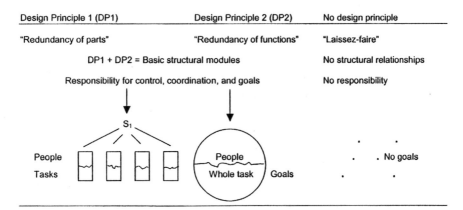

Note: S_1 = first-line supervisor.

Figure 5.1.   The Genotypical Organizational Design Principles.

technical name of DP1 is "redundancy of parts" because there are more parts—that is, people—than are required to do the productive work at any given time (F. Emery, 1967a). DP1 yields a supervisory or dominant hierarchy. A dominant hierarchy, or hierarchy of personal dominance, is one where the people, at least one level above where the work is being done, have a legal right and responsibility to tell the people below them what to do and how to do it. Its second critical feature is that responsibility for coordination and control is located at least one level above where the work, learning, or planning is being done (Emery & Emery, 1974). In DP1 structures, responsibility for control, which is the vertical dimension, is vested in S_1. It is S_1's responsibility to ensure that each person does his or her job on time and up to specifications. It is also S_1's responsibility to ensure that coordination, the horizontal dimension, is adequate, that all the outcomes of the separate jobs plus all the interdependencies between them add up to the section's goals. The master–servant relationship is at the heart of DP1. Relationships between masters and servants are not symmetrical, as the servants are dependent on the masters for their jobs and the masters regard the servants as redundant, replaceable parts (F. Emery, 1980b).

Figure 5.1 also shows that the basic module flowing from the second design principle (DP2) is a self-managing group without an S_1. The technical name of DP2 is "redundancy of functions" because there are more skills and functions built into each individual person than they need to do the productive work at any one given time. DP2 yields a nondominant hierarchy of functions, or a functional hierarchy. A hierarchy of functions acknowledges that different types of work need to be done at different levels of the organization, certainly in large organizations. For example, in large organizations, considerable productive work needs to be done everyday at the overall organizational, strategic, or policy level. This is the case in a school district office. Similarly, no organization can survive without having people working at the operational level, the level at which the core work or business of the organization is performed. In schools, this is the daily teaching and administration of a school. In a DP2 structure, nobody has the right to tell others what to do and how to do it. All communications are conducted as negotiations between equals. DP2 structures are open information systems.

The second critical feature of DP2 structures is that responsibility for coordination and control is located exactly where the work, learning, or planning is being done. In DP2 structures where multiskilling is possible, responsibility for both coordination and control is vested in self-managing groups at different levels of the functional hierarchy. It is the group's responsibility to manage themselves as people and to ensure that the group's goals are met on time and up to specifications. Once the goals are drafted, negotiated, and agreed with the authorizing group, it is up to the group to decide how to allocate different pieces of the work to different people at different times.

At times, the group may ask an individual to tell them what to do, for example, if a fire breaks out and only that individual has experience with fire. An observer of this situation may conclude that that individual is the leader, that is, that the structure is DP1. That conclusion would be wrong. The structure is still DP2 because the group has allocated the responsibility and can remove it at any time (Emery, 1990). This example shows that DP1 can exist within DP2 but DP2 cannot exist within DP1. The design principles are asymmetrical (Herbst, 1990).

The basic modules can be reproduced laterally and vertically. DP1 structures tend to grow wildly in good times, but their growth tends to be based on more areas of specialization, the technocratic bureaucracy (Trist, 1977). People complain about the growth in the number of chiefs relative to the Indians. DP2 structures may grow in terms of functions and people but tend rather to be limited in the number of levels in the hierarchy.

Relationship Between Design Principles and Six Criteria

In analyzing how the design principles affect the six criteria, one can begin to see why DP2 structures produce intrinsic motivation whereas DP1 structures do not. In DP1 structures, if the S_1 is doing his or her job properly, few decisions will be left for the people to make and, therefore, little elbow room. Similarly, those below S_1 (or below any level of S) will have little room to set goals, as again S_1 will set these to ensure that the goals are met on time. As each person has only one set of tasks, variety is limited by the set.

In DP2 structures, the situation could not be more different. In a self-managing group the group must make the decisions so that people who like making decisions can get in there and help make them. People who would prefer not to make decisions can sit back and let the others make decisions for them. The same logic applies to goal setting. For variety, every member of the group now has a range of tasks open to him or her. Each person is no longer constrained by a single job.

When it comes to feedback, DP1 structures have great difficulty providing it because they are inherently competitive. Even at the most trivial level, people must compete for the job above them. If somebody is making a mistake, it is simply not in the interests of their peers to give them feedback to correct the mistake. By leaving the mistake in place, the others are making themselves look better than the mistake maker. When promotion time comes, the mistake maker will be passed over.

DP2 structures, on the other hand, encourage cooperation, as it is the group as a whole that takes responsibility for meeting its goals. Punishments and rewards are awarded not to individuals but to the group as a whole. If a member of the group is making a mistake, it is in the interests of other members to correct it immediately so that the group meets its goals.

Competition in DP1 also negatively affects mutual support and respect. People with mental health or drug and alcohol problems are likely to be avoided rather than helped because of guilt by association. In DP2 structures, these same people are helped, as self-managing groups often become close and do not want to lose a colleague.

Meaningfulness is also enhanced in DP2 structures because the group now does a whole task instead of a fragmented part of it. People can therefore see the product of the group, whereas in DP1, they may see only their own component.

In DP1 structures people often have little chance of a desirable future because their skill set is constrained by the narrowness of their jobs. DP1 structures also de-skill those within them. People who enter a DP1 structure with a range of skills can practice only those relevant to a narrowly defined job. The old rule of "use them or lose them" applies. DP2 structures by contrast increase skills, as each member has the opportunity to learn all the skill sets available in the group's whole task.

The nature of the relationship between design principles and six criteria has held in every country and culture tried so far. It is a good example of a species-specific, or human, law. The six criteria provide a highly reliable measure of intrinsic motivation, and DP2 works well regardless of the nature of the industry or the purpose of the organization. This includes schools and universities (Davies, 1993a; M. Emery, 2000c; Williams, 1975, 1982).

There are some practical matters that must be considered in DP2 structures. One important one is the size of groups. The minimum group size for stable functioning is four people. Two people tend to take on the characteristics of an old married couple, which can be disruptive for others. Three has been found to be an unstable number, as three people rapidly evolve into shifting coalitions of one and two. The maximum group size is still unknown. It used to be thought to be about 19, but there have been well-functioning road maintenance crews of 27.

Varieties of DP2 Structures

Figure 5.2 shows that DP2 structures come in three forms that can be mixed and matched. The first form is that described earlier where there can be full multiskilling (Model A). Multiskilling does not mean that everybody in a team can do everything; it means that there is a sufficient distribution of skills and knowledge for responsibility for all goals to be shared.

Model A Medium to large organization where all groups are multiskilled (double lines indicate negotiations between peers).

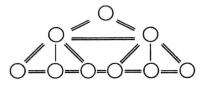

Model B Small to medium organization with specialists at the strategic level. Specialists share organizational goals (G_o) but individually oversee departmental goals (G_d).

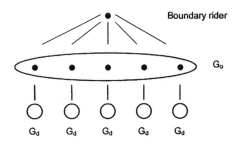

Model C Small, so-called knowledge-work organization—a one-level organization where the whole is the decision-making body, composed of temporary, overlapping project teams.

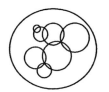

Figure 5.2.   Varieties of Second-Design-Principle (DP2) Systems.

Full multiskilling is not possible, for example, with doctors and nurses where there are legal restrictions on what nurses can do. Model B in Figure 5.2 can be used when, for reasons of specialization, people cannot share all of each other's work. In these cases coordination and control are split. The specialists at the strategic level of the organization retain control of their individual functions, say finance or marketing, but all specialists must coordinate across the organization to achieve the organization's strategic goals.

In this form, an individual is above the specialists who functions not as a supervisor but as a boundary rider (F. Emery, 1989b). In other words, that person moves backward and forward across the boundary of the organization and the outside world, bringing new intelligence to the senior team. The boundary rider will have to intervene in the case that the specialists cannot effectively coordinate or achieve the goals. Failing to coordinate is as much a dereliction of duty as is the failure to control the function or department. Sometimes, of course, the specialists cannot coordinate because the strategic plan or policy framework is out of date. In this case the specialists approach the boundary rider to consider a new plan or policy set.

The third form is appropriate when work is unstable. Unstable work usually takes the form of projects where every project is different. Model C in Figure 5.2 shows a single-level organization composed of temporary, overlapping project teams. When a new project comes in, as many people as possible from the existing project teams come together to decide who best should work on the new project and for how much time. The whole is therefore the decision-making body. Model C yields a highly flexible, dynamic organization.

As seen in chapter 1 the design principles underlie all organizational structures, from committees to conferences to multinationals to governments. The principles have also been discovered independently by Eisler (1995), who gives them different names but recognizes that they are extremely powerful and affect organizational life as well as male–female relationships.

The Assumptions Groups Make About Their Leaders

The 1938–1940 study noted that in autocracy the boys were prone to become dependent on their leaders or aggressive toward them, either actively or passively—states that are called *dependency* and *fight/flight*. Also noted was the case where a boy in laissez-faire took over the leadership of the group, a phenomenon called *pairing*. These reactions to the leader were intensively explored by Bion (1952, 1961).

Bion ran groups to rehabilitate people who had been mentally damaged by World War II. He noted that people form a group quickly but are insecure and lacking in self-confidence in the early stages. Further, he observed that the groups made assumptions about their leader, not as individuals but as a group. He concluded that there were two types of mental function. The first he called the *working-group mode*, a conscious way of functioning characterized by cooperative participation in the group task. The second was instinctive and governed by the assumptions that the group was making about its leader at the moment.

Bion identified three basic assumptions made by the group. The first assumption was that a great and powerful being (a leader) exists to look after the group. The group can therefore behave irresponsibly, as the leader will provide security. This phenomenon Bion called the *assumption of dependency*, and when the group has made this assumption, it feels no inclination to learn. The second assumption was that the leader is working against the best interests of the group and must therefore be resisted, either actively (fight) or passively (flight). When the group is in the grip of fight/flight, it is more concerned with fighting the leader than it is with getting on with the task. The third assumption Bion called *pairing*, as he observed two people, usually a male and a female, holding an animated conversation. Bion assumed that pairing was for the purpose of building a sexual relationship, the excitement of which allowed the couple to take over the leadership of the group. Practitioners now know that this is not the purpose, as we have observed many instances of pairing in the last 30 years. The leadership can be taken over by an individual, a couple, or a small group within a large group, and pairing comes in a negative and a positive form (M. Emery, 1999).

We also now know that, contrary to what many believe, the basic assumptions that groups make about their leaders are not an inevitable part of working with groups. In the 1938–1940 experiments and in Bion's therapy groups, there was always a leader. The same is true of all the experiments reported in the classic paper by Tuckman (1965) that established the theory that all groups must go through the stages of "forming, storming, and norming" before "performing," or Bion's creative working-group mode. Armed now with our knowledge of the genotypical design principles, we can see that the basic group assumptions are a product of a DP1 structure. Literally hundreds if not more search conferences, which have DP2 structures, have swung into the creative working mode and have never experienced a group assumption. Self-managing groups do not have supervisors, team leaders, trainers, or coaches as a separate level of the hierarchy (M. Emery, 1992b).

How then did the democratic groups in the 1938–1940 experiments work so well when they had group leaders? Did the basic group assumptions arise in these groups? The democratic leaders were reasonably successful in attempting to be on "the same level" (Lippett & White, 1943, p. 498), as they showed more than eight times as many "jovial and confident" behaviors as other leaders. However, the democratic leaders did at times have to give orders, although fewer than those given by the autocratic leaders. Similarly, the boys in the democratic groups did show some "leader-dependent actions," some "critical discontent," and demands for attention, although they showed less of them than did the boys in other groups (Lippitt & White, 1947). Therefore, while the democratic leaders produced fewer group assumptions, they did not entirely disappear. This is the critical difference between friendly, communicative leaders and genuine DP2 structures.

No matter how friendly or how communicative, the followers are always aware that there is a gap between the leader and themselves, that the leader holds responsibility for coordination and control. In genuinely self-managing groups, there are no basic assumptions because there is no leader to make them about. The self-managing group immediately goes into the creative working mode and stays there.

Adults in a variety of workplaces show all the typical Bion dynamics, defense mechanisms, and negative feelings (Zuboff, 1988). Many organizations and rural communities in India showed exactly the same phenomena, positive and negative, in relation to the design principles (De, 1984, 1991), and some of these organizations were big and high-tech (F. Emery, 1984). Teachers inevitably experience the same range of emotions in DP1 structures as do workers in other industries, and a teacher's emotions affect the knowledge, motivation, and behaviors of other teachers and students. However, there has been only limited research in this area (Sutton & Wheatley, 2003).

In terms of learning, a continuum exists from dependency through fight/flight to pairing (M. Emery, 1999). However, people in these basic assumption states do not show anywhere near the amount of learning that occurs in DP2 structures. If learning is a purpose of an organization as it is in schools, it is always more productive to have people organized into a self-managing structure than hope that helpful leaders will overcome the barriers to learning that are inherent in DP1 structures.

Communication in DP1 and DP2 Structures

Communication problems are often cited as one of the most frequent problems in organizations. Because communication is widely believed to be a primary property of behavior and organizational life, problems with it are dealt with directly. People are trained in additional communication skills because it is believed that once these skills are increased, the organization will work better. Others create communication channels that bypass the bureaucratic structure (Pajak & Hairston, 2001).

However, communication is not a primary property of behavior but a secondary one, a consequence of other factors. Often, communication channels exist but are not used, or communication reduces social activity (Emery & Emery, 1976). Because communication is affected by the emotions (Thatcher & John, 1977; Tomkins, 1962), it can be maladaptive as well as adaptive for an individual or organization. The organizational structure significantly affects the emotions and therefore significantly affects the quality and quantity of communication.

Communication is between individuals in DP1 structures and between groups in DP2 structures. This radically cuts down the total number of communications (Emery & Emery, 1976). An increase in communication skills does not translate into improved communication unless the person is motivated to use the skills. As seen here, in DP1 structures people are less likely to enjoy satisfactory levels of the six motivational criteria, so they will be less likely to use the communication skills they have. This is readily observed by watching the same people communicate in other settings where they are motivated to communicate with others, for example, in a voluntary organization.

DP1 structures reduce the quality of communication because they induce competition. Competition produces the adversarial characteristics of asymmetry, egocentrism, and "them and us." Asymmetrical relations between superiors and subordinates result in instructions or reactions, not conversation or negotiation. Egocentrism is expressed in statements such as "I want this by Friday." *I* versus *we* was one of the most distinctive language differences between autocratic and democratic organizations (Lippitt & White, 1943). A status gap between people is always a potential barrier to communication. It creates instability as people may omit or distort messages in ways that have everything to do with self-interest and nothing to do with organizational purpose (Emery & Emery, 1976). DP1 structures amplify errors whereas DP2 structures reduce them (Beer, 1972). Errors seep in from the environment and are subject to the influence of competition (F. Emery, 1977).

Regardless of what observations and measures are made of these two fundamentally different structures from DP1 and DP2, the only conclusion is that participative democracies are more appropriate for people, organizational health, and prosperity. If a community wants to implement its goals, it is important that it have a DP2 structure.

THE PDW AFTER A SEARCH CONFERENCE

The form of PDW used to design an organization from scratch is much the same as that used to design greenfield sites or turn project or research "teams" into cohesive, effective groups (M. Emery, 1999). It consists of the following steps.

Phase 1. Analysis

- Workshop management gives briefing 1 on DP1 and its effects.
- Action-planning groups from the search complete the matrix for the six criteria, using a previous experience similar to the implementation facing them, followed by reports.

- All members list the major essential skills required to implement the action plans and then complete the matrix in terms of who holds what skills on the list.

Phase 2. Designing a Structure

- Workshop management gives briefing 2 on DP2 and its effects.
- Action planning groups design a DP2 structure within which to implement the plans. Designs are reported, and a final design is chosen or negotiated.

Phase 3. Practicalities

- Groups consider the skills matrix and what other resources they may need, if any. If additional skills are required, they may need to do further action planning on how to acquire them. Timetables for progress reports and other practicalities are also decided.

The PDW for Commerce City Community

Following a single search, as was the case in Commerce City, the PDW need take only about 6 hours or less. It is often an advantage to give the participants at least a night off before they reconvene for the PDW.

The PDW begins with a briefing from the managers about the six criteria and DP1 and its effects, the same information as described here, using overheads to visually convey the nature of DP1. The organizational form is immediately recognizable, but it is essential that participants understand the design principles and their powerful effects. There are so many misunderstandings about the reasons for the dynamics in organizations. For example, conflict in DP1 structure is often put down to personality clashes without realizing that these structures amplify personality differences, whereas DP2 structures attenuate them. Competition always stresses differences whereas similarities are minimized. Without conscious conceptual understanding of the design principles, people are left to guess what has gone wrong in their organization. Their efforts to rectify the situation may worsen it if they mistake the symptoms.

It used to be commonplace for search conference managers to get a call about 3 to 6 months after the event telling them that people had stopped coming to meetings and that nothing was happening. Usually, the participants had set up committees, but they are DP1 structures with all their negative consequences. The two-stage model of the search followed by the PDW was invented to stop this problem of failed implementation. Once people have conscious, conceptual knowledge of the design principles, they can understand and fix problems for themselves. Better still, they can prevent them.

Completing the Matrix for the Six Criteria

With about 30 participants, I would form three or four groups, give them the scoring system, and show them how to draw up the matrix on one flip chart, with names or initials across the top and the criteria down the side, as shown in Table 5.1.

The groups are asked to think of when they were engaged in a previous similar experience to that of implementing the plans from the search. Most people have some experience of working for a church or Parent-Teacher Association or other voluntary organization. It does not matter that they did not share these various experiences, as when they put their scores on the matrix, they explain to the group what it was about that experience that caused them to score it this way. Through discussing their experiences, participants learn about the realities behind the six criteria and start to see what to do and what to avoid while they are implementing their plans. They work across the rows, giving themselves scores on one criterion at a time. They are learning to do an analysis of how organizations affect the people within them.

There is no need for any elaborate reporting of the matrices. Groups may just pick out some highlights to share with other groups or make a short summary.

Completing the Skills and Knowledge Matrix

The participants complete the skills and knowledge matrix as a total group. The first step is to go back to the action plans and list the major classes of skills and knowledge required to implement them.

With this list forming the lefthand side of the matrix, as many flip charts as needed to include the initials of all participants across the top are pasted on the wall as in Table 5.2. There is a simple scoring system that consists of putting a dash (—) for no skill or knowledge, one x for a little or backup level of skill, and two x's (xx) for a high level of skill. Participants then take a pen and mark what level of skill or knowledge they have for each item on the list. An honor system works well, as participants have no reason to deceive in such an event.

When the matrix is complete, the participants peruse it carefully. They can see immediately if there are any items where skills and knowledge are lacking. In such a large diverse group, most categories will be covered, but there

Table 5.2.   Completed Matrix of Essential Skills and Knowledge for Implementation

	JG	WA	DS	ME
Report writing	—	x	x	xx
Negotiation	x	x	—	—
Gardening	x	—	—	x
Arts and crafts	x	x	—	—
Computing	xx	xx	x	—
Fund-raising	x	x	—	—

Note: Initials represent the names of the participants filling out the matrix. A dash (—) denotes no skill or knowledge; *x* = a little skill or a backup level of skill; *xx* = a high level of skill.

may be one or two specialist skills missing. If there is anything missing, the participants discuss possible sources known to them and may do another little action plan to acquire them at the right time in the implementation process.

One of the big advantages of completing the skills matrix is that all participants now know where the high levels of relevant skills and knowledge are in their search community, making it easier to share those between groups as they are required. Groups can consult the matrix and contact people anytime so that the search community functions flexibly and communicates easily across action-group boundaries.

The Second Briefing

The PDW managers then give the second briefing on DP2, the various forms it can take and its consequences. Again, participants must fully understand how the design principle works and how to use it.

Designing the Organization for Implementation

Participants are again put into three or four groups and asked to design their organization for implementation using DP2. This is a simple task, but because most people are not used to designing organizational structures, participants may find it difficult to get to grips with it quickly. Rather than waste time, the managers can give them a few hints and talk about the groups that participants formed as they were working on the action plans. As these groups are responsible for implementation, they will be the basis for the design. Participants can then begin to see the nature of the structure they will need (see Figure 5.3).

To weld these action-planning groups into one organization requires a mechanism for coordination and convening progress meetings of the whole

Coordinating group

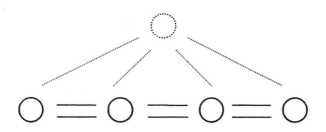

Action planning groups for strategic goals

Note: Dotted lines indicate nonpermanent level of organization. Double lines indicate self-managing groups cooperating and sharing responsibility.

Figure 5.3. Organizational Design for Commerce City Community.
Source: Adapted from M. Emery (1999, p. 218).

search community. This mechanism is shown by dotted lines in Figure 5.3, indicating that the coordinating group is not a permanent level of the organization. It is a function that a few participants will perform as required. The double lines between the self-managing groups implementing the plans indicate that these groups are cooperating and sharing responsibility for the total set of goals. The whole search community remains a single-level cohesive organization working toward its most desirable future.

Participants have several choices for this mechanism for coordination, all in the spirit of DP2. One of the most popular is to pull the names of a few members out of a hat to serve a term on the coordinating group. Participants may ask for a few volunteers, or people may be rotated in and out of the coordinating group on some reasonable schedule. Once these decisions have been made, only a few issues remain to be sorted out. These include items such as the frequency of meetings to check progress and solve problems, if any, and the nature of the report to be written. This latter question will involve discussion of what should be in the report, who should draft it, and the date by which the draft will be returned to all participants for checking. There may be other matters to be discussed by an individual community, and these will be included in this last stage, which is generally known as "next steps." The next steps are the points of transition between the two-stage model and the implementation.

By the time the participants in Commerce City have decided on the next steps, they have welded themselves into a learning, planning community; have designed an effective democratic organization though which they can implement their plans; and are well on their way to revitalizing the broader community of their school district.

The PDW for Huntingdon Area Community

In Huntingdon Area there are two searches. Because of this, the actual steps participants perform stay the same, but the design they arrive at will look slightly different.

The focus is still on one community with a set of goals that will be implemented in both halves of the community as it was split for the searches. The halves may also have some goals that are unique. There is no reason why all members of the two search communities cannot come together in one PDW. Depending on numbers, there could be six or seven small groups to complete the matrices for the six criteria. Each group would consist of some people, picked randomly, from each of the search communities. This provides an opportunity to work, share, learn, support, and get to know others from a different part of the area.

The skills matrix will be done as it was in Commerce City. It will just be broader across the top. When it comes to choosing the groups to work on the design of the whole organization, I suggest that each group consist of the two groups working on a shared goal. Those working on unique goals could also be grouped together. This has all the advantages of working together before the implementation proper begins.

The final organization design needs to reflect the whole area. Rather than have one group per goal, as was the case in Commerce City, in the Huntingdon Area there are two groups per goal, with the exception of the unique goals. This means the two groups who share a particular goal need to work together to implement it. This will give a slight variation of the design for Commerce City in that each group working toward implementation now consists of two groups, one from each half of the area, working together as one group. Although they may still basically implement in their half of the area, sharing the action across the area will give much greater flexibility with a greater range of skills and knowledge to share and more heads to put together if problems arise.

Having the groups with shared goals working together provides great opportunities for really getting exciting action going across the whole area. If there are two groups working together on some form of environmental goal, perhaps beautifying the area, the groups can cooperate to get the total community involved in a big day of action, with families out in the sun working together with their neighbors. These sorts of major events are memorable and satisfying for all involved. They can lead to rapid diffusion of a goal and a widespread escalation of action.

There will still be the same need for an overall coordinating and convening function, as there was in Commerce City. In the Huntingdon Area, however, there is also the need for meetings between the two groups implementing each shared goal if they have been working separately for part of the time. Nobody wants to be overloaded with meetings, so careful consideration will need to be given to the timing of joint meetings of the whole for monitoring overall progress.

It is probably best if meetings of the two groups implementing a shared goal are left to the discretion of the two groups, with a rule that says that either group can call a joint meeting if the need arises. Another rule could say that if a meeting has not been called in about three months, one should be arranged. The same rules could apply to the original search community meetings that are needed to keep the search community spirit intact. These too need to be held at regular but not frequent intervals. There will need to be coordination of both these types of meetings with the joint meeting of the whole. The rule could be that both shared goal group and search community meetings need to be held in the couple of weeks before a scheduled meeting of the whole. In this way, the meeting of the whole is guaranteed to have before it the most up-to-date information about progress toward goals and coordination on the ground.

Participants will also need to discuss whether everybody needs to attend the joint meetings of the whole or whether rotating a couple of members of the groups would be sufficient. Those attending the meeting of the whole will then need to report back fully to their groups so that everybody is kept well informed of progress plus any emerging problems or bright ideas.

The PDW for Tucson Community

In Tucson there were 30 search conferences, so again although the steps of the PDW remain the same, the overall form of the PDW and the organizations that come out of it will be different from those in Commerce City and Huntingdon Area.

With about 1,000 people involved, there is a theoretically best possible design for the PDWs, but logistically it could present many problems. Rather than risk confused and ultimately frustrated people, it is better to revert to a simpler model that will still ensure the coordination of all efforts in Tucson.

The simple model for Tucson is to use the process described for Commerce City and treat each search community as a separate entity with its own group to perform the coordination function. In addition, there needs to be a second level of coordination that will cover each of the 30 units. Each PDW will also select one person from those chosen to coordinate, to attend the second-level coordination meetings.

The first second-level coordination meeting should be held as soon as the 30 search communities have finalized their own organizations. This meeting should review goals, as inevitably, there will be goals in common. Action on these can be coordinated across the city, ensuring that there is strong mutual support for all during implementation. Those attending the second-level coordination meeting need to agree on their own timetable for meeting. They would also need to report back to their communities on coordination and support at the level of the city of Tucson. The final design of the organization for implementation of Tucson's community strategic goals would then look similar to that for Commerce City and Huntingdon Area, only with more groups and two levels of coordination.

A special point needs to be made here about the skills and knowledge matrices, as it is impractical to have a single matrix covering over 1,000 people. The best way of handling this would appear to be keeping the original records in a central place, under the care of those coordinating, so that they can be referred to when a need emerges. In a city the size of Tucson, it should not be difficult to access most skills and knowledge sets, either from within the original search communities or through knowledge of friends and colleagues.

A NOTE ABOUT PROGRESS MEETINGS

It is critical that meetings called to monitor progress and solve problems are structured from DP2 and are open and task oriented. This means that those who run the meetings need to act as process managers rather than as chairpeople and to use open, flip chart records. These processes ensure that participants stay involved in creative work, continue to share and support each other, and can see that all are still engaged in working for their most desirable community. Any reversion to DP1 would result in dependent or fight/flight behavior with a corresponding reduction in productive work. Attendance at meetings would drop off, and implementation would falter.

With well-designed meetings, motivation, creativity, and energy will continue to be generated; support for community action will grow; and more people will enjoy the excitement of working with others in their community for the good of all.

· 6 ·

Planning and Organizing to Improve the School District—Steps 4 and 5

$\mathcal{T}$he last two chapters have discussed processes that result in vibrant and active communities around a school district. Revitalizing the communities within which school districts are embedded ensures that as the school district begins to change, it will find energetic support from the broader community. In this chapter I look at the steps involved in planning a most desirable school district and designing an effective organization to bring it into being. This is the stage at which the broad-based sectors of the community and school district come together to learn, plan, and take collective ownership of the process and its outcomes. The steps follow those discussed in chapters 3, 4, and 5:

- Preparation
- Running search conferences to the point of deciding a set of strategic goals for the most desirable school district
- Conducting an integration event in which the strategic goals are integrated into a final list for the school district and community
- Resuming the searches to deal with constraints and to do action plans
- Running PDWs to ensure an effective organization for implementation of the plans

Throughout I note the differences between the steps for the broader communities (chapters 3, 4, and 5) and those for the school district.

PREPARATION

The SLT will have had progress meetings between the first meeting, discussed in chapter 3, and this step. Also, by the time that this step takes place, the results of the first two-stage model for the community will have become widely known. This round of two-stage events, searches followed by PDWs, for the school district is therefore informed by this previous work and its outcomes to date. All the processes, including those of preparation, will now be more familiar.

For this second round of events, the appropriate people to organize them are those in the group or groups that accepted responsibility for the community's strategic goals for the school district and learning. It would not be appropriate for them to be participants again. Working together with perhaps one or two professional designers and managers, these people will use the CRS across the three areas of community, school district staff, and students to select participants and call meetings for briefings, problem solving, and spreading the effects. This is why the participation of a sizable contingent of school, school district office, staff, and senior students is essential for the mix of participants.

Participants in the first search frame their goals for education and learning from the melding of the perspective of parents and citizens and their ideals. The goals for the school district starts from the same foundations but needs to be supplemented by the firsthand knowledge of those who work and learn within the school district on a daily basis. The ideals expressed in the search conference will be the same, but how they are framed as goals will depend on more detailed insider knowledge of how the system works or, in some matters perhaps, how it does not.

The inclusion of teachers and other staff in the improvement process is critical. After all, it is the teachers who have to implement change in the classroom and in teaching practices (Phillips, 2001). Teachers have been blamed for many of the problems in schools, but to ignore teachers is to treat them unprofessionally as they are expected to implement changes imposed upon them. "We have probably alienated our most important ally in renewal" (Bruner, 1996, p. 84). Rather than getting better teachers, we need to trust and support the teachers we now have (Dillon, 2001). Some teachers have become reluctant to believe that their input is valued (Shelby & Musgrove, 2001). The most likely reason is that the purposes of education have been narrowed from producing fully developed democratic citizens to producing vehicles for economic advancement and national economic competitiveness. Schools are now judged by test scores, and teachers are seen as technicians. "But no sustained improvement will occur without qualified and experienced teachers working together with the larger community to improve schools" (Harvard Graduate School of Education, 2004).

So far, I have used the terms *groups* and *goals* because it is quite common in community searches to have two or more goals relating to the school system or learning. One goal may relate to the quality of learning and education; another may relate to partnerships between the business community and the school system; or other goals may reflect the unique requirements of learning in that community. All groups with goals relating to learning and the school district need to come together to help with the preparation of the second round of events.

I use the schools and the district office as the basic units of the district, as each has its unique identity and character. This gives staff and citizens the opportunity to make unique goals for each school as well as for the school district as a whole. The basis of the overall process is therefore some number of units, each of which takes the whole school district as its focus.

The participants for this second round of events are a more complex mix than that for the first round because the process has moved from the community to the school district, its schools, and learning. The mix must now contain community members, school staff using the word *staff* to cover faculty and administrative staff, and students where appropriate. As all will focus on the school district, so again there needs to be an integration event. This time around, responsibility for the set of strategic goals for the school district will be distributed to individual schools, to the school district office, to the community as appropriate, and perhaps in some cases to the state. This meets the need for a comprehensive district strategy that is flexible enough to account for the uniqueness of individual schools (Anderson & Cascarino, 2001; Grasmick, 2001).

The first major difference therefore lies in the administration of the CRS. In this second round, use of the CRS will be more complex, as there are three quite separate populations from which to select participants. It would not be appropriate to have the community selecting school or school district office staff, nor would it be appropriate to have the school staff selecting students. Each population needs to select its own people. Nor would it be appropriate for any of the same community people who participated in the first round to participate in the second. They have their own goals and plans to implement in other parts of the community. Selecting a new sample of the community to participate in the second round adds to the number of community members directly involved in the efforts and helps spread knowledge of and interest in the changes underway.

It may be asked why there needs to be community people in the second round of events at all. Why not just leave them to a variety of staff and students? In chapter 1 I review the evidence for the fact that schools belong to the community. School districts serve their community and the district, and community cultures influence each other. In addition, there is the obvious advantage of having community and district people learn more about each other.

It is always educational for the different parties to share their perceptions of the same phenomena. A community may emphasize technology for personal student learning whereas the staff may see it as only another teaching tool. Students may have a different perception altogether. There are also serious issues related to the nature of the relationships among the school district, its schools, and its general community. Schools are richer for being deeply embedded into their communities.

The community component consists of parents and citizens from the geographical area surrounding the school. The relevant criteria for selection by the CRS include an adaptation of the one used in the first round, namely, that participants have a track record of being active and concerned about the school district. Potential candidates for reference in the community include members of the Parent-Teacher Association and various action and reform groups, those members of the business community who have supported the school and others who have worked for the school district in different ways. The community knows who these people are. Other criteria will be added if relevant. Demographic factors will again be taken into account.

The staff component consists of all staff of the school in point and the school district office. In cases where the school district office is small, some staff may have to attend more than one event, as it is important that someone from the office be present to inject knowledge of the system as it looks from the district office perspective. Staff will discuss other criteria for selection.

The organizers for education from the first round could split themselves into three or four groups, one each administering the CRS in the populations of school district staff, the community, and students. If there are many staff, this population may be further split into teaching and other staff. In other words, each population selects its own participants. Then the system proceeds within each of the populations, as described in chapter 3.

As the unions and staff associations are already involved in the process as discussed in chapter 3, it would be most unusual if union members were not selected among the participants. Selecting to give a range of union membership has the advantage of keeping unions in touch with the nature and direction of progress through the personal perceptions of their members, in addition to being formally informed.

Whether students participate in the second-round events is very much a question of age and judgment. Children of high school age have successfully participated in search conferences and similar events along with adults (Blick & Bradshaw, 2001; Davies, 1993a). Children as young as 14 years have had no difficulty in understanding the six criteria and working with the genotypical design principles (Butterfield, Dale, Ninham, & Travis, 1976). Much younger children have participated in similar events, such as planning and designing children's playgrounds, with only a degree of modification for age (Williams & Watkins, 1974).

It is probably safest to limit student involvement to those in high school. Here again, though, other issues arise, not of age but of other criteria such as ability to take responsibility for implementing plans over time. Students in their last year of high school are probably too busy and have limited capacity to continue to work on implementation if in the following year they move away to college or university or take full-time employment. Although they may have been chosen for their interest in the school district while they were part of it, there is no guarantee that this interest would survive a move out of the system. It may be best to concentrate the student sample on the middle years of high school. This would achieve the best balance of knowledge of the system with time remaining to help implement the change. This is spelled out in more detail as I consider criteria for selection in the CRS.

In considering the proportions of staff, students, and community among the participants, it would seem most appropriate for elementary and middle schools to set staff at about two-thirds the total number of participants, with the community forming a third. For high schools, the proportions could look more like staff, contributing about half with students and the community contributing about a quarter each. These ratios of staff to others indicates that the great bulk of the day-to-day work to be done in changing the school district will necessarily involve the staff within the district. They will, of course, be doing it in partnership with the community and their students, under the umbrella of the goals set originally by the community.

The criteria for selecting participants in the three areas of staff, students, and community need to be considered carefully. The universal criterion of being active and concerned about the future of the school district or any of its schools always applies, but in the case of students, this criterion may need to be supplemented by being active and concerned in student affairs. In some schools, this may be the only avenue through which students have been able to express their interest.

In each of the areas, the question of availability to implement the plan is central. As discussed in relation to students, leaving the school in less than a year or even less than two years can create problems if the change program has not spread rapidly through the student body. Similarly, staff who intend to leave a school or school district in the near future will be less likely to be enthusiastic about participating in planning and implementing the plans. If they are successful in readily procuring positions elsewhere, their participation will be lost early in the change process, even if they had been enthusiastic.

The second major difference between the first and second rounds lies in the information required by participants and, therefore, the briefings that need to be given. It is always useful to ensure that all participants have up-to-date information and basic statistics about the school district and its schools. This prevents many misunderstandings that may arise if people are working from incompatible understandings of their school district. Many of the staff may have current and intimate knowledge of the district and its schools whereas some of the students and community do not. An open flow of information must be available to all so that all participants can start off on equal footing in regard to knowledge of the school district.

The organizers of the preparation phase should consult with those in the school district early on in the process and build a database of essential information to be shared. It may be found that some information about the school district is not locally available, in which case some research may need to be done to extract it from other sources. Somebody will be delegated to search the national educational databases or the original census figures.

When everyone is sure that the database is adequate and the participants are selected, organizers need to call a meeting in which the information is shared with all participants, followed by group discussion. The participants may wish to take the information package away for further study so that a meeting and further discussion can be held. These face-to-face forums are not to replace the discussion that will take place in the search but are only to guarantee that participants will be working from a common baseline of data. Do not send material through the mail or rely on websites. Even if people do skim through or read the information, they simply do not absorb it as they do when they hear and discuss it with others whom they know share their purpose of improving their school district. The face-to-face discussion has an immediacy and a relevance that can never be approximated by more distant and impersonal communications.

In some cases, participants may decide that they would like more up-to-date information from the community about its attitudes toward or knowledge about its schools. They may be concerned that the community sees a different range of issues in the school district to those perceived by school district staff and take the opportunity to test this difference. They may decide to gather the information by methods such as surveys through the community surrounding the school district.

The third major difference between the first round of searches for the community and this second round for the school district flows from the nature of the organizational structures throughout the school district. It must be stressed in the preparation stage for these second-round events that it is critical that all participants behave as peers, equals. This matter did not need to be so pointed for the first round because communities usually do not experience problems with status differences. A problem may arise, however, which organizations such as schools have formal and dominant hierarchies. There are status differences between staff and between staff and students.

Organizers need to explain the importance of all participants' acting as equals in the search, where participants collectively share the responsibility for the content work, the outcomes, and the implementation of the ensuing plans. The special meeting described in chapter 3 was one opportunity to discuss the design principles and their consequences. The principles and the use of the second principle to structure the search conference need to be emphasized again in the educative phase for this second round of events. There is a need for honesty and effective communication in the search and PDW, and this is best guaranteed by people putting away their status differences, looking at the operation of their schools and offices fairly and squarely, and moving on to bring about improvements. The matter must be discussed, as the major dimensions of the event must be known to all.

As all participants have an interest in seeing how their school district can serve the interests of its students, its staff, and its community as well as possible, organizers can also reassure participants that the process and management of the search work to damp down tendencies of personal dominance. In particular, organizers need to mention that the ground rule for the first session, which is that "all perceptions are valid," is an effective equalizer. Additionally, the rationalization of conflict and integration reassures everyone that differences will be handled calmly and coolly.

Another reason that status differences should not cause too much of a problem is that all parties will be aware that a draft agreement is in preparation for the school district to move to the second design principle. As stated in chapter 3, this allows the parties to move forward with planning for the most desirable school district, with confidence that the changes planned will come to fruition.

THE STEPS IN THE SEARCH
CONFERENCE FOR SCHOOL DISTRICTS

The fourth major difference between the two rounds is that the search planning the future of the school district needs more steps. Whereas the first round of searches, focusing on the community, could use the most simple and minimal steps, that is not appropriate for this round, dealing with school districts that are organizations. In community searches people agree that change toward a more desirable future is desirable. However, it is to be expected that some organizational staff—and school districts are no exception—will resist some changes, particularly a change from the first to the second design principle.

Some will simply not believe that such a change is possible or could work in schools. Some will oppose it because they believe personal authority is necessary in organizations. Others may not believe that they will be involved in deciding and implementing the changes. Much of the resistance will fade away as people learn more about the changes through the educational briefings and discussion, but there may still be some residual resistance by the time of the two-stage model.

Participants with doubts about the change will be less enthusiastic than others and may positively resist it. In these cases, it is useful to include another step after the analysis of the school district as it stands now. This step is that of looking at the most probable future of the school district if nobody does anything differently, if nothing changes.

To do this most probable future of the school district, the search returns to the lists that were compiled for the analysis of the school district, concentrating on the Drop and Create lists. The question with respect to the Drop list becomes "What will the school district be like in 5 years time if we don't get rid of the things we have put on the Drop list?" As the things on the Drop list are things that are holding the school district back or disadvantaging it, not addressing them means that the school district will continue to be disadvantaged or that its decline may accelerate.

A similar question is asked about the Create list. In discussing the implications of not creating the items on the list, the more reluctant or resistant participants begin to see clearly that changes are required if the school district is to be improved.

The session need not be long or difficult; it is merely a reality check for all participants and serves the purpose of raising the probability that everybody sees the need for change and the directions in which this should occur. This session further sets the scene for constructive work in the next session, in which participants decide on the most desirable school district, outlining a set of strategic goals for that district.

A fifth major difference between the steps for the general community searches and those for the school district is the amount of time spent dealing with the constraints to creating a most desirable school district. A school district differs from a community in that there is a much higher level of regulation. School districts are subject to a range of other forces, from the local level to that of the state and the nation. This frequently means that many lobby and pressure groups are operating at any time to influence regulators, school districts, and other groups.

Some of the regulatory pressures on a school district are then going to constitute constraints on the ease with which school districts can implement their strategic goals. Plenty of time should be left for the search to work on how school districts will deal with those pressures. One common strategy is that of teaming up with other neighboring districts who are feeling the same pressures. This can become an action plan in its own right, as participants realize the power of numbers and the advantage of presenting a common front.

Another result of the analytical work on school districts, dealing with barriers and deciding goals for them, is the realization that so many of them spring from within the school district. As discussed in chapter 4, many if not all of these concerns will automatically be dealt with in the next step of the process, which is to change the design principle of all organizational structures in the school district and then enjoy the benefits that flow from this change. The sixth difference is that, in this case, there may be more barriers and goals that need to be held over to the next step to await solution. Constraints or goals that concern job satisfaction, morale, motivation, communication, or cooperation are primarily a consequence of working in a DP1 structure and will be affected by the change in design principle (chapter 7).

Again, as in chapter 3, the process managers will reassure participants that these constraints and goals can be safely left to the PDWs, by explaining how these problems arise from the design principles and do not require action plans to fix personality differences or communication skills. After this discussion, participants will be even more motivated to get on with the process, as they do not have to face the tricky, if not impossible, task of changing the behavior of some of their people. The behavior will change when the structure changes.

Overall, more time should be allocated to each of the steps in these second-round searches than for the same steps in the first-round searches, as a school district is far more complex than a community and may generate more heat. The exception is the first phase, of exploring the world.

The minimum steps in the searches for the future of the school district are as follows:

- Changes in the world around our school district
- Most probable and most desirable worlds
- History of our school district—what has made it look the way it does today
- Our school district today—what do we want to keep, drop, and create
- The most probable future of our school district—if nobody does anything differently
- The most desirable future of our school district, and then after the integration event
- Major constraints and dealing with them
- Action planning

The search is not limited to these steps, however. The process managers, together with the participants, may decide that other steps are required.

MANAGING THE PROCESS

The seventh major difference between the community searches and those for the school district may be summed up as a heavier involvement of the process managers because the search is organizationally based. This means that (a) some of the parties involved in the process may have experienced conflicted relationships in the past and (b) the structures within the school district are hierarchies of dominance so that there is always a chance that negative dynamics, particularly dependency or fight/flight (chapter 5), may enter the process despite the best design and management possible.

Under these conditions, random processes for selecting the membership of small groups are not appropriate. Nor can the groups be left to select themselves. Either of these options may yield a biased group composed almost entirely of one constituency, such as administrative staff, teachers, parents, or unions. If for example parents and teachers are in conflict about an issue, these groups would provide an opportunity for the different parties to "stand on their soapboxes" rather than cooperate to find a constructive solution to the conflict.

In cases like this, the safest way to select a group is for the managers to consult the list of participants and specifically design the groups for the most heterogeneous mix in each group. This guarantees that all sides of and perspectives on an issue will be heard and that the group stands a good chance at finding a new, creative solution for the issue. By avoiding soapboxes and preventing the reignition of a conflict, the new solution can be taken to the reporting session and subjected to the normal processes of rationalization of conflict and integration in a calm and productive manner. This helps everyone to continue to build trust and cohere as a community throughout the rest of the event.

When designing the small groups in this way, managers must avoid another potential problem. If a group stays together for two or more sessions, it tends to take on a life as an entity in its own right rather than simply be a part of the scaffolding for the work of the whole search community (M. Emery, 1999). If this happens, the community breaks down into separate groups with the potential for intergroup conflict. It is important to keep the community together in one large room rather than use breakout rooms for groups at any stage. Having small groups work in different corners of a large room keeps everyone in physical contact, facilitates communications between the groups, and reinforces the idea of a community working together for a set of shared purposes.

In general, process managers need to be more on their toes in a search involving an organization or in any search with a potential for conflict or negative dynamics. Process managers need to be more interventionist in designing each of the steps as the event proceeds. By preventing these potential problems, managers can be confident that by the time the participants self-select around the set of strategic goals, enough trust has been generated within the total community to overcome any tendencies for it splitting apart.

It is at this point that I need to discuss the three examples one by one, as the size of the district determines the steps to an effective process.

THE SCHOOL DISTRICT OF COMMERCE CITY

Commerce City school district has an elementary, a middle school, and a high school, so these schools are the basis for the overall process. The three processes are all called the "Future of the Commerce City School District."

Students would participate in only the high school events, as other students are too young to successfully participate as equals with adults in these events. However, other events can be designed in before the searches and PDWs to involve these younger students and gauge their views on how their schools can be improved. These smaller events, designed explicitly for the age groups involved, could be fun half days held at weekends with parents and other citizens, listening to the children and questioning them in informal ways.

After each of the searches has a set of strategic goals for the most desirable school district, an integration event needs to be held as soon as possible to allow the searches to get back to action planning. With approximately 30 participants in each search, the final step, after deciding on their goals, would be to select a number of participants to attend the integration event.

This event needs to take only 2 to 3 hours and can be held anytime convenient to its participants. The three sets of goals will be put up on the wall, reported, and discussed. They will then be integrated into one list, simply putting together those goals that are identical in meaning or belong together as parts of a goal and leaving those that have no equivalent as stand-alones. The set of goals will probably need to be rewritten to remove the redundancies. The redrafted list needs to be checked by all participants in the integration event to ensure that it stays true to the original concrete statements.

The integrated list of goals will then be sorted into

- those that are unique to a particular school and community, which will take responsibility for them;
- others that all schools and their communities in the district can take responsibility for;

- those that only the school district can take responsibility for; and
- possibly others that only the state can take responsibility for. If this is the case, there needs to be discussion about and selection of a special group who will take these goals to the SLT and then onto the relevant state officers to initiate negotiations.

The searches then need to reconvene so that participants can select around the goals that remain, deal with constraints, and do action planning. Once the action planning is complete, a PDW needs to be scheduled to design an effective organization for implementing goals in the Commerce City school district. The steps that participants perform in the PDW will be the same as those discussed in chapter 5. With about 90 participants in Commerce City, 9 or 10 small groups can be formed to complete the matrix for the six criteria, with a mixture of the three search participants in each group to promote networking, mutual learning, and sharing. Again the matrix for the skills and knowledge required for implementation of the action plans can be done in the total group.

Using the same logic as that used in chapter 5, the groups doing the final organizational designs can be those who are working on the same or similar goal. Again, those groups working on unique goals for their particular schools can be grouped to do the organizational design work. This will yield about 10 to 15 groups in all.

The final organization design needs to reflect the whole Commerce City school district in its community. If the basis for the design is "one group, one goal," which ensures cooperative work across the school district, all that remains is to select a coordinating group from the membership and decide timetables and rules for meeting as a whole, as goal-based groups, and as a coordinating group. If it is decided that 90 people are too many for progress meetings of the whole, some mechanism needs to be put into place for selecting or rotating people through meetings. As many people as possible need to experience progress meetings of the whole, reporting back to their goal group and to their search community.

THE SCHOOL DISTRICT OF HUNTINGDON AREA

Huntingdon Area school district has six schools, a senior high school, a middle school, and four elementary schools. Again, each school forms a unit, resulting in six searches with about 180 engaged. Assuming that some community people have been trained to manage the processes involved, all six searches can be held on the same days. The process managers from the community need to go out in pairs, as having joint management results in less stress as they share the decision making. The professional managers can act as supports and possible troubleshooters to the community people, visiting each of the six searches and being in mobile phone contact.

The integration event can follow shortly, keeping the momentum going and allowing participants to return quickly to their search communities for action planning. About five to six people from each search can attend, giving adequate coverage of each search but keeping the total number of participants manageable. Because there are six searches, rather than integrate all six sets of goals at once, which could become logistically difficult and confusing, it is easier to integrate the goals in two steps. In the first step, two clusters of three searches could integrate their sets of strategic goals into one list, giving two sets of strategic goals. All participants then are present in the second step as the final two sets of goals are integrated. This two-step process is clear, simple, and not much longer than the one-step process. Responsibilities can then be assigned as those described for Commerce City.

Schools and their communities take home their set of goals, deal with constraints, and do action plans and then are ready for the PDW that welds all participants from the six subunits back into a school district–wide organization.

With this number of people involved, there are many possible configurations for the PDWs, but some are complex. To keep the process simple and effective, a single PDW can be held. This means that all participants receive exactly the same briefings but then break up into four groups based on the location of responsibility of

- the goals unique to the particular school and community, which will take responsibility for them;
- others that all schools and their communities in the district can take responsibility for;
- those that only the formal school district can take responsibility for; and
- possibly others that only the state can take responsibility for.

It is quite possible that there may be quite different numbers in these four categories, so I cannot prescribe a formula for breaking the groups down further. But each of the four large groups needs to be arranged into smaller groups to work with the matrices and do an organizational design.

Once the designs have been finalized, they can be integrated for each large group. Each of the four or fewer resulting designs can then be taken to a session of the whole (180 people). Here the four designs will be reported and discussed. One may be chosen, or a new integrated design may emerge.

The resulting organizational structure may have either one or two levels of coordination depending on what the participants believe is manageable. Again it would be advantageous to rotate people through both the coordination function and the attendance at the progress meetings of the whole. Using the PDW in this way produces a high probability of enthusiastic cooperation and coordination across the units.

THE TUCSON UNIFIED SCHOOL DISTRICT

Tucson Unified School District has 115 schools in four large neighborhoods so that using school-based searches means involving approximately 3,500 people. It is not a good idea to have the searches spread over many weeks or months, as those involved in the early ones would become frustrated at having to wait for integration. Nor is it feasible to deal only with a small section of the Tucson Unified School District at a time. That option would destroy the integrity of the school district as a holistic system. Choosing parts of a system to begin processes is similar to setting up pilot or demonstration sites, which have invariably resulted in failure or less-than-optimal results (M. Emery, 1999). Such partial solutions generate the "guinea pig effect," where the people in the parts chosen find the experience of being watched unpleasant and uncomfortable.

In dealing with school districts with big numbers of schools, it would appear that there is little option other than to spend time and resources at the beginning to train enough members of the community to permit successful processes. These trained community members are not wasted, as they are available to assist with any further work that the school district or indeed the city may require. They become a valuable asset into the future.

With about 50 trained community members doing one search per week with two managers, the series of searches need only take 4 to 5 weeks, a period that most people should be able to wait without undue frustration.

Rather than one integration event for 115 schools, there could be four, one for all the schools in each area of Tucson Unified School District. Each search could send two people. Approximately 25 sets of goals would be brought to that event, with a large degree of overlap among them. In the first round of integration, five clusters could integrate five sets of goals each. In the second round, all participants would come together and integrate the five sets. A little later, a final integration event, involving a few people from each of the preceding four area integration events, could meet to integrate the final four sets into one for the total school district. This is manageable.

Once the goals are integrated and the responsibilities allocated, the search communities reconvene to perform the final tasks of dealing with constraints and devising action plans to meet their goals.

For series of PDWs in large school districts, planners have an alternative to involving everybody at once. This alternative uses a selection of people from each search to attend the first round of PDWs. When using PDWs, participants adhere to a basic rule that "designs may not be imposed." This means that although the teams that attended the first round of PDWs may have come up with wonderful designs, they cannot be imposed on those who did not attend. They must take back the process of the PDW as well as their draft design.

The team who attended the PDW now reconvenes the search community. It re-creates the workshop, gives the briefings, puts the others to work on the matrices for the six criteria and skills, and engages them in the design work. The total search community finalizes a design. Using this method avoids the danger that a design will be imposed, as imposition always carries the potential for lack of commitment and possibly resistance.

Sample size for selected teams should not drop below four people, as this is the minimum number that constitutes a stable group. With four people attending, there is a guarantee that what one forgets, one of the others will remember. Between the four, they should be able to re-create the major points of the briefings and guide people through the rest of the process.

Again I can use the four areas of Tucson Unified School District. Within each area, a PDW will consist of roughly 100 participants covering all the schools in that area. People can be selected into smaller groups to do the steps in the PDW by such devices as grouping schools by type. At the end of the workshop, the smaller groups can integrate their designs. The participants would then return to their search communities and run them through the PDWs. Each search community would then agree on a design. Designs may show some variation but they are usually quite similar because they are so simple and basic.

The final step is a meeting of all the 115 searches to agree on a final design. This meeting needs to be kept manageable in terms of numbers, and as there are only a few possible designs, it is reasonable that each search send only one member of its previous PDW team.

The final organizational design for Tucson Unified School District will probably have goal-based groups as in the other examples but with one or two levels of coordination, depending on the ease with which participants believe that they can coordinate and communicate across the school district. If it is considered necessary, there may be coordination at the level of the four areas and at that for the whole school district.

Two-stage models for a school district present many more challenges than do those for communities, but they are worth the effort. They confirm both the open boundaries and the partnership between the community and its school district. Through their goal setting, they set the stage for the exciting redesign work that transforms a school district into a healthy, creative place for working and learning.

· 7 ·

Redesigning Staff and Student Structures—Steps 6 and 7

Education and democracy have gone hand in hand at the societal level in America (Delbanco, 2005; Madrick, 2005). However, since the beginning of the twentieth century, the compulsory, secular education system has prepared young people to serve in the master–servant relationship in industry. As that relationship is disappearing around the world, why is the education system still producing people for it (F. Emery, 1983)? What we need is an increasingly progressive vision of education based on social justice, civic responsibility, and democratic participation (Down, 2001).

To strengthen the education–democracy relationship and improve the school district as a place of work and learning, this chapter deals with the process and results of achieving democratic school districts. Through the PDW, staff and students practice democracy as they learn to redesign their current bureaucracies, DP1, into participative democracies that flow from DP2. Representative democracy does not work in schools (Schmuck & Schmuck, 1992) anymore than it does in industry (Emery & Thorsrud, 1969). Elections held to decide representatives have little to do with determining the direction that the organization or society will take (Megill, 1970).

THE NEED FOR DEMOCRATIC SCHOOL DISTRICTS

The dangers and dehumanizing effects of working within DP1 structures in manufacturing have been well illustrated by two lightly written but true stories: *The Unknown Industrial Prisoner* (Ireland, 1971) and *The Assembly Line* (Linhart, 1981). It is probably less well known that the consequences of today's white collar work in DP1 structures are just as serious. DP1 has long

129

been associated with lower self-esteem (M. Emery, 1988) and poorer physical health than that found in DP2 structures (Gardell, 1977; Gardell & Gustavsen, 1980; Williams, 1975, 1993). Inequalities at work are a major factor in ill health and premature mortality (Marmot, 1999; Marmot et al., 1999; Wilkinson, 1996). People in poor workplaces and in conferences in which the basic assumptions are operating often feel tired, even if there is little physical reason for that feeling. The reason is that fatigue is in the mind, not the muscles. Feeling tired is an emotional response initiated by the brain to defend the person against any possible damage (Lovett, 2004; Randerson, 2004). The fight/flight response is particularly dangerous when it becomes frequent or chronic (Brunner & Marmot, 1999). Perhaps even more disturbing than the relation of work organization to workers' health is the finding that spouses of professionals in high-stress jobs are subject to high levels of stress and dissatisfaction caused by the same source (Pavett, 1986). DP1 organizations are a health hazard.

Not only are DP1 structures dangerous, but they are also failing to meet their original purposes. Within the bounds of the classroom, teachers set standards for teaching, learning, and interpersonal relationships (Pepitone, 1990), but unfortunately for the success of autocracy in the classroom, the boundary of the classroom is permeable. The outside world invades and disrupts classroom proceedings, reducing the teacher's power. The anarchy that arises from weakened guardianship is, however, overcome by the persuasion and negotiation practiced in democracy (Knight, 2000). Teachers can make their classes more democratic by negotiating decision making with students who then feel greater belonging, ownership, and authority to increase their control over what happens to them at school (Mills & Gale, 2002). "Only by including students as meaningful participants in the learning community of the school are we likely to resolve issues of decreasing motivation and academic performance amongst young people in the secondary school years" (Wilson, 2002, p. 98).

Rather than ask how we can arrange a school so that teachers can deliver their messages, we should be asking how to arrange learning environments and provide resources so that students can master learning tasks (Montuori & Conti, 1993). Rigid educational structures restrict creativity (Mills & Gale, 2002) whereas democratic classrooms are inclusive and encourage everyone to reach his or her potential (Knight, 2000). The ultimate aim of a democratic society is the production of free human beings relating as equals (Dillon, 2001).

It is of greater benefit to the performance of a school to concentrate on work processes, social architecture, and the organization's relationship with its broader environment than on supervising individual intellectual enterprises, as these are difficult to supervise in knowledge organizations such as schools

(Duffy, 1997). Social architecture includes culture, communication patterns, reward systems, pay schedules, career ladders, and organizational design (Duffy, 2004), but as seen later, organizational design given by the design principle is the most powerful. The other factors are consequences of the design principle and are difficult to change without a change in design principle.

Organizational factors are prominent in two outstanding examples of school reform in Oregon. These include staff working together on changes, teams of teachers working with groups of students, a career pathways system, teacher planning time, flexibility for students, and support for families to help their children (Blum, 2003).

However, many of the changes that are made in schools are often not connected to the way that knowledge is constructed, the division of responsibility between or interaction of teacher and student. In other words, the changes are superficial and do not affect learning. Significant changes relating to educational practice are less likely to be adopted, and, conversely, the further an innovation is from core practice, the more readily it will be adopted on a large scale (Elmore, 1996).

"Why, when schools seem to be constantly changing, do teaching practices change so little?" (Elmore, 1996, p. 6). Changes in U.S. schools are almost entirely teacher centered, and schools routinely undertake reforms for which they are ill prepared. They also trivialize reforms, changing their language and doing anything but changing teaching practice. Elmore concluded that we must find a way to overcome collectively bargained seniority agreements that, at the moment, are a major inhibitor of participative, democratic change.

Elmore (1996) found a widespread belief that good teaching lies in the motivated individual rather than in professional learning. This belief is holding back reform, thereby creating a need to push hard for change in a few strategic places in the system. Elmore suggested externalizing standards of good practice, such as those put out by the National Council of Teachers of Mathematics. However, external accountability is less closely related to a school's effective capacity than its internal accountability (Newman, King, & Rigdon, 1997).

Schools do not have the appropriate structures to increase intrinsic motivation for better practice. For example, only 12% of teachers base their lesson content on cooperative work with other teachers (Association for Supervision and Curriculum Development, 2003). In large schools, the knowledge of front office staff is frequently ignored, yet they hear about a child's domestic circumstances through such matters as reasons for late arrivals and can relate these to the classroom behaviors. This is a major loss of the capacity of the whole school to work as a team. Best practice organizations are those in which face-to-face relationships dominate impersonal, bureaucratic ones, in which people routinely interact around their practices and focus on the results of their work for students (Elmore, 1996). These are, of course, the DP2 structures discussed herein.

A NOTE ABOUT COMPUTERIZED TECHNOLOGY

Many have placed their faith in the adoption of computerized technology as the road to either higher profit or a DP2 organization. It is a misplaced faith. Technological innovation is not clearly linked to profit (Schroy, 2004) and democratization will not be achieved by any "technological fix" (Mathews, 1989). Management systems are key in determining the relationships at work (Maccoby, 1976). Many technologies do not support democratic working, as their underlying assumption is that "most people are lazy, stupid or hostile" (Garson, 1988, p. 262). Even those technologies that do support democratized work will be assimilated into the status quo unless the organization changes its design principle (Williams, 1988; Zuboff, 1988).

In chapter 5 I explore the design principles and the PDW to create an organization for implementation. In this chapter, I use the PDW to redesign the existing structures of the school district, producing a school district that is a "learning organization," an organization "structured in such a way that its members can learn and continue to learn within it" (M. Emery, 1993a, p. 2).

PREPARATION FOR THE PDWS

Changing the formal legal structure to replace the master–servant act, the default option for our organizations (M. Emery, 1997), will ultimately require the redesign of virtually all subsystems because those subsystems have been designed for DP1 structures. Because of the nature of these changes, the preparatory work concerns drawing up a labor–management agreement for the change and educating all staff about the change. Nonunionized school districts can have an agreement between management and staff, but this carries less weight.

An agreement is necessary because in the early days of democratization, many organizations that had successfully changed to DP2 were reversed on the whim of a new CEO. Despite excellent business figures, some managers could not believe it possible for some "uneducated" operators to do something that an "educated" manager could not understand (Zuboff, 1988). Resistance to democracy in general can involve educational qualifications (Bartel & Emery, 1999). Many other organizations regressed (Miller, 1993; Trist & Dwyer, 1993) partly as a result of the absence of an agreement. Labor–management agreements are guarantees that the changes cannot be wiped out at whim. They must stay in place until the agreement is renegotiated.

The outcomes of the PDWs are practical but simple, elegant, democratic organizational designs with a flat hierarchy of functions. Everybody in them will understand that groups at every level are held responsible for their own coordination and control, for meeting a comprehensive set of measurable goals, and for negotiating change as equals.

Making an Informed Decision

As mentioned in chapter 3, an educative process needs to take place before the PDWs. This starts as soon as making real change in an organization is mentioned. It is the responsibility of the process managers to educate both senior management and the union executive about what is involved in the process and its consequences. It is not enough to have an enthusiastic management. The union must also be convinced (Bluestone, 1983).

Learning must begin at the top in bureaucratic structures (Maccoby, 1976), as only they have the power to authorize the change. It is essential that both parties fully understand the process and its ramifications. They must understand the nature of the commitment they are making, the industrial issues involved, and the contingencies that may arise. Nobody should have to make such an important decision before being fully informed. The concepts and principles that all staff learn and use may be foreign; therefore, bringing in democratization requires "sincere, steadfast commitment on the part of both management and labor" (Bluestone, 1983, p. 36). American automakers finally started to catch up with the Japanese use of groups (Zimbardo, 2004) after the union became involved.

The educative phase may be both intensive and extensive. It sometimes involves visiting other school districts or studying research reports, whatever learning is required to produce confidence that the chosen path is the right one. It is necessary because so much of what is written about "teams" is not about genuinely self-managing teams. Take, for example, a comment by the *Economist* (2003) in relation to corporate leaders that "meetings are the cornerstone of teams, which in turn are the basic building blocks of corporate existence" (p. 13). Genuine self-managing teams do not have frequent meetings, because they do not need them. There may be a quick meeting at the beginning of the week or perhaps a longer intergroup meeting for coordination once a month or so. But most matters are quietly sorted out on the job as people work together to get the work done and meet their group goals. A reduction in meetings is frequently cited as one of the most dramatic increases in efficiency.

Most senior managements are organized as dominant hierarchies with individual managers reporting to the manager above or to the CEO. Nothing further from a team can be envisaged, as these senior managers frequently exhibit the worst possible dynamics of intense competition, which causes endless meetings. Self-managing groups avoid the frustration and grind of unproductive meetings (Haskell & Prichard, 2004).

The term *self-managing group* has been corrupted, has degenerated into a fashion whereby anything other than a lone person can be called a "group." A common example is the introduction of so-called self-managing groups with team leaders. It is a pseudochange, purely cosmetic. It is related to the still prevalent belief that investing in human relations alone will lead to higher commitment, productivity, and quality. Some executives hope to build a more exciting, highly motivated team. They want a flexible organization without losing control, so they do not change the hierarchical structure of dominance (Maccoby, 1976). Modern examples are no more successful than the early ones (M. Emery, 1992b). Like all cosmetic changes, they may produce short-term gains as staff give it the benefit of the doubt, but they quickly realize that once again nothing has really changed.

As seen in chapter 5, a self-managing group or a DP2 structure has no team trainers, leaders, or coaches. There may be one or more self-managing groups of resource people to train in the short term, but they are not a separate level of management and do not supervise. Everybody in a DP2 structure does productive work. Nobody manages other people.

Once the change has been decided upon, the union will usually request two guarantees. The first is that of no involuntary layoffs as a direct result of the process of change. This means that all will be employed but not necessarily in their previously specified jobs. The second is that no one will go backward in terms of pay and conditions. These guarantees are discussed in more detail later.

The Agreement

The Australian national debate about workplace reform led management and labor away from conflict and toward accepting responsibility to search for win–win solutions (F. Emery, 1996). By 1993, negotiating an agreement at the level of the enterprise was the route to workplace reform (Morris, 1996). Because school districts are employing organizations, there must be a labor–management agreement that the design principle will be legally changed

(M. Emery, 2000b) from the first principle (DP1) to the second (DP2). The agreement should state unequivocally that responsibility for coordination and control will shift to those who are doing the work or the learning.

It is important that the wording use these precise terms. Agreements have been drawn up with a variety of other wordings, such as "the work will be done by self-managing groups," which sounds fine, but as mentioned, these words are now meaningless. For example, an agreement with an organization in Sydney stated, "The re-organization is from the existing arrangement of people, i.e., independent job activity or informal group association of jobs, to a formal identification of people called workplace groups who will perform a measure of work" (Llewellyn, 1996, p. 42). That change process failed. The concept of "teamwork" was enthusiastically adopted in the automotive industry as a means of motivating employees and increasing efficiency; however, the teamwork was not fully implemented (Lansbury, Bamber, & Davis, 1996). Firms have also been urged to become "high-performance workplaces," but nobody can agree on what these things are (*Economist*, 1994).

The first labor–management contract for a democratic greenfield site in North America resulted from collaborative work between management and the union right from the start. Both parties saw the opportunity as one of "providing for satisfaction of quality of working life needs for workers" (quoted in Davis & Sullivan, 1993, p. 537). Those designing the new organization understood that the design was a "skeleton structure" that would evolve over time. The agreement stated that employees were responsible and trustworthy, capable of working together and making proper relevant decisions. It did not explicitly state the location of responsibility for coordination and control, and it also did not contain the traditional statement of the Management's Rights clause.

Despite excellent business results, the agreement was held to be inadequate, as the design did not evolve, nor did it spread further. Managerial support for these changes was lacking (Davis & Sullivan, 1993). This finding not only confirms the importance of a precise agreement but also underlines the importance of having a self-managing organization rather than simply self-management at the operator levels. It is much safer for all concerned that the location of responsibility for coordination and control be spelled out explicitly. When the words are explicit and clear, so is the meaning. It also means that anybody can look at the organization and immediately see if the structure conforms to the agreement or not.

Because school districts are legal entities employing a variety of staff, the change of design principle raises many issues with industrial relations implications. Changes are already afoot to acknowledge the professional status of teaching in collective bargaining for wages, hours, and working conditions, requiring extensive negotiations (Dale, 2001). Experience has taught us that it is best if all parties have agreed on ways of equitably resolving these issues before they arise during the process. Among these issues will be the need for a new pay system.

Pay for Skills and Knowledge Held

As the structure changes from a dominant hierarchy, where pay rises with position in the hierarchy, to a much flatter, nondominant hierarchy of broadly based functions, individual pay for position and seniority system will not work fairly and equitably. As the structure at every level is composed of self-managing and increasingly multiskilled groups where the group accepts responsibility for a comprehensive set of measurable goals, the only fair form of compensation that has been found so far is the "payment for skills and knowledge held" system. From here on, I refer simply to the *pay-for-skills system* or *skills ladder* for brevity.

These skills and knowledge are objectively measured "competencies" that are recognized within an industry and certified by accrediting agencies such as colleges, universities, and professional associations. There are lists of competencies in major industries such as the North Carolina Technology Competencies for Educators. These competencies are designed to "support and enhance professional productivity, information access, collaboration, and communication among educators." The advanced sets "enable educators to use multiple forms of technology to enhance learning in their classrooms" (North Carolina Department of Public Instruction, 1996).

As each skill, piece of knowledge, or broad-banded set of skills and knowledge is acquired, so an individual receives additional pay. This has several advantages. First, the individual has the choice of whether or not to move up the skills ladder. Some young staff will be full of ambition. Older staff may decide to move slowly up the skills ladder or not at all. The first-ever agreement in North America included a pay-for-skills system, designed by team members, where advancement was at the discretion of the individual (Davis & Sullivan, 1993). The second advantage is that one can continue to be a teacher and not have to move into full-time administration in order to make more money (Dale, 2001). Administration relies on a separate skill set, and many teachers are simply not interested in administration. With pay for skills held, these teachers can pursue their vocation and still enjoy pay rises. The third advantage is the flexibility that the system provides for the organization. Many schools are struggling with the organizational structures to support ever-increasing societal expectations of them (Dale, 2001). As staff become more multiskilled, they can handle more tasks, and in a rapidly changing environment, new skills and knowledge can quickly be imported into the organization to keep it adaptive. Once employees are used to the pay-for-skills system, the introduction of new skills is seen as an opportunity to advance.

A recent set of proposals to ensure increased teacher effectiveness covers several aspects of career paths with pay for skills. It envisages all teachers as having multiple career paths that guarantee expanded roles within the school or within the community. Teachers would have ongoing, professional growth that incorporates daily time to encourage collaboration, planning, and reflection. High standards are maintained through performance-based accountability where advancement is determined by academic achievement, examination, and demonstration. The scheme includes independent review by peer experts outside the district (Milken, 1999). However, the proposal envisages these changes as being welded onto a dominant hierarchy so that the results would be patchy at best. Systems designed for different design principles do not weld easily.

It is important, however, that initiators of school reform remember that the change of design principle must precede the introduction of the new pay system (F. Emery, 1989a). In Australia in 1987, the new terms *multiskilling* and *broadbanding* became common (Morris, 1996), and there were examples where people were multiskilled without other change. This change, even with new laws and levies regarding levels of training, did not produce a more educated workplace (Still & Mortimer, 1996). Training on its own does not produce the "learning organization," as staff do not have the motivation and structures to use the new learning. Training simply allows organizations to evade the real challenge of building participative democracies whose members would demand additional skilling (F. Emery, 1996).

When pay for skills is initiated, additional funds are required for the first few years until inequities are removed. This means that in the short term, more money may be required because some staff may be currently earning more than their knowledge and skills would indicate. The most effective way of overcoming this difficulty is to institute a program for updating the relevant knowledge and skills of these people so that the organization is receiving value for its money. The increased productivity and efficiency that flows from the change of design principle more than offsets the additional short-term funds required.

Barriers do exist to successfully introducing pay for skills, the first of which is delayed introduction. In a greenfield organization designed for self-managing groups, workers were promised a pay-for-skills system. Productivity initially increased, but as operators' skills improved, so did their dissatisfaction. As dissatisfaction increased, so did productivity fall back to the original level. It was only when the new systems were developed and accepted that production once again began to increase (Zuboff, 1988). The second barrier is to introduce the changes in only one part of the organization. Zuboff observed the growing psychological distance between management who remained in the normal DP1 configuration and the operators worked within DP2 with a pay-for-skills system. Managers were frustrated by their attempts to direct and control subordinates, and as efforts at control increased, operators reduced their commitment and responsibility. This example reinforces the need for a self-managing organization, not an organization with some self-managing groups.

Group Goals Replace Individual Performance

Along with the old pay system goes the individual performance appraisal system. Its replacement lies within the new system itself and its regulation of the group by performance in relation to a comprehensive set of measurable goals. Because individual jobs do not exist in a DP2 system, the focus shifts to group performance. For example, in the Australian auto industry, managers in all companies surveyed claimed that they had moved away from general duty descriptions toward defining the outputs required from the work group. These outputs included quality requirements (Lansbury et al., 1996).

If a group has met or exceeded its set of goals and has no group members complaining about other members, then there is no need to make any additional measure of an individual's performance. Work groups rarely break down for internal reasons (Trist & Dwyer, 1993). A group member will be directed outside the group in only the most serious cases that the group cannot solve on its own—for example, those involving mental illness or drug and alcohol problems.

Sharing Increased Productivity

Before the change takes place, negotiators will need to decide how to share up the increased productivity. At the beginning of *Productive Workplaces*, Weisbord (1987) described his surprise when he first introduced self-managing work teams. Output shot up by 40%, and quality improved to levels that the industry considered unattainable. The teams surged with energy and commitment, and antagonists made friends. Absenteeism and turnover dropped to nearly zero, as people loved coming to work. That has been the story from the earliest examples (Trist & Bamforth, 1951). A selection of references documents this over different cultures; industries, including education; generations; and measures (Aughton, 1997; Bain, Crawfor, & Mortimer, 1996; Baird & Grey, 1996; Bluestone, 1983; Davis & Sullivan, 1993;

de Guerre & Noon, 1998; F. Emery, 1983; Emery & Phillips, 1976; Emery & Thorsrud, 1976; Fells, 1996; Glaser & Halliday, 1999; Passmore, Francis, Shani, & Halderman, 1982; Purser & Cabana, 1998; van Eijnatten, 1993; Vaughan, 2003; Williams, 1982).

Staff will be aware of the increased productivity because they will be producing it. Although pay for increased productivity has led many organizations to such techniques as "the balanced scorecard" and "productivity accounting" (Parsons, 1996a, 1996b), schools also have several productivity measures, not simply that of student achievement (Hanushek, 1996; Leverich, n.d.; Lockwood, n.d.; North Central Regional Educational Laboratory, n.d.-b). Productivity gain-sharing systems should distribute gains equitably to all parties (Parsons, 1996c), and a flat rate of monetary return across the paid workforce works best in practice. The formula may also include a percentage held for organization development, training, or other matters that concern the school district and its community.

Teachers and teachers' unions often oppose bonus systems, as is shown by recent cases in Florida. In 2001, in an effort to recruit and retain teachers, the legislature's budget included a bonus of $850 per teacher who met a set of criteria. Unions believed that it was an attempt to circumvent collective bargaining. It did not raise teachers' base salaries, nor did it figure into their retirement (Rado, 2001). The issue was raised again in 2003 when the Florida legislature offered teachers a bonus if they could show that they were doing an outstanding job. School districts reported that only 2% to 4% of eligible teachers had applied for the bonus. In Pasco County, only 4 out of 3,600 teachers applied. The program was seen as being "very divisive," and teachers did not like the idea of "taking money from all teachers to give bonuses to a few." The executive director of the Pinellas Classroom Teachers Association described it as "a bad pay system based on a bad set of criteria" (Hegarty, 2003).

From Jobs to Employment

When the design principle shifts from redundancy of parts to redundancy of functions, fewer people are required. Some jobs disappear. The school district is then faced with the creative work of finding productive work for staff whose jobs have become redundant after the redesigns.

However, this may not create a problem, as many school districts argue that they are now understaffed (Evans, 2004; Feldman, 2002; Hill, 2003; Hiller, 2002; Ingersoll, 1999; Merrow, 2004). Hiller documents the consequences of the No Child Left Behind Act on Hawaii's schools, where more than a quarter of Hawaii's public school children are eligible to transfer because their schools need improvement. Understaffing appears to affect all areas of school function, including that of athletics (Evans, 2004). Many creative efforts have surfaced to overcome the joint problems of poorly funded and understaffed schools, including increasing resources through volunteerism (Hill, 2003).

The problem is exacerbated by underqualified teachers in secondary schools—in particular, "out of field" teaching, where teachers are required to teach subjects in which they have no qualifications. This is primarily an organizational problem (Ingersoll, 1999). There is a need for improved learning for teachers, but teachers need to be paid more and schools need to be restructured to enable teachers to maximize learning opportunities for their students as well as themselves. Without these changes, even the most highly qualified and dedicated teachers will continue to leave the profession (Feldman, 2002). All these reforms are accomplished by a move from DP1 to DP2, as multiskilled groups of teachers would learn from each other and have a say in teaching assignments. The power pyramid can be turned upside down (Merrow, 2004).

For those fortunate school districts that do find themselves overstaffed after the change, there are solutions, and groups often come up with their own in the PDW. The union guarantee of no direct involuntary layoffs does not preclude voluntary retirements. Nor does it preclude creative solutions such as inviting those whose jobs have been made redundant to list the work that has been neglected (because everybody had been too busy to get around to it), including developmental work. Displaced staff consult their skills and knowledge matrices and allocate themselves into groups to do this work.

Educating All Staff

Once there is an agreement, at least in principle, all staff are informed, and education about the change process begins. This involves briefings on the content and the process of the PDWs and takes the form of management–union presentations, followed by extended question-and-answer sessions. Staff come to understand the nature of the change and the implications of it for everybody in the school district.

These comprehensive presentations use the same overheads that are used in the PDWs to follow. One of the advantages of these briefings is that issues such as the loss of supervisory positions can be handled well before the workshops begin. They are discussed with reference to the agreement so that possible anxieties can be put to rest early. In this way, they will not interfere with the creative design work that will be done in the workshops. When all staff have been briefed, the PDWs begin.

THE PDW FOR EXISTING STRUCTURES

The form of PDW discussed in chapters 5 and 6 is to create an organization. School districts contain structures, so a different form of PDW is required. It uses the same components but with additional tasks in the third part. These PDWs take about 2 days, or separate parts can be done at different times.

PDWs are as participative in formal workplaces as they are in communities. Without full participation, there is not full psychological ownership of the product (Emery & Emery, 1974). And without full ownership of the product, there is no intense intrinsic motivation for high quality and productivity. The danger of "experts" or management-designing organizations for other people leads to resistance and misunderstanding about teamwork (Lansbury et al., 1996). Similar problems exist with the method called STS in North America (M. Emery, 1997). There can be "a relatively high degree of cynicism about the change to team working"; managers may become frustrated by "the pace of change" and tend to blame key individuals as well as deficiencies in the STS process (Macintosh, 1996, p. 224).

Participants in the PDWs

The rule for PDWs is "no imposition": the people who work in an organization or a section of it redesign their own structure. The units for the first round of redesigns are natural sections of the existing structure—the bottom two, three, or four levels of the hierarchy depending on the total number of levels. The top two or three levels are redesigned at the end, when these levels come together in a final "management PDW." The management PDW integrates (but does not change) the first-round designs, and it designs the management structure for a coherent organization. One or two of the middle levels may attend both rounds of workshops for maximum flexibility (M. Emery, 1993b). It is usual for one or more managers to either sit in on the workshops or listen to the reports. Sometimes, the groups need information that is known only to management.

If organizations cannot send everybody to a PDW, sections will select a "deep slice" team (Emery & Emery, 1974). This team will contain people from every level of the hierarchy in similar ratio to the number of people in the section and from as many skill groups as possible, to avoid bias. These teams take back to their section a draft design and the process. They then involve everybody in the section in completing the process and agreeing on a final design.

It is essential to involve everybody, as "an equitable and democratic education will not become a reality by some top down dictum, nor will it emerge by 'steering from afar.' It will emerge, as all successful democratic movements have and should, from the development of a grounded organization building on small successes" (Knight, 2002, p. 105). "Unfortunately, for the last decade or so policy has been done to teachers rather than with them" (Lingard & Mills, 2003, p. 2), which explains low motivation to reform practices or consider "alternatives to the existing flawed institutional arrangements and incentives structures" (Elmore, 1996, p. 25).

Differences Between the PDWs for Creating and Redesigning

The only difference in the first part of the PDW between that shown in chapter 5, for creation, and that for redesign is that in redesign, the six criteria are rated for the participant's own work. From the matrix for the six criteria, people can immediately see the effects of the structure.

The difference in the second part is that the participants will draw up the existing structure and a rough and ready workflow. They redesign the structure, not the workflow. The workflow is for information, as sometimes people in different small sections may not know each other's work. Yet in DP2, those sections may become a self-managing group. The workflow is not redesigned, because it cannot determine the design principle, but a change of structure changes the workflow. The only criterion for the new design is that it provides the best possible quality of work for everybody in that section.

The major differences occur in the third part of the PDW, which includes all the additional work that guarantees that the design will work in practice. The tasks are as follow:

1. Participants draft a comprehensive set of measurable goals for each group and the section as a whole. *Comprehensive* means covering every aspect of the work, productive, quality, environmental, and human or social. All goals must have hard numbers attached. For example, an environmental goal for a school could be a 20% increased usage of recycled paper per year. This set of goals is later negotiated with management, as they must fit with the organization's strategic goals. Once the design has gone to implementation, these goals control the work of the groups and the section.

2. Participants then check their skills matrix for requirements for training that need to be complete before the design can be implemented. The groups spell out who requires what training, whether it can be done on the job, how long it will take, and how much it will cost. Again these training requirements must be checked with manage-

ment. It is usually found that most additional skills can be learned on the job within about 3 months at most. The longest training time commonly determines the date of implementation, or "start-up day."

3. Participants then draft a career path or skills ladder as it applies to their section. After all the PDWs, a professional career path designer builds these fragments into a career path for the whole organization.

4. Participants then consider what else needs to be done to make the design work well in practice. The first two items are mechanisms for coordination within groups and between groups. These may be nothing more than a quick Monday-morning meeting. Other changes may include networked computers, changes in layout, or anything the design may indicate. Many different requirements have been addressed in this category, including finding productive work for people whose jobs have disappeared. As much as possible of this work is done in the workshop; it is not just listed.

5. Finally, participants must show how their new design improves scores on the six criteria. If a design cannot improve psychological satisfaction, it is an inadequate design.

The work done in the third phase of the workshop is implemented over the next few weeks so that everything is in place before start-up day. Before start-up day, the whole organization works as a DP1 structure. On start-up day, the whole organization works as a DP2 structure. When there are several PDWs, this day is determined largely by the longest training time required to bring groups up to the minimum skill requirements for safe, effective, and efficient work. Large organizations may have different start-up days for different areas or branches, depending on the overall organization design. Regardless of organization size, this process ensures that confusion and the possibility of reduced productivity are kept to a minimum.

PLANNING PDWS FOR THE THREE SCHOOL DISTRICTS

The appropriate unit for redesign in a school district is the individual school and district office, not including the boards, which are discussed later. Process managers study the organizational structures of the schools and district office to plan one or a series of PDWs to give a self-managing organization. Larger schools or offices are broken into effective sections for redesign, each one sufficiently large and complex to provide everyone in that subsection with high-quality work.

One powerful technique available for cases such as those involving school districts is the use of mirror groups in the PDWs. In a mirror-group workshop, two teams from two different units, say a school and a district office, work together as one team. On the first day of the PDW, both teams work together to redesign the school. On the second day, both teams work together to redesign the office. Mirror groups ask hard questions and help explore many more opportunities for learning than does a single team (M. Emery, 1993b).

Commerce City School District

PDWs always provide options with pros and cons as they can be used flexibly.

Option 1. For Commerce City, the first option is to redesign each of the three schools and district office as separate units. The disadvantages are, first, that the high school may be too large and complex, requiring it to be broken into subsections followed by a management workshop. The second disadvantage is that the school district office is too small to present staff with opportunities to learn how to design.

Option 2. The second option is for elementary and middle schools to hold their own PDWs and for two deep-slice teams to attend a high school PDW where they redesign the whole school in parallel, then choose one design or integrate features of the two. This workshop could include the school district staff who redesign their office and gain more design skills through seeing the high school teams at work.

Option 3. The third option is for all four establishments to send a deep-slice team to a PDW where the elementary and middle schools mirror each other and the high school and district office mirror each other. This is an efficient use of PDW time and has the advantage that the establishments get to know their work and each other much better. Another advantage is that the PDW reinforces the feeling that they are all in it together (the broad-front approach). It has the disadvantage that all four teams need time to take the designs and process home, but then again, each establishment will be doing this at the same time. In such a small district, all establishments could share a start-up day for the DP2 structures.

I would choose the third option, as quickly welding the four establishments into a cohesive district prevents possible problems down the track. Especially in large districts, differences may appear between schools, or units may get seriously out of step. Also, at the end of this workshop, everybody can work on mechanisms for coordination, heading off one potential problem. This need add only an hour or two to the total workshop length.

Huntingdon Area and Tucson Unified School Districts

Huntingdon Area—with its four elementary schools, one middle school, one high school, and a district office—can use basically the same design as in option 3 for Commerce City. With two teams from the high school, there could be a PDW with eight teams mirrored up to provide maximum opportunities for learning across the district.

In Tucson, mirror group workshops would again provide the best base for the series. Schools could be grouped by the four geographical areas and then divided to keep the sizes of the PDWs manageable.

For large complex high schools, PDWs for the individual school might be more effective, sacrificing the advantages of mirror groups to the need to involve many different staff in a formal workshop. The school district office in Tucson will attend one workshop to redesign itself, but it needs to consider sending a member of staff to hear design reports from the schools. This is strictly for purposes of mutual learning, and attendance can rotate around the office.

Once the series of PDWs is complete, there needs to be a meeting of people from all schools and the office to decide mechanisms for coordination and problem solving across the district. The dates for start-up days can be discussed and kept as close to each other as possible. Given that enough people have been trained to run the PDWs, the interval between the first and last PDWs should not cause too many problems. Then all staff can enjoy the excitement of being caught up in a wave of change that promises benefits for all.

THE DESIGN OF SCHOOLS

The DP1 structure in Figure 5.1 can be elaborated to show a principal at the top with individual teachers and other staff in the middle, with individual students at the bottom. Conventional classes are DP1 structures. The DP2 equivalent is groups of teachers and other staff working with groups of students, with the principal functioning in the boundary-rider role. There will be variations, with perhaps large schools having a group of senior managers at the top and groups of teachers and groups of other staff reporting directly. Some may have mixed groups—for example, classroom teachers and teacher librarians—as this increases learning for both as well as leads to higher student achievement (Australian Council for Educational Research, 2003).

In DP1 structures, teachers and students are often stuck with each other, suffering the "bar magnet" effects of personality whereby a teacher and a student may attract or repel each other. There is no easy way to cope with favoritism and the often unconscious rejection of individuals. DP1 accentuates the role of individual personalities so that the focus of attention is on the teacher's personality rather than his or her message (M. Emery, 1976). Given that teachers are engaged in one of the most meaningful of tasks, encouraging the development of young human beings, they have shown low job satisfaction (Emery & Phillips, 1976).

Groups of teachers sharing responsibility has become known as *team teaching* and has become more widespread since the 1960s, particularly in middle schools (Cromwell, 2002; Murata, 2002). However, team teaching means different things to different people. Shafer (2001) has identified DP2 models where all instructors are jointly responsible for course content and grading but take turns at presenting material according to their specialty or discuss specific topics from divergent perspectives. Other forms, where a coordinator takes responsibility for course content, are still DP1 and do not create genuine teams. Unfortunately, the DP2 models discussed by Shafer are grafted onto the existing DP1 structure, and attempting to mix the design principles inevitably causes problems. Several authors give tips about team teaching in an attempt to make it work better:

- Do careful planning to ensure compatibility and mutual respect (Shafer, 2001; Tan, 2002); recognize and appreciate the skills and strength of others, and create and enforce a common code of conduct (Glencoe Online, 2004).
- Take the responsibility of the team leader seriously (Cromwell, 2002), and should disruptions arise, ensure that the coordinator exercises internal control (Tan, 2002).
- Require attendance of each faculty member (coordinator) at other's classes (Beavers & DeTurck, 2000; Tan, 2002).
- Limit teams to no more than three members because reaching consensus is difficult with many diverse personalities (Cromwell, 2002; Tan, 2002).
- Have a dedicated coordinator with a clear vision of the class (Tan, 2002).
- Make teamwork a top priority; do not hold grudges against team members; use humor; stay positive (Cromwell, 2002; Tan, 2002); have or establish trust and a spirit of adventure (Beavers & DeTurck, 2000; ResearchWorks, 2002).

These tips show that the conflicts inherent in DP1 remain when team teaching is grafted onto a DP1 structure. Another example is if an open critique is seen as being risky, teachers learn to limit what they say. Developing trust takes time and is a difficult and continuing task (Bishop, 1999). "Working in teams is not easy" (ResearchWorks, 2002).

When the structure is legally DP2, no special efforts are required to build a cooperative positive team with a sense of humor because the structure itself encourages these behaviors. The detailed attention to skills and the set of measurable goals agreed on beforehand ensures that the structure is workable and well controlled.

Even talented, well-trained teachers flounder without support on the job. Teachers are the most undersupervised professionals in America, with a typical supervisory ratio of about 1 to 20. This ratio amounts to virtually no supervision (Rothstein, 1999) so that schools are among the large number of DP1 but effectively laissez-faire organizations in North America (de Guerre, 2000). To solve the supervisory problem and provide an adequate mentoring system would require a 10% increase in school professionals at an annual cost of $13 billion at 1999 salaries (Rothstein, 1999).

Forget ineffective supervisory systems and costly mentoring systems. Self-managing groups of teachers mentor and monitor each other as part of their daily work. Each group has been designed to achieve diversity of skills and experience in each group. Because it is in each group member's interest to cooperate, help and advice are freely forthcoming to raise the skill level of each teacher, as any teacher left behind would lower the group's performance. For a term, perhaps, some teachers may be allocated particular teaching or mentoring responsibilities by the group to enhance the overall group performance. The system would be flexible and require no more teachers than that of the current system. The teachers would simply be more effective and supportive without additional cost. Because it is built into the normal structure of everyday work, the advantage of this form of employee involvement is that it does not cut into family time (Drago, Caplan, Markowitz, Spiros, & Riggs, 1996).

Groups promote mutual learning (Hodkinson & Hodkinson, 2003) and much needed collaborative enquiry (Carter & Francis, 2000). These features are needed because teachers' initial training counts for little compared with on-the-job learning where learning for beginner teachers becomes "more and more a lonely process" (Flores, 2003, p. 18). Teachers need shared goals and a sense of self-efficacy through opportunities to participate in decision making. Team teaching is flexible, allows students to see a variety of approaches, is collaborative, and enables teachers to more accurately meet students needs (Gambill, Pfaff, & Yates, 1995b).

SCHOOL BOARDS

Boards have different functions to the staff and students in school districts and are typically elected. They are a form of representative democracy. To democratize boards, the constitution must be legally changed, first, so that members may be selected rather than elected and, second, so that members may work in an open search-type mode.

The best way of selecting members is to put the names of all eligible citizens of the district into a hat and draw out the required number, a form of jury system (F. Emery, 1976a, 1976b). Once selected, the members work as a one-level structure, ensuring that the competitive negative dynamics associated with DP1 structures are avoided and that all can work toward the best possible directions and policies for their school or school district. Changes to the constitution and function of the boards can be left until other more pressing changes are in place.

ORGANIZING STUDENTS INTO GROUPS

When school staff have finalized their group structure, they can discuss how best to involve students in achieving self-managing learning groups. Some different approaches to group formation are discussed here and often vary by age, but regardless of approach, student group working increases learning and individual growth.

Groups Work Best and Learn Most

The Longitudinal Surveys of Australian Youth project looks progressively at the performance of thousands of students as they move through the school system. It has consistently found that "positive school climate helps students achieve positive results" (Rothman & McMillan, 2004, p. 16). The more positive the feeling within the school, the higher the scores on reading comprehension and mathematics. Positive feelings and learning have gone hand in hand from 1939 to today's international studies (Rothman & McMillan, 2003). And as seen in chapter 5, there is a much more positive feeling in democracy than in autocracy and laissez-faire.

In Britain in 1986 a widespread practice involved seating children in groups around tables and expecting that they would work on their own without interacting with other children in the group (British Psychological Society, 1986). Of course, the children were not a "group" at all, merely individuals around a table. There was the appearance of groups but not the substance. In this section, I look at the effects of substantive student groups, the associations of social relationships, motivation, positive feeling, and achievement.

An early series of experiments in America compared the power of groups, lectures, and one-to-one discussion to change food habits. All participants received the same information. Group decision making about changing behavior was superior to lecturing and talking individually, and the effects were longer lasting (Bennett Pelz, 1947; Lewin, 1947).

Another series of experiments compared groups and individuals in problem solving. Groups achieved many more correct solutions than did individuals. The reason was that the groups were more likely to reject incorrect solutions and check for errors in their work. Contrary to the worries of some about the development of "groupthink," most of the incorrect solutions were rejected by somebody other than the person making the suggestion (Shaw, 1947).

These experiments have profound implications for schools, for even today, a great deal of information that the child is expected to absorb is imparted by the lecture. The National Assessment of Educational Progress found that American students can recall simple facts more than they can apply their knowledge to solve problems. Teachers are in control, are the center of activity, and do three-quarters of the talking. There is little student participation, cooperation, and peer learning, meaning that one of the major resources in the classroom—other students—is neglected (DeMiranda & Folkestad, n.d.). Similarly, it is still often assumed that the best way to help students is to work with them on a one-to-one basis, but since the 1930s, research has shown that this is among the least effective method for learning.

Two particularly troublesome classroom behaviors are "talking out of turn" and "hindering other children." Seventy percent of primary classroom talk is not work related (British Psychological Society, 1986), and one of teachers' most frequent admonishments is "Sit still and be quiet." By insisting on these most unnatural forms of behavior in children, teachers are discouraging learning, as learning is definitely associated with talk, activity, and noise.

"To be active, intellectually, physically and socially is the most characteristic feature of childhood" (Oeser, 1955, p. 11), and schools can create environments in which children's natural activity patterns and interests are put to work toward learning. All that is required is to break the class into small groups, allowing them full freedom of speech with the restrictions that discussion within the group must be relevant to the work and that the level of noise must not prevent other groups from working. "The second restriction soon becomes unnecessary, since the groups themselves will see to it that others do not unduly disturb them" (p. 12).

Groups multiply the output of work many times. Learning is speeded up, better retained, and better liked. Whenever a teacher helps a group, that teaching is spread (Oeser, 1955). Tensions between students are diminished below those considered to be normal in playtime. In a group with a clear set of goals, everyone cooperates. Leadership in the group will be different for different tasks.

Schools work like the rest of society. When group activities are not rewarding, they die out. Motivations arise when people experience the excitement of discovering something (Presser, Boyd, & Lea, 1955). If a behavior is sustained only by threats of punishment, interest is directed toward avoiding the punishment. "This is undoubtedly one of the factors which is responsible for the great majority of children leaving school as soon as it is legally permissible" (Oeser, 1955, p. 3). Motivation is essential for learning and "is generated and sustained by social interactions more than by intellectual insight." This applies to social relations between students as much as it is between students and teachers. When peer relations improve, so does children's learning improve.

Ward and Murphy (1955) found that the advantages of groups over classrooms included students' accepting opportunities to achieve individual goals and cooperating to achieve group goals. They communicate freely, and communication skills grow rapidly with self-discipline, unselfishness, getting along with others, and helping others. Isolated or rejected children are better absorbed into a group, become accepted, and make more contributions. Students with high ability receive great satisfaction from being recognized and are encouraged to work to the fullest extent of their capacity. Group work dramatically improves social relations with peers and teachers, emotional and mental health, and motivation.

Another advantage is that while groups are getting on with their work, teachers have time to spend with children who need special attention (Ward & Murphy, 1955). This freeing up of teachers' time significantly reduces the frustration that teachers feel when surrounded by large classes including difficult children. Assessment can also be used less frequently as it is easier to see what has been accomplished and learned.

"Jigsaw classrooms" were invented in Austin, Texas, to avoid the negative consequences of desegregating schools. Jigsaw classrooms contain groups where each member chooses one piece of the topic to learn. The students return to their teams and teach other members the piece they learned. A whole picture emerges from the pieces of the puzzle. Soon after its introduction, remarkable things happened. All children started to listen to each other—especially minority children, who used to be ignored or disparaged—

because such attention and cooperation are essential to getting a good grade. Self-esteem and achievement rose (Zimbardo, 2004).

A thorough comparison of jigsaw and traditional instruction was carried out in eight German elementary schools. It showed that self-esteem and achievement rose in Germany as well as in America (Steffens, n.d.). The results were measured before, directly after, and 4 months later. The students in the cooperative jigsaw classes learned more than did those in traditional instruction classes. Most strikingly, the students in the cooperative classes had the same amount of knowledge gain after 4 months as students in the traditional classes had immediately after the instruction. The increased achievement applied regardless of whether a student had been a teacher of or a listener to a piece of knowledge and covered students across the ability range (Borsch, Jurgen-Lohmann, & Giesen, 2001; Institut fur Padagogische Psychologie, n.d.).

Small groups of students mixed in intellectual ability in East Lyme Middle School (Niantic, Connecticut) have raised achievement scores, self-esteem, and intergroup relations (National Middle School Association, 1999). Groups provide a focus for identity as members educate each other, balancing ethnic or racial identities and the sense of the larger community of which they are a part: "We have known for years that if you treat people, young kids included, as responsible, contributing parties to the group, as having a job to do, they will grow into it" (Bruner, 1996, p. 77).

When team teaching is combined with multiage groups of children in high school, the benefits of teaming are multiplied. Students in multiage classes and groups are more likely than their peers to have positive self-concepts, high self-esteem, and good attitudes toward school: 58% of students in multiage classes performed better than their peers; 33% performed as well; and only 9% did worse (Gambill, Pfaff, & Yates, 1995a).

When the older children taught information and skills to their younger classmates, their academic performance, even their IQ scores, dramatically improved, allaying parental worries that they may drop behind. Teaching and learning become relative concepts, as all involved come to see themselves as colearners as they solve problems and complete tasks creatively. Underachieving high school students improved their reading scores by 2 years after acting as reading tutors for younger students for 6 months (Gambill et al., 1995a).

An experiment in Canberra, Australia, at a secondary college where 16- to 17-year-old students complete the last 2 years of high school involved students choosing group projects within a stipulated curriculum. The college wanted a general studies curriculum to educate "the total person for survival in an unpredictable, turbulent future" (Davies, 1993a, p. 258). The college wanted to develop and maintain group support and morale but realized that the goals could not be met within the existing school structure and instructional modes.

The starting conditions were that students would be volunteers, would be prepared to work outside both the college timetable and the school premises, and would participate in the planning and management of the course. The research team met with 25 students five times over a term in an open and exploratory process. The students worked between 58 and 70 hours.

The students began by spelling out their view of the future and the skills, knowledge, and experience they would need to adequately equip themselves for that future. They selected two important skills and then identified the activities that these implied. They then self-selected into three groups called Communication, Survival Skills, and Helping Others. They were briefed on the importance of group coordination, control, and planning.

Each group experienced some difficulties but found that learning can accrue from negative experiences and is not always associated with books. By the fifth meeting, the groups had collectively become self-managing and assessed their own performance. There was active, intelligent questioning between groups and intense involvement in the whole session.

Students then used the six criteria (chapter 5) to compare their learning satisfaction with that in English. The general studies course scored higher than the conventional classroom approach by an order of magnitude, as did a participative university course (M. Emery, 2000a). Groups agreed that the most valuable outcome was the mutual support and respect that they had generated, which other structures within the college had been unable to provide. Therefore, the course achieved its major objective.

More generally the evaluation showed that students of this age are capable of managing their own learning even when they have no experience of taking responsibility for their learning and self-management. Staff were impressed by the students' responsibility, creativity, and initiative, as the students had learned to deal with interpersonal conflict and a variety of difficult situations outside the school. However, the students believed that the school staff would not support the wider application of self-management because of a belief that students were not responsible.

A similar group process conducted with three self-managing university courses showed that learning can be increased considerably (Williams, 1975, 1982). Collaborative groups are also as essential to scientific creativity as they are to other areas of learning (Levine & Moreland, 2004), so it would appear that groups are the way to go at any stage in life.

The Composition of Groups

Although the group method is simple enough, a question arises about how to break the class up. A combination of children's friendships, their intellectual abilities, and any special characteristics that they may have is most common. Using different groups for different subjects has advantages, as children who are good at mathematics may not necessarily have the same level of competency in English. The students can choose who they want to work with within their ability level (Ward & Murphy, 1955). Others have had success with mixed-ability groups (National Middle School Association, 1999).

Children who are isolates, not chosen by anyone, are best placed into groups of children who are well adjusted. The social acceptability of these children can be improved by giving them special responsibilities that suit their talents and make them useful to the group (Ward & Murphy, 1955). Isolation, rejection, and unequal status can more generally lead to conflict that occasionally escalates into full-scale tragedy. It has been suggested that the killings at Columbine High School were fueled by an extreme hierarchical system of social rankings and labeling, with the murderers at the bottom. One student said, "They were hated, so they hated back" (quoted in Hari, 2004, p. 15). Moving a school to groups would gradually reduce the culture of hierarchical dominance with its inherent potential for conflicts.

The Promise of Groups

The promise of groups is not simply to achieve more learning and satisfaction; they can also more fully exploit new technologies for learning in schools. To make the most of our new technologies, "the traditional roles of teaching and learning will need to undergo significant change . . . and the very climate and structure of education must be transformed" (NFIE, 2000, p. 20). Introducing new technology into the current structures requires much time and effort, which is to be expected, as DP1 is inefficient, wasteful, and does not mix with DP2. When teachers and students are organized into groups, there is a resultant saving. For example, staff do not need to spend time after hours providing support, as they are prividing it during hours. The same logic applies to calculations for additional time required for coaching, collegial learning, team training, and professional development. This additional time is simply not required, as all the functions mentioned here are built into a normal working day.

The literature about the use of virtual or online groups contains a caution, however. Although face-to-face teams have long been known to have major benefits, Napier and Hasler-Waters (2003) found that it was necessary to prepare groups to work online. Some of the factors in the face-to-face situation are missing in virtual groups, and support from the instructor is "the most essential ingredient for satisfying team experiences" (p. 14). Students experienced less frustration with team assignments if they met beforehand in online team-building chatrooms.

At this stage of the process, staff and students are now organized for creative work and learning within a school district community that is actively working on improvements in all aspects of the district and community. Chapter 8 adds the final ingredient, learning directly from perceptions and experience.

· 8 ·

Balancing Teaching and Learning—Step 8

In chapters 5 and 7, I review the power of groups and redesign both staff and students into groups for productive and energy generating, work and learning. These are necessary steps toward adaptive schools and their districts, but as Fred Emery (1980a, 1999) realized, they are not enough to complete the transformation. He saw that the debates about reform centered on two competing theories of how the human mind works. Behind these theories lie assumptions about how humans perceive and learn.

THE TWO THEORIES OF LEARNING AND KNOWING

Fred Emery (1980a) tracked the development of both theories through history. The first theory is based on a Newtonian view of the universe as a mechanical system. The second flows from the very different universe described by Einstein. The first theory is a central strand in the development of Western scientific culture and is the basis of our education system. The second theory has roots extending back into history and has recently been boosted by discoveries in psychology and neurophysiology. Its has long been applied in adult/continuing education (M. Emery, 1999).

The first theory uses a logic derived from believing that the perceptual system functions like a machine. It rests on the assumption that people are born tabula rasa, blank slates on which knowledge must be written. People can obtain knowledge from a set of sensory organs, their eyes, ears, fingers, and the like, but those senses deliver only fragmented and inadequate knowledge of the world.

155

This theory contains assumptions about how the brain works after it receives this fragmented knowledge. To create at least some meaningful knowledge, the mind must be capable of associating and inferring relationships between pieces of knowledge to make meaning of them. But because the knowledge is inadequate, it must be topped up. To function well, people need injections of information from those who have it. This, of course, is the reason for teaching. Our current school systems are predicated on the faulty assumption that children are empty vessels, sponges, who need to be filled with facts, information, and skills (Dillon, 2001).

The knowledge considered useful and relevant in this theory, and hence the knowledge transmitted by teachers, is of a certain type called *abstract knowledge* (F. Emery, 1980a). A lot of abstract knowledge today is collected by instruments such as radio telescopes and relates to things such as black holes, which have never been seen directly by anybody. It is knowledge divorced from the concrete world around us. Much of the core task of schools today is the transmission of stores of abstract knowledge, everything from learning to read to absorbing the periodic table of elements. After years studying such abstract knowledge, people understand and can create new theories about how the world works. These theories are called *scientific theories*.

The second theory starts from a different set of assumptions. It assumes that the world contains information structured in an orderly manner and that people are adapted to this planet, having evolved to absorb this information from their daily lives. In other words, their perceptual systems directly extract this information from their environments without mediators of any kind (F. Emery, 1980a; Gibson, 1966).

In particular, people make meaning from noticing that the same things are happening in different places at different times. These unvarying events allow people to build increasingly reliable and comprehensive theories of how the world works (Gibson, 1977, cited in Reed & Jones, 1982).

Both the physical and social environments provide people with certain knowledge. The match between these environments and people's evolved abilities to use the knowledge they offer is the key to learning and further adaptation (Gibson, 1967; Michaels & Carello, 1981; Reed & Jones, 1982). The form of learning arising from this match between our capabilities and our environments is called *ecological learning*.

As people mature, they note more and more unvarying features and build these into larger, more coherent theories. "Knowledge emerges as the individual perceives the world" (F. Emery, 1983, pp. 131–132). These theories are sometimes derided as being "primitive" or simply "common sense," reflecting the undervaluing of direct learning from experience. This learning is, however, the bedrock on which the human race has progressed.

Indigenous people still use a powerful form of learning and knowing quite distinct from that recognized in today's Western world (Knudtson & Suzuki, 1992). In both these forms of learning, nature is accessible to inquiry, but one is based on direct perception whereas the other is at least one step removed from it. This is a clear statement of extraction and abstraction. Native knowledge is practical and extremely sophisticated. Many myths and legends have been found to be based on a "profound, enduring sensitivity to the real workings of the natural world over great expanses of time," and their detail conforms to scientific findings (Knudtson & Susuki, 1992, p. 135).

Both theories appear to have served us well, and we need not abandon either form of learning. We cannot abandon ecological learning anyway, as it is what we do naturally. However, we can make much better use of our propensities for both forms of learning, reforming our educational practices to give a better balance between the two. In so doing, we can realize the potential of people and make our schools productive, creative, and satisfying for students and teachers alike.

Assumptions and Evidence From Babies

Fred Emery (1980a, 1983) observed from many experiments in the education system, and from many failures, that there were two layers of assumptions about education. The first layer contained the assumption that bureaucratic structure was necessary. The second layer contained the assumption that people are unable to learn from their experience.

Others, too, have noted that the assumptions on which the education system is based have become beliefs. It is now an axiom that "learning is the result of teaching. And institutional wisdom continues to accept this axiom, despite overwhelming evidence to the contrary" (Illich, 1971, p. 28). Freire (1972) discovered that adults begin to read in about 40 hours if they choose words charged with political meaning for them. But such discoveries have not been "strong enough to overcome the dominant understanding that learning consists of the consumption of objective facts by individuals" (St. Julien, 2000, p. 269).

Polanyi (1958) called the knowledge gained by ecological learning "tacit," or unconscious, knowledge. He described knowledge as "an activity which would be better described as a process of knowing" (1969, p. 132) and saw learning as the personal experience and training of perception. He maintained that all knowledge must be either tacit or rooted in tacit knowledge before people become consciously aware of it. De Bono (1976, 1979) has shown that knowing or thinking is a function of perception.

Growing evidence supports the assumption that people are adapted to this planet with the ability to directly extract meaning about how it works.

Babies are not born blank slates but already have many capabilities. Newborns look at the edges of things, exploring them. They also prefer the complex to the simple, the patterned to the plain. They combine the perception of two activities (Friedrich, 1983). They crave novelty and become bored with familiar things.

"Children are more able intellectually than previously acknowledged" (British Psychological Society, 1986, p. 124). They develop this ability by actively interacting with the world. They build "intuitive" and "powerful theories" about how the world works (Bruner, 1996, p. 45; Gardner, 1991), showing a breathtaking range of knowledge and skills without teaching. After a few months, infants mentally cluster objects that are similar in some ways. By age 3 or 4 years, children are observing the functions of things and putting them into classes. The developing mind is always making connections between the knowledge it discovers and creates (Thompson, 2004). This is the "child as builder" (Papert, 1980, p. 7).

Starkey, Spelke, and Gelman (1983) showed that infants 6 to 8 months old could extract information about numbers across vision and hearing. The researchers had to disregard sensory inputs to detect the learning. "In other words, meaning is extracted by a single, organized, perceptual system." People are mobile, unitary perceptual systems (M. Emery, 1999). Whereas abstraction must necessarily involve remembering, extraction is pure perception.

Direct learning is not confined to perception of the physical world but extends to all realms including human and social behavior (Loveland, 1991; van Acker & Valenti, 1989). This includes such things as the tempo of action, emotional information (Walker-Andrews, Bahrick, & Raglioni, 1991), and gender (Berry, 1991). Young children can also detect intentions as well as intentions to deceive (Valenti & Good, 1991). Newborns have a "seek" operation that is not dependent on external stimulation. They actively search their environment for meaning (Haith, 1980). "Babies are ecological learners" (M. Emery, 1999, p. 59).

There can now be little doubt that by the time children arrive for their first experience at school, they already have working theories of how the world works. As they mature, they cluster knowledge differently. Young children find it easier to grasp sets of facts related to the attainment of goals that are related to specific topics and they therefore cluster them this way. As children become older, they are more likely to cluster knowledge by discipline. However, even in sixth grade, some children still predominantly cluster knowledge by topic.

The age at which children move from clustering by topic or goal versus clustering by discipline varies from subject to subject. Clustering by discipline happens at an earlier age in the area of physics than in areas of social psychology (Danovitch & Keil, 2004). Children probably hear more about why people behave as they do than they hear about why the physical world works as it does. Because they know more about people than physics, they keep their theories longer.

With the exception of highly abstract domains such as mathematical physics or cosmology, it becomes evident that people spend their lives accumulating relevant knowledge about their world. This makes the idea that a teacher needs to explicitly tell or show learners everything they need to know an "impoverished conception" of education (Bruner, 1996, pp. 20–21). Little learning is a one-way street, and in an institution that specializes in the learning of its members, it is more appropriate that learners help each other learn. The assumption underlying the promotion of mutual learning is that the mutual learners have some knowledge of the subject of the learning.

This means that one of the most effective solutions to accelerating learning is to assemble children into diverse and particularly multiage groups so that each realm of knowledge can be discussed and absorbed. The students' own theories and the abstract knowledge can be aired and compared through a medium that encourages learning. If these groups are of mixed gender, they will help both girls and boys who differ in the ease with which they comprehend different subjects (Cox, Leder, & Forgazz, 2004). Montessori schools are based on multiage groups.

The belief that children are born blank slates has been so strong that new information about the function of the human perceptual systems has been slow to diffuse. In a textbook on child development, Baldwin (1981, p. 3) stated, "In the first few years of children's lives they indulge in no theory building, they modify their behavior on the basis of the consequences of their acts." It is time to correct this view.

The Process of Skill Acquisition

Dreyfus and Dreyfus (1986) established that there are five stages of skill acquisition. These stages are qualitatively different perceptions of the task or decision making as the skill level improves. They labeled the stages from *novice* to *advanced beginner* to *competent* to *proficient* and then to *expert*.

Novices learn to recognize various facts and features relevant to the skill, and these are so clear that they need not take the context of the behavior into account. Novices judge their performance by how well they have followed the rules.

Advanced beginners have learned about meaningful elements through practical experience in concrete situations. They recognize elements and rules that apply to both context-free and situational elements. In this process experience is much more important than any form of verbal description. For example, teachers distinguish between two wriggles, one when the child is bored and one when they are excited, without being able to describe the difference precisely.

As learners advance to the competent stage, they see particular patterns in the world with definite conclusions or decisions attached. This is often called "making a decision by instinct." Many ancient peoples recognize this process by saying that "a decision arrives."

By the time learners have reached the stage of proficiency, a task or situation is so recognized that certain salient features will stand out whereas others will fade into the background. There is recognition of a holistic similarity. It is the product of a deep situational awareness and experience of invariances. Proficient learners supplement their unconscious understanding of the task with thinking how to go about it. Task involvement is interrupted by periods of analyzing the choices to be made.

When learners have reached the stage of expertise with a skill, doing tasks and making decisions simply become part of life. This is why people can recognize whole words faster than single letters (Dreyfus & Dreyfus, 1986). The human mind has the capacity to immediately recognize and understand whole situations. Experts do not see problems in some detached way or make conscious plans. They use their skill without being aware of it, involve themselves totally with the task, and perform skillfully without analysis or choice. "When things are proceeding normally, experts don't solve problems and don't make decisions; they do what normally works" (pp. 30–31).

Now it becomes apparent that requiring conscious, rule-based decision making can be counterproductive. Many complex installations, such as defense systems, require operators to follow a set of computer rules. This may look like competent decision making, but skilled operators know they must sometimes break the rules when a slow process of detailed decision making may turn an emergency into a crisis.

Young disadvantaged students may know how to quickly and accurately give change because they have worked on the streets but cannot explain the arithmetic behind their expertise. Experienced teachers help these students to identify the clues and make explicit their tacitly held knowledge. They design practice sessions with abstract knowledge using concrete examples that the students understand. This allows them to pass from the early stages of learning to the higher, more holistic levels.

Dreyfus and Dreyfus (1986) have shown that as learners move through the five stages in formal learning situations, the evolution of skill is from the abstract to the concrete. This is the reverse process that people use in their everyday ecological learning from the world around them. The conclusion is obvious: high levels of proficiency and expertise are dependent on experience and the direct ecological knowledge that flows from it, regardless of the type of skill or knowledge involved. This has great implications for the design of processes for helping children and adults learn new skills and knowledge. Once students have reached a level of competence, they should be taken off any rule-based procedures involved in drill- and computer-based learning. Human beings show flexibility, judgment, and holistic learning, none of which can be decomposed into specifications and rules. These features have proved difficult to build into logic machines such as computers.

Dreyfus and Dreyfus (1986) have stressed the difference between education and training. Education involves drawing out the abilities of the students whereas training involves learning a particular area of knowledge. They saw that computers have a role in assisting training. Computers may provide essential information about an area where students must conform to a specified body of knowledge but fail to provide the experience that students need to see connections and similarities for themselves.

International assessment programs recognize that in today's rapidly changing world students need higher-order thinking skills to be able to use their literacy, numeracy, and other skills effectively. These higher-order skills are required in two particular contexts: where the thought processes are needed to solve problems and make decisions in everyday life; and where mental processes are needed to benefit from instruction, including comparing, evaluating, justifying, and making inferences (Forster, 2004). Over the life span today, it would appear that people begin learning directly and are then constantly in a process of alternating between (and merging) ecological and mediated learning.

Effects and Implications of the Two Theories of Learning

The high value placed on knowledge that cannot be derived from experience has two effects: it devalues the experience of the ordinary person, and it has to be taught. This automatically led to the "don't knows" and the "knows," an educated, highly literate elite who specializes in knowing abstract knowledge and transmitting it to others. This led to specializations within abstract knowledge, or the disciplines. As the ideal within Western democracies became "mass education," so it has been found that more and more people need more and more injections.

Another effect of the high valuation of abstract knowledge has been the necessity to disabuse individuals of any faith in the validity of their perceptions. It has also required stressing the importance of memorizing and knowing the rules of classification of abstract knowledge. It logically follows from this that discipline, silence, sitting still, and literacy are high priorities. It is possible to track—from the original assumptions to the major features of the Western education system—the teacher–student relationship, the time-tables, the standardized curricula, and the nature of the reward and punishment systems.

Difficulties with such subjects as mathematics become the first step of a process through which people see themselves as bunches of aptitudes or their lack thereof. They accept the labels associated with the aptitude or lack of it, for example, musical or not musical. In this way, "deficiency becomes identity," and learning moves from being free exploration to "a chore beset by insecurities and self-imposed restrictions" (Papert, 1980, p. 8). This process creates people labeled as failures.

"All children are naturally and inherently motivated to learn" (Dillon, 2001, p. 59), but unfortunately, one of the first things that many children learn at school is that they do not want to be there. For many children, the in-built urge to be effective, competent, and independent; to understand the world; and to act with skill becomes thwarted partly as a consequence of their school experience (British Psychological Society, 1986). It is quite common to hear that little Johnny could not wait to get to school, was ready to go at 7:00 a.m. on the first day, and rushed in without saying good-bye. Three months later Johnny cannot get out of bed in the morning, often has tummy aches or headaches, and dawdles. Johnny's motivation has disappeared.

One reason intrinsic that motivation dwindles is that the theories preschoolers develop allow them to make provisional sense of most of what they encounter in the world but not necessarily in school. They answer questions in class from their ecological learning, which often results in wrong answers. Teachers then refer the children back to their books. This experience, repeated often enough, creates the thought in children's minds that they do not know anything. The children immediately begin to lose confidence in their theories and knowledge and in themselves. Frequently, neither children nor their elders are conscious of these theories and therefore do not acknowledge them when school begins (Gardner, 1991).

The propensity to answer "nothing" when asked the question "What did you do in school today?" appears to be a phenomenon worldwide. I regularly receive that answer from my grandchildren as much as I did from my own children. This answer contains a grain of truth, as school is typically done to children as it is often done to teachers (Gardner, 1991). To escape from the "nothing" phenomenon, students need to take responsibility for their learning as soon as possible. And there is no reason why this should not start happening as soon as the children enter the formal education system. The "five-year old is in many ways an energetic, imaginative, and integrating kind of learner"

(p. 250). It is also a well-established fact in psychology that children must be active in the mastery and application of intellectual skills (British Psychological Society, 1986). Educators can exploit the cognitive and affective powers of the 5-year-old mind and help keep it alive. By working with the child's mind rather than against it, the educator's task will suddenly become much easier and far less frustrating and distressing.

Teaching is inevitably based on beliefs and assumptions about the nature of the learner's mind (Bruner, 1996), but the debate about schools has been so focused on standards and assessment that the crucial questions about how teachers teach and learners learn have been neglected. Understanding the relationship between teachers' theories of minds and their teaching practices is fundamental to school reform.

The challenges many children and teachers experience at school can be overcome by a clear understanding of how people learn. This knowledge can then be taught to trainee teachers and applied in classrooms. Groups mixed for age, ability, and experience can engage in projects that are based in common experiences and that involve the learning of abstract concepts. This group work can overcome many of the problems springing from lack of awareness of ecological and mediated learning. Such reality-based introductions to abstract knowledge may also help deficiencies in understanding. Even when students have performed well in the tasks that school tests require, they do not always have adequate understanding of the materials and concepts with which they are dealing (Gardner, 1991).

The Purpose of Schools

Papert (1980) compared listening to a teacher or a television program with learning to program a computer. With the computer, the learning becomes more active and self-directed. Knowledge is being acquired for a recognizably personal purpose. The child does something with the knowledge, seeing it as a source of power. The reason is that meaning does not come from memorizing information; it comes from making sense of it (Dillon, 2001). The most central human concern is for meaning, and the process of extracting meaning from the surrounding world is that process called *learning* (M. Emery, 1993a). Both Dillon and Papert want to see children being supported as they build their own intellectual structures with materials available in the surrounding culture. They have argued that students are best served by engaging in open dialogue with each other, with the teacher acting as facilitator rather than instructor or lecturer. Teachers who ask open-ended questions that do not have a "correct" answer promote critical thinking and help the development of meaning.

When students and teachers work together around projects, all the relationships improve and the experiences are more positive and motivating. Papert (1980) mentioned examples such as the samba schools in Brazil where learning is not separated from reality. The samba schools are clubs organized as learning environments in which people congregate, primarily to socialize. But each year the club chooses a theme for the next carnival; lyrics are written; stars are selected; the dance is choreographed and practiced. All members dance and learn together, although the age ranges from children to grandparents. Much of the learning is deliberate, as a star dancer may gather a group of children around to learn something specific. There is a strong sense of social cohesion, belonging, and common purpose.

Learning directly from perception eliminates the possibility of the knower as outsider or bystander. It acknowledges that knowledge is in the world, not something divorced from it or outside it (Montuori & Purser, 1996). Once this is understood, it opens the way to learning as equals. As people live in the same world and the knowledge is in the world, there need be no barriers to mutual learning. Once people engage in mutual learning, they share their perceptions, and with the creativity inherent in group work, they multiply the amount of meaning that can be made from it.

As the central human need is to learn and make sense of the world and as meaning is generated from shared perceptions, then it follows that the purpose of schools should be the education of perception (F. Emery, 1980a; M. Emery, 1999; Polanyi, 1969).

Are teachers (and parents for that matter) aware of the relationship between theories of learning and school practices, and are they equipped with the best available theory? Based on the classrooms of most schools in the Western world, the answer to those questions would have to be no. "Perhaps the time has come for an entrepreneur to start schools based on what we know about learning" (Drucker, 1985, p. 110). The rest of this chapter looks at ways in which schools may reconcile the best theory with their practices.

APPLICATIONS OF ECOLOGICAL LEARNING

Using ecological learning in reality-based projects can have humble beginnings but big payoffs for the students, the school, and the partnering organizations. In Norway a teacher developed new relations between his school and a research group (Thorsrud, 1977). His students developed a new teaching/learning situation from working both in the school laboratory and in local community firms. As a result, the firms invested in some expensive equipment, which they installed in the school for common use by firms, students, and the school. Other school projects followed, and some students created new work roles for themselves before they had finished school. As this example shows, using ecological learning integrated with learning abstract knowledge is nothing particularly new. There have been several major studies of this method over time, and the most recent findings from these studies simply confirm the results of the earlier research despite advances in computer technology.

Discovery Methods

There has always been a range of discovery methods with and without tools. All discovery methods rely on ecological learning, and most are or can be adapted for group work. They confirm that much learning does not involve memory (F. Emery, 1993).

Many earlier reformers made suggestions designed to promote discovery learning. Illich (1973) discussed technologies that serve interrelated individuals at all levels of an egalitarian society; ordinary, everyday things could be used as basic resources for learning by webs of people who would be supported by professionals acting more like reference librarians than teachers. They would refer people to other "experts," such as elders in the community with special knowledge and skills.

Illich (1971) also described children in a Mexican market playing a game called Wiff 'n' Proof, which consists of dice with 12 logical symbols. The children were shown the best two or three combinations, and "within a few hours of playfully conducting formal logical proofs, some children are capable of introducing others to the fundamental proofs of propositional logic" (p. 81). Such games are liberating, also simple and cheap. Children do not need expensive software to play learning games.

New opportunities for learning lie in old institutions such as apprenticeships and in new ideas such as children's museums (Gardner, 1991). In apprenticeships, students learn from skilled adults, and the learning is relevant to its context. The reasons for the learning are obvious, and the skills and knowledge contribute to earning a living and being of service to society. It is meaningful work. In many countries apprenticeships are widely used. In Germany, over half of all adolescents participate in some kind of apprenticeship where the scholastic competence is tied closely to the needs and demands of a workplace (Gardner, 1991). Many of the most demanding professions in society, such as that of medicine, still employ a form of apprenticeship. Many short-term projects, such as producing a stage play, amount to providing apprenticeships for many skills and knowledge. Apprenticeships can build on the natural learning of young people, yet apprenticeships are in decline in America, as they have been seen as being less effective than teaching.

The master introduces the apprentice to tools, such as mathematical equations and books, only as the need for them arises in the course of a genuine problem, a challenging project, or the production of a valuable product or service (Gardner, 1991). Apprenticeships could be integrated into classroom practices and the school day. For example, students can share responsibility for maintenance of a school's physical plant. In a democratic community of learners, acknowledging rights and accepting responsibilities increase self-esteem (Bruner, 1996).

When the goal is simply to increase knowledge of the three Rs, it is often found that the students cannot read for understanding and may not want to read at all (Gardner, 1991). Students are not presented with challenges or projects that could show the usefulness of the three Rs. "The three literacies sit like religious icons on the shelf of a tourist shop, reasonably decorative, perhaps, but out of place in this casual context" (p. 187). Dewey's progressive education emphasized context and involved hands-on learning. Children visited farms, factories, and forests and brought their observations back to the classroom, where they were used in various ways to capture and consolidate learning. Children were also expected to help each other and contribute to the disadvantaged in the community. Although the instruction was indirect rather than direct (Saskatoon Public School Division, 2004), graduates of progressive schools performed as well as or better than those who attended traditional institutions (Gardner, 1991, citing Aiken, 1942; Minuchin, 1969).

Some progressive education tended toward laissez-faire and worked best with children from well-endowed homes with interested parents and motivated children. However, as seen in chapters 5 and 7, there is no need today to confuse laissez-faire with a genuinely democratic approach. And as detailed in the next chapter, although the problem of overcoming the achievement gap is far from being solved in America today, there are long-term solutions to this problem. Progressive education is still an "alluring educational vision" (Gardner, 1991, p. 199).

To realize this vision, we need no more than self-managing groups of students working with self-managing groups of teachers on projects that encompass ecological learning integrated with abstract learning. Such "mutual learning cultures" do not reduce the teachers' role nor their authority (Bruner, 1996, p. xv). The teacher groups function as the masters to the apprentices, and the projects can be drawn from the students' everyday lives or from today's new generation of science museums.

There does not appear to be any basic subject that cannot be approached by ecological learning and by changing the role of the teacher. The tools devised to help children learn arithmetic, for example, work to encourage the child's discovery of the properties and relationships between numbers. The "children learn arithmetic by insight and not by drill" (Stern & Stern, 1971, p. 15). The teacher introduces the child to the materials, may demonstrate a task, but does not correct errors, because the tools themselves are designed to provide feedback to the child. If the child fails on a task, the teacher restructures the task so that the child can succeed and learn the principles involved. The method is the same as that recommended for the learning of reading (Gibson & Levin, 1975).

The advantages of this teaching method are that children of any age and ability show "an active enthusiasm" for working with it (Sawyer, 1971, p. viii) and the process does not depend on memory. Once the principles have been grasped, anything that has been forgotten can easily be reconstructed (Stern & Stern, 1971).

Ward and Murphy (1955) reported on a series of studies in three grades of boys and girls aged about 10 to 12 years in social studies, arithmetic, and English. In English, many aspects of the subject worked well with groups. Groups can each be assigned a part of the reading and can prepare a summary for the rest of the class. Debates, short "lectures," and the writing of plays and stories are among those activities most appropriate for group work. In social studies, the children filled in a questionnaire about radio programs and discussed it, generating so much interest that they suggested topics for projects to learn more about radio. Groups formed around a topic. The teacher spent some time with each group and was accepted as a group member, contributing to the group goal. Thus, he gave guidance without autocratic control.

The groups experienced feelings of achievement and satisfaction as they presented their projects and new knowledge. There was a marked increase in the number of personal acceptances and a decrease in the number of rejections. There were friendly relationships between the students and between teachers and students. Some of the groups initially sought direction and were noisy, but all soon settled down, asking each other to be quieter because "we want to work" (Ward & Murphy, 1955, p. 98).

Although teachers often doubt that work groups can be used in arithmetic, it is in this subject that the most striking academic results were obtained (Ward & Murphy, 1955). Two grades were tested on standard tests before the experiment and showed no significant differences. After 4 months, the grade doing group work had made significantly greater gains than those of the other grade on all parts of the test. In this experimental grade, three children had raised their arithmetical age by over 12 months, and five children had raised theirs by 9 to 11 months.

In the group condition, the teacher put arithmetic exercises on the board for all children to attempt. Each group set itself a goal, but each child was allowed to work at his or her own pace. The teacher found that it was impossible to put enough work on the board to keep the brighter students fully employed, and they were allowed to work out of textbooks and to correct their own work from answer books. Students could ask help of any other student or go to the blackboard to solve a problem. The teacher was able to give his time to the slower students.

Students in groups that were homogeneous in terms of ability levels kept pace with each other, stimulating each other to higher levels and overcoming the frustrations of being left behind or getting bored as others caught up with them. Having a chart for each group, where students record their individual as well as group output, proved a strong incentive to improve both.

One particularly interesting finding in the group-based grade was that several times these young students, no more than 12 years old, requested examinations to assure themselves that they were making progress. The researchers found that the best procedure was for the teacher to set an exam and leave the students to it. They marked their own work and then discussed the results. "Often they are too strict" (Ward & Murphy, 1955, p. 104). "Kids are tougher critics than teachers" (Bruner, 1996, p. 94). This has been a typical result of group-based work throughout its documented history, regardless of whether it has been in education, industry, or voluntary work. Democratic groups are much harder on themselves than a teacher or a supervisor would ever be. The control exercised by self-managing groups is far more powerful than the tenuous control exercised by teachers and supervisors.

In Edison Elementary School, the teachers connect the curriculum to experiences that actively involve children in order to make the learning meaningful to their own lives. A simple activity such as learning about letter carriers involves children writing letters and delivering mail through the school. Through these activities the children learn math and language skills as well as develop competence and a sense of community. This school's performance has exceeded that of comparable schools in language and math. Teachers no longer approach problems by blaming others; instead, they discuss better ways of using the curriculum to solve problems. There is now a solid infrastructure for solving problems in which everybody is happy to be involved (Blank & Cady, 2004).

A new program for secondary science was brought into being in the United Kingdom in 1986. Rather than just teach theory, "Science and Technology in Society" aimed for an understanding of science by relating the theory to the realities of industry, technology, and everyday life. It covered nearly 100 units in physics, chemistry, and biology with comprehensive kits for both students and teachers. The units included "Test-Tube Babies," "Recycling Aluminium," "What's in Our Food?" and "The Bigger the Better," which introduced the idea of economy of scale. Some posed problems in which the groups had to work out a solution. Teachers were encouraged to develop their own local materials to suit local needs and issues, and students responded with enthusiasm. "Discussion is rare in science lessons, yet many children respond positively when asked for their opinion. Students who feel they have nothing to offer in an ordinary science lesson often become involved and committed" (Holman, 1986, p. 46).

To increase motivation and provide variety, science teachers need to include different approaches to their subject matter, including such techniques as oral presentations and simulations that are focused on socially relevant science. But because science cannot provide all knowledge relevant to any particular issue, transdisciplinary team teaching can be used to help students understand the complexity of any given socially important issue of the day (Dawson, 2000).

Using current controversies such as "mad cow disease" and genetically modified food can generate learning through opportunities to promote thinking and the skills of arguing and debating. These issues revealed links between science and other forms of knowledge, showed how disputes can arise in a community and how progress toward resolution takes place. They proved extremely valuable in promoting a healthy skepticism, although some students wanted certainty and some found the science difficult (Thomas, 2000).

When students engage in projects drawn from their experience, they see their lives as being relevant to their learning and success at school, particularly encouraging the more disadvantaged students. These projects produce closer relationships between students and teachers and between different students (Mills & Gale, 2002). The simplest way of beginning this process is to ask the class what has struck them recently as being novel or significant, a question borrowed from the first phase of the search conference, and to sort out what three or four items they would most like to learn more about. This procedure can be adapted for just about any subject.

Educational innovators can be sensitive to what is happening in the surrounding culture and "use dynamic cultural trends as a medium to carry their educational interventions" and content (Papert, 1980, p. 181; Carter & Berreth, 2001). Educators can be cultural anthropologists who find what children of a certain age relate to and then find a way to use it as a medium for generating learning and knowledge. Any attractive cultural trend can be grist to the learning mill. The health of the planet can encompass a range of learning. Many schools have established gardens where the produce is used in the school canteen or sold at school fetes. Some schools have established

or currently maintain tree plantations that encourage native birds and animals. These can be used as tools for learning in every conceivable way involving the obvious basic disciplines of mathematics, science, and biology.
Other skills and knowledge are also involved. Even local preschool children
are involved in water projects in times of drought. They keep a diary of
things they have noticed about water and its usage, discussing the implications of them and suggesting bright ideas for saving more water. Not only are
these youngsters learning to observe, write, think, and work creatively on a
serious issue, they are also becoming educated citizens who realize that their
actions, far from being irrelevant or powerless, contribute in significant ways
to the health and vitality of the places in which they live.

Using Computers

President Clinton's technology and literacy challenge stressed the need for
"computer skills and the ability to use computers and other technologies to
improve learning, productivity and performance" (U.S. Department of Education, 1996, cited in Snyder, 1999, p. 287). Computers in schools can rapidly accelerate learning and motivation (Gardner, 1991; Gibson, 2005;
NFIE, 2000). As students begin to assume different roles when working
with computers, including teaching, they are preparing to take responsibility for their own learning. Virtual communities provide a sense of place and
support through the creation of a "social presence" that facilitates learning
(Harris, 2004).

New technologies have the power to improve learning and productivity,
but these powers may not be effectively deployed. Classrooms with networked
computers demand different skills from teachers and different relationships
with students. Teachers of computer programming see a need for moving
from teacher- and subject-centered learning to student-centered learning
where teachers facilitate and encourage collaborative project work (Yuen,
2000). There has not been widespread change in this area (Wiske, 2000). For
new technologies to be used effectively, they must meet real and current
needs, and teachers must be prepared to use them effectively (Russell & Russell, 2001).

However, Cuban (1986, 1993) concluded from his studies of technology
use in American schools for about a hundred years that computers are mainly
incompatible with or irrelevant to teaching requirements and not worth the effort that teachers must expend in order to use them. Although computers have
been placed in classrooms with the expectation that they will become part of
a teacher's tool kit, the teachers have not requested them, nor have they specific plans for using them, nor have they been trained to use them effectively.

Although Cuban's conclusions were relevant at the time of publication, computers today bear little resemblance to those of 15 years ago. Are his conclusions correct today? Becker (2000) specifically tested Cuban's conclusions through the 1998 Teaching, Learning and Computing Survey. Over 1,100 schools across the United States and more than 4,000 teachers were surveyed with measures of educational philosophies, teaching practices, and the use of computers. Among these schools were those that had participated in identified educational reform programs.

American schools now contain over 10 million computers, and despite their sophistication they are infrequently used by students to acquire information, analyze ideas, and demonstrate and communicate understanding in secondary-school academic classes. Most frequent use was found in separate courses in computer education (80%), preparation for business and vocational education (42%–70%), exploratory uses in elementary schools (43%), and the use of word processing for presentation of work. The highest rate of academic use was in English, at 24%. This dwindled down to 12% for social studies and 9% for fine arts (Becker, 2000). The reasons given for this state of affairs included those of scheduling and time limits on classes, pressures to cover the information in a course, and the convenience of access to computers. Teachers are more likely to use computers if they are in the classroom rather than in a lab.

Another important factor in determining the use of computers was the teacher's educational philosophy: 40% of teachers favored being a facilitator rather than an instructor (30%) whereas 30% favored some of both. The "facilitators" are more likely to use computers effectively as they attempt to make content meaningful to a student and thereby develop deep understanding and the ability to communicate this understanding. These motivations spring from a view that understanding cannot be transmitted; it is the result of efforts to integrate new with prior learning.

Those favoring the instructor mode were more oriented to the sheer transmission of information and were more likely to use the computer for tasks such as skills reinforcement. Those favoring the facilitation mode often experienced practical difficulties that interfered with their intentions. However, some teachers had changed, particularly those who used a variety of software, who used the World Wide Web, and who tried to get students to work collaboratively. Teachers made more change when technology was readily available and they had participated in a program of technology-based instructional reform.

Becker (2000) concluded that Cuban was right in that "computers have *not* transformed the teaching practices of a majority of teachers, particularly teachers of secondary academic subjects" (p. 29). For technology to have an important educational effect, teachers must be able to see that it offers an educational advantage. It must also be readily affordable, networked, and portable. All aspects of practice must change, and if these remain unchanged, a new technology will be used simply to enact traditional practices (Wiske, 2000, p. 70).

For the introduction of graphing calculators, the National Council of Teachers of Mathematics worked collaboratively with all its constituent groups through the 1980s and 1990s to develop new standards for mathematics curriculum, pedagogy, and assessment. All new materials, educational goals, and supports were in place to make maximum advantage of the new technology. But there was one factor that was lagging: U.S. classrooms, the critical interface between context and the day-to-day experience of math, did not change quickly to use this advantage. International comparisons showed that U.S. schools were still relying more than German or Japanese schools on memorizing rather than on understanding. Japanese schools had changed their cultural assumptions and practices through a systematic process that began with groups of teachers meeting to develop, test out, and assess different kinds of math lessons (Wiske, 2000). When a group had developed an effective lesson, they shared it with other groups. This led to a new culture of teaching based on teacher-led research and collegial exchange.

Transformation with technology requires student interest (Becker, 2000), and to promote science understanding a technology must connect to personal or relevant experience. Other criteria include encouraging links to other topics, supporting peer learning, promoting autonomous inquiry, and enabling lifelong learning. These are all part and parcel of group working. For further progress there needs to be trustful school–community relationships that translate into partnerships in learning technology, and it would help if the entire education system was changing to meet the needs of students in a knowledge-based global world (Linn, Slotta, & Baumgartner, 2000).

Computers may function as "tutors" or "tutees" (Dreyfus & Dreyfus, 1986). The computer as tutor may provide students with information and instruct them as they work through structured exercises. Or, for example, students may learn mathematics through programming computers. The programmer instructs the computer, reversing the role of the student from one who is instructed to one who instructs. The activity is so varied, so rich in discoveries even in the first day of programming that the student may achieve something the teacher has not seen before.

When the computer is tutee, the flow of ideas and instruction between teachers and students is back and forth because students and teachers are instructors of the computer. The line between the status of student and teacher becomes blurred, and the relationships among students and between students and teachers are radically improved. However, the teachers are still professional teachers and in charge, despite the fact that they may not be acting as authority figures.

Writing programs for computer graphics or music is an activity found in the real world, and children are attracted to the products of it. Put children to work on programs for their favorite cartoons. Such examples exploit the child's natural desire to explore the world and learn all they can about it. Through them, the child's ecological learning is merged with the educational task, which is to learn mathematics. This contrasts sharply with doing sums, which is not a part of an exciting adult activity and is "boring" (Papert, 1980). It arouses no interest or intrinsic motivation, as it fails to exploit ecological learning about the real world that the child knows. With intrinsic motivation, anything can be gained; without it, much is lost.

The computer as tutee has both power and limitations, as skill acquisition moves from abstract rules to concrete cases (Dreyfus & Dreyfus, 1986). This means that Papert's computer model (1980) works perfectly for learning such items as arithmetical algorithms. However, once a student has passed the early stage of skill acquisition or learning, the computer would begin to get in the road of new learning. Advanced learning needs to be based on reality, as it requires diverse examples from the real, diverse world. When learners must see and remember whole patterns, analysis can impede their progress and risk their staying forever beginners.

There appears to be less hope for extended learning with the computer as tutor, although, again for beginners, there is value in it for drill and practice for tasks requiring memorization of facts, rules, and procedures, such as spelling and subtraction (Dreyfus & Dreyfus, 1986). The human mind is not a "smart" machine, and children need to be encouraged to nurture, grow, and value their capacities for ecological learning. "There is more information available at our fingertips during a walk in the woods than in any computer system" (Weiser, 1991, p. 75). "To confuse the common sense, wisdom and mature judgement of the expert with today's artificial intelligence, or to value them less highly, would be a genuine stupidity" (Dreyfus & Dreyfus, 1986, p. 201).

The children Papert (1980) worked with in his mathematical programming experiments were of elementary school age. However, some members of his team worked successfully with children as young as 4 years old. As our preschoolers show, age is no barrier to the use of projects employing ecological learning. As long as the project is geared to the developmental age of the children and expresses an immediate and real-world issue and interest, it is an appropriate vehicle for a range of learning opportunities. There is no end to the possibilities that the world offers for learning.

The opportunities include disasters. At the Oakland project in California, students studied the aftermath of the *Exxon Valdez* oil spill (Bruner, 1996). Their goal was to come up with a plan. Students worked as a collaborative community of learners, engaged in producing a joint product. All ideas were welcome. As well as learning a relevant part of the curriculum and learning empowering ways of using their minds, students were also learning about participating in an enabling community—a participative, democratic community.

In 2000, the National Foundation for Improvement in Education (NFIE) reported on the program called the Road Ahead for school technology. It showed that simply placing computers in classrooms does not guarantee improved student achievement. However, information technologies can help change teacher and student roles, as such technologies support project- and team-based learning, diminish lecture-based methods, and transform uninvolved and at-risk students into active learners. Students became better prepared for the modern world of work as they worked in teams to create multimedia projects. Teachers acquired the skills of web designers and information managers: students acted as teachers for other students, adults, and sometimes their teachers. Blurring the boundaries between teachers and learners is one of the conditions for producing learners who want to spread their learning to others (M. Emery, 1999).

With Internet access, the world becomes the curriculum (NFIE, 2000), and the spread of motivated learning becomes worldwide. As the technology and its content are ever changing, there is always something new to learn and the community of learners spreads ever outward like ripples on a pond. In some schools, students took the lead in providing technical support for maintenance and upgrade. This also multiskills the community. The NFIE sees a long road ahead for these changes, but with self-management, changes happen quickly and cleanly and groups continue to innovate.

There are, however, needless worries built into much of the thinking about computerized technologies. Consider the following.

Example 1. When people consider the role of technology in school, they encounter a seeming paradox. On the one hand, they read that computer technologies demand flexibility and blur the boundaries between teacher and student toward a growing community of learners. On the other, they read of the challenges involved in integrating technology into "instructional programs," that is, teaching. There is no paradox. Both statements are true. Instruction by its very nature is a top–down process, from the one with the information to the one without. The very language of instructional programs tells us that the authors have not escaped from the "teaching" model. Therefore, they can only see the use of flexibility-demanding technology as a challenge. Were these authors to understand the second design principle, they would see only an opportunity.

Example 2. How can teachers determine how much students understand of the principles involved when students use computers for calculation (NFIE, 2000)? Teachers allow the use of only pencil and paper until they are sure students understand. When they do, they may progress to using the new technology.

Example 3. How can teachers set goals for ecological learning through projects when there is a fixed and often lock-step curriculum? Teachers can work in collaboration with students to design projects in such a way that they become relevant to the students' lives and incorporate the curriculum goals. Final goals can be broken down into subgoals that students can use to guide the project work and that teachers can use to introduce new knowledge and skills when they are required.

If teachers know that a particular piece of learning has not yet been raised by the students' work, they can simply introduce it by saying, "Here is something new that might help you." Teachers do not abrogate their responsibilities with the advent of technologies, nor do they cease to bring "a lifetime of knowledge" to their students or influence their social development by example (NFIE, 2000, p. 35). There is no dilemma or conflict. Students need democracy, not laissez-faire.

Connecting the Bits (NFIE, 2000) gives many examples of projects that cover grade-specific competencies as determined by the National Educational Technology Standards. The projects are simple in concept but through their parts encompass the different skills and knowledge required. For example, as students research rocks and minerals on a CD-ROM encyclopedia, communicate with geologists via e-mail, and create hypermedia presentations, they show that they can collaborate with experts, peers, and others using telecommunications. They also show that they can use collaborative tools to research and develop solutions or products for audiences inside and outside the classroom. Students learn to generate and test their own hypotheses.

Students of any age or stage have knowledge, skills, and interest to work on tasks that involve substantive real-world problems (NFIE, 2000). Projects may cover several different ages and grades or different remote sites, as the technology facilitates coordination. These types of projects, particularly if they address real-life problems within real-life contexts, help students develop the higher-order thinking skills that are required in their postschool lives and work. As there is no specified role for each individual, those who like to play with technology can investigate its further potential for the project without detriment to its progress. Imagine the excitement and motivation of a student who has discovered something that can vastly improve the work of the team.

Such a discovery can add immeasurably to the overall creativity, learning, and excitement of the whole team.

Among the benefits of projects using computers are increased motivation as shown by such measures as punctuality and lack of absenteeism, as well as collaboration, as shown by students teaching and evaluating each other as part of a cooperative effort to reach the group goal. There is also an increase in problem-solving ability, research skills, and research-management skills, as shown by students taking responsibility for allocating time and resources to meet schedules (NFIE, 2000).

Students in projects generate confidence in themselves and their fellow group members. Because these projects fulfill the criteria for openness, awareness of living in a shared world, and recognizing each other as human beings, trust is generated. This trust creates a framework for approaching the rest of life in an active, adaptive manner.

SUMMARY

There is a commonality between what the human mind requires and what the technology encourages (DeMiranda, 2004). People need to be active, motivated, and engaged with their environments and others in order to learn. Computer technology transfers many of the functions of teachers to students, encouraging them to be active in questioning, collecting, and analyzing information. Group projects based on real-life experiences are a perfect mix with the new technologies. The teacher's role changes from transmitting information to blank slates to nurturing student learning (DeMiranda & Folkestad, n.d.). Moving to groups will fuel supportive research and spark the debate about teaching and learning that is required if teaching is to become a "true profession" (Wiske, 2000). Ventures such as Education with New Technologies, developed at Harvard University, are explicitly designed to do this.

When teachers themselves work as groups, project work for student groups' merging ecological and abstract learning will spread easily and rapidly. A combination of all these factors will result in effective and exciting learning for all as the boundaries between school and the world outside fade. Project-based learning enjoys so many advantages for teachers and students alike that one wonders why it has not been, and is not now, the primary vehicle for learning.

· 9 ·

Icing the Cake for the Future

In previous chapters I look at building participative, democratic communities and at changing the major internal features of school districts. These changes taken together will have a profoundly beneficial effect on all those who work within the district. They will also have a profound effect on the quality and quantity of formal student learning and achievement.

One of America's abiding concerns yesterday and today is the achievement gap between rich and poor, black and white. The reduction of this gap has been the subject of many well-intentioned creative endeavors. However, there is one way of narrowing this gap that appears to have been almost entirely overlooked. It is a way that follows directly from research evidence about the causes of the gap. It is also a way that can be addressed, in part at least, by schools districts and their communities acting together.

Nothing in this chapter is meant to deny the importance of early childhood interventions, Head Start, after-school programs, economic reforms to narrow the gap between the haves and have-nots, or social reforms that may improve understandings between various subcultures within America. All these factors are vitally important but have been dealt with in detail elsewhere (Rothstein, 2004c). This chapter adds one critical element to the solution.

THE CAUSES OF THE ACHIEVEMENT GAP

In 1986, Fred Emery wrote an article on secondary education and possible directions for its improvement. I have extracted some of that research. In the sections preceding this extract, Emery presented and analyzed the historical and then current statistics about secondary education in Australia. These

177

statistics showed "that the characteristics of the Australian educational system and their inter-relationships are remarkably persistent. They have persisted during long periods of overall growth. The evidence suggests that it is a highly integrated system and one that is to a considerable degree self-perpetuating" (p. 29). As demonstrated here, this could just as well be a description of the American education system.

If we know how the system works, we can make change to the most influential parts of it. This offers a greater chance of desired change than making change to less influential parts. However, professional educators have typically planned from the "simplistic assumption" (F. Emery, 1986) that in the educational system "many factors interact—students and their backgrounds; staff and their skills; schools and their structure and ethos; curricula; and societal expectations"; hence, "there is no simple prescription of the ingredients necessary to achieve high quality education" (Karmel, 1985, p. 144). Working from Karmel's assumption, a change in any part is as likely to produce effects as a change in any other part. It then becomes a matter of intervening where it is most convenient or cheapest.

The assumption that a national educational system can be viewed as "an aggregate of interacting parts" was proven false by James S. Coleman and his team in the study reported in *Equality of Educational Opportunity* in America in 1966. That is an unusually strong claim to make of a single study, but then, this was not one of the usual kind of studies.

Emery reviewed and reanalyzed Coleman's findings with a more modern and powerful statistical technique. He presented data from similar studies from 1966 to 1986. I have added in studies since 1986. All studies confirm Coleman's findings. There is no review here of major studies contradicting Coleman's findings because no such studies have been found in the literature.

The Findings of the Coleman Study

In 1964, the U.S. Congress was disturbed by the lack of progress following the Supreme Court desegregation decision of 1954. It was also concerned by the vigor of the Black civil rights movement, particularly in the South. It passed the 1964 Civil Rights Act, Section 402 of which specified that a survey should identify where there was a lack of equal educational opportunities in public educational institutions. The legislators intended to use the results of the study as a guide to the allocation of federal funds toward rectifying inequalities. It was that study that Coleman and his multitude of collaborators undertook.

The legislators assumed that inequalities could be rectified by changes in school composition and by pumping funds into facilities, curriculum redesign, and texts, as well as teacher development programs. Following the intent of the legislators, Coleman's study (1966) "concentrated on the educational opportunities offered by schools in terms of their student body composition, facilities, curriculums and teachers" (p. 22). This was a strong bias in the study, and it makes Coleman's findings even more significant.

The Coleman study was not in any way stinted for want of funds and, hence, was on a scale that has not been seen before or since. At the high school level alone some 689 randomly selected schools returned completed survey forms and tests for their pupils, their teachers, and their principals and superintendents. Some 356,860 pupils completed the forms and tests. They were divided into eight subsamples for Grades 6, 9, and 12: White North, White South, Black North, Black South, Asian Americans, Native Americans, Puerto Ricans, and Mexican Americans.[1]

The findings of the Coleman study showed that the assumptions on which it was based were wrong. Students' learning did not depend on such matters as the provision of good school facilities, low pupil–teacher ratios, well-designed curricula and texts, provision of stimulating extracurricula activities, and well-trained and well-paid teachers.

Contrary to the aforementioned assumptions, the Coleman study found that the overwhelming influence on student motivation and achievement came from nonschool factors. The researchers did not anticipate "the variability between individual pupils within the same school: this variability is roughly four times as large as the variability between schools" (Coleman, 1966, p. 23). In other words, schools had little to do with student achievement. Achievement depended on the social class of the family.

Up until then, the influence of the socioeconomic status of the parents on pupil achievement was accepted as fact. However, that influence was largely ascribed to superior genetic inheritance or to the ability of well-to-do parents to get their children into the best schools. Nobody believed that social class itself was the critical factor.

Because the study was so large and well funded, Coleman (1966) had included measures to cover this unexpected finding. As a result, he was able to explore at length the sources and nature of the differences between students. He concluded that "one implication stands out above all: that school brings little influence to bear on a child's achievement that is independent of his background and general social context; and that this very lack of an independent effect means that the inequalities imposed on children by their home, neighborhood, and peer environment are carried along to become the inequalities with which they confront adult life at the end of school" (p. 325). If schools are to ensure equality of educational opportunity, they must be able to have a strong effect that is independent of the child's immediate social environment.

However, "that strong independent effect is not present in American schools" (p. 325). This conclusion was a bitter blow for those who believed that government policies on school funding could be a major tool for creating equality of educational opportunity. Coleman's conclusion, however, was not arrived at lightly. He took into account all his findings, including

- the great importance of family background for achievement;
- the fact that the importance of family background to achievement does not diminish over the years of school;
- the small effect of school facilities, curriculum, facilities, and staff on achievement; and
- the fact that attitudes toward the social environment, such as a sense of control of it, are highly related to achievement but appear to be little influenced by school characteristics.

Coleman (1966) made two further discoveries that deepen knowledge of the educational process. He detected (a) that parental education, a literate home, and parents' desires for their children's further education have a more direct influence than family wealth and (b) that some minority groups have been so deprived of education in the past that the schools are a much more important influence on their learning. On this latter point, Coleman noted that 20% of the achievement of Blacks in the South is associated with the particular school they go to, whereas only 10% of the achievement of Whites in the South is. This general result is found in all minorities except Asian Americans. When White students from homes that strongly support education are put into schools where most students do not come from such homes, their achievements will be the same as if they were in a school composed of similar students. But if minority students from homes without much educational strength are put with students with strong educational backgrounds, their achievements are likely to increase. Coleman did not strongly follow up these findings, but they become relevant in some of the results reported here.

The major finding of the Coleman study (1966) was not that expected by Congress. It was a finding that stressed the relative impotence of politicians to bring about short-term results in the upgrading of an educated community, one that had gone past simply providing elementary education to the mass of its citizens. It was also a finding that challenged all those who had a vested interest in having more resources allocated to education, teachers' unions included.

Quite understandably Coleman's report (1966) was heavily attacked. The most serious attacks were directed at the way the study was conducted, although further work by other experts confirmed the correctness of Coleman's conclusions. However, the damage appears to have been done. Many walked away from the issue not wishing to accept its implications. Many still like to think that it never happened or, in any case, that it is now outdated and can say nothing important about the educational systems and processes of today. However, Coleman's conclusions are just as relevant today as they were in the 1960s (Rothstein, 2004c).

Findings From Further Analysis of Coleman's Data

Soon after the Coleman report (1966) appeared, new statistical methods were devised. Fred Emery (1986) used a modern method of "causal path analysis" to reanalyze Coleman's data for Grade 12 in all of the eight ethnic and social groups. This method yields a unique and nonsubjective graph that takes account of all interrelationships in the data. The graph of the causal path showing these interrelationships can be read just like a road map. The arrows show what leads to what (Emery & Phillips, 1976).

The study data consist of three clusters, or groups of factors—those of school, achievement, and family—plus two variables that linked the school measures to achievement.[2] The overall pattern showed that both the school and the family determine educational achievement but that the influence of the family is the strongest. The family also has an influence on verbal scores and the proportion of students preparing for college, but it is smaller than its direct effect on achievement. The school makes a small contribution directly to achievement but mainly acts through the scores for average verbal ability and the proportion of students preparing for college.

As the following list shows, the family was comprehensively measured. From this detail, it is possible to tease out which factors proved the most influential in determining achievement. The family cluster consisted of

- Reading material in the home—which included dictionary, encyclopedia, daily newspaper, numbers of magazines, and numbers of books at home
- Parents' education—which was a combined score for father and mother, ranging from some grade school to graduate school
- Parents' desires for child's education—combined score again for father and mother
- Student interest in school and reading—which included variables such as number of books read over the summer, feelings about leaving school, desire to achieve at school, measure of staying away from school
- Student self-concept as scholar—included perceptions of self as being "bright" compared to other students, learning ability, and teacher as hindrance through speed

- Homework—average time per school day spent studying outside of school
- Parents' interest—time the child spent with parents talking about schoolwork and time the parents spent reading to children before they started school
- Household possessions or poverty index—television, telephone, record player, refrigerator, automobile, vacuum cleaner

Parents' education and the amount of reading materials in a home are the most powerful factors. They lead to parents' desires for their children's education and the student's interest in education. Parents' interest in their children's learning also contributes to these factors. Parents' desires and student interest then lead to the student's concept of self as a scholar. Parents' education and reading materials in the home also lead to the number of household possessions; that is, education influences material wealth.

The Key Family Factors in Achievement in Eight Groups

Fred Emery (1986) then reanalyzed the causal path between the family and achievement for each of the eight geographical and racial groups in order to discover how families can best change themselves to increase the achievement of children. In the following figures, *P* stands for *parents*, *S* for *students*, and "reading materials" has been shortened to *books*.

The White North pattern (Figure 9.1) is most likely typical of developed societies at a time when some secondary education was the minimal acceptable standard for entering adulthood. Parental education and reading materials in the home lead to parental desires for the student's education and his or her interest in education. These factors then lead to achievement, the student's concept of self as a scholar, and to homework. Parental education has a secondary link to interest (dotted arrow), but parental interest also makes an

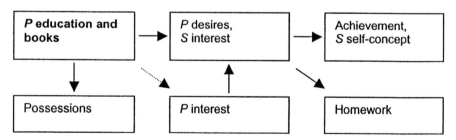

Note: **P** = parents, **S** = students, dotted arrow = secondary link to interest.

Figure 9.1.   Causal Path for White North.

independent contribution to achievement. The reason is probably that some parents who lack education see opportunities for postcompulsory education and occupational opportunities for the better educated.

The figure for White South is almost identical to that for White North. The only difference is that the degree of parental interest was dependent on parental education. When the Coleman study (1966) was done, the economic boom in the U.S. South and Southwest was in its early years. People could probably not yet see economic opportunities. The Black North pattern is, too, essentially the same as that of the White South. With most of the participants living in urban ghetto areas, the schooling system and labor markets offered little to encourage any parental interest that did not arise from their own education. The Mexican Americans are rural South but with a large minority from cities such as Detroit, San Diego, and Los Angeles. Their pattern is essentially the same as that from the Northern Blacks and Southern Whites, except even more dependent on the parents' having escaped from their roots and "made it" in terms of education.

The pattern for the Asian American (Figure 9.2) is unique among all of the eight social groups that Coleman (1966) compared. The features are twofold:

- Asian Americans, basically Japanese farmers in California and Chinese small business people throughout the central areas of the cities, appear to be strongly disposed toward more education for their children, regardless of the education the parents received. Having a good family income (household possessions) appears to be the only critical determinant.
- The student's self-concept as a scholar is dependent on his or her achievement. In other words, the student does not develop this self-concept until he or she has done well at school. It does not come directly from the home, as was the case for the other groups.

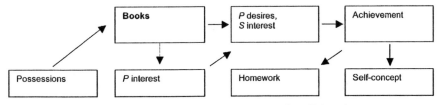

Note: P = parents, *S* = students, dotted arrow = secondary link to interest.

Figure 9.2.   Causal Path for Asian Americans.

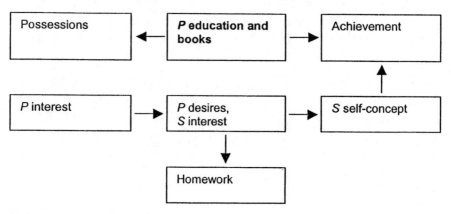

Note: P = parents, *S* = students.

Figure 9.3.   Causal Path for Black South.

The pattern for the Black South (Figure 9.3) is indicative of a rapid transition from a backward educational system, where the basic goal was usually some primary education, to a system that aimed at achieving some secondary education. Parents' education still directly affects the achievement of their children but a similar role is played by "parental interest" and the translation of that parental interest into parental educational desires for the student's education and student's interest in school. These then lead to the student's having a concept of self as a scholar, which then leads to achievement. This would appear to presuppose a considerable pool of untapped student talent.

The Native American pattern (Figure 9.4) shows a high dependency on continued pressure from parents who had more-than-average education. A clear response from their children is not observed until after parental interest is concretized into parental desires or plans for their children's education, and

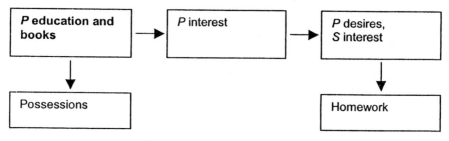

Note: P = parents, *S* = students.

Figure 9.4.   Causal Path for Native Americans.

even then, the only consistent outcome is in their children's trying harder through homework. For Native American children, a family background conducive to achievement did not lead to a concept of the self as a scholar, nor did it show up in achievement.

The only other group whose efforts did not result in achievement was the Puerto Rican Americans. Parents' education and reading materials in the home lead to the student's self-concept as a scholar, which is probably a realistic reflection of ability. This self-concept then leads to student interest and doing homework, that is, trying harder. But this was not rewarded by achievement.

The comparison of these eight groups clearly shows which family influences produce educational outcomes. Despite differences between the groups, an overriding pattern in the data shows that when the driving forces are high, educational achievement is high. When they are low, achievement is low. The most powerful drivers are those of parental education and reading materials in the home. With the sole exception of the Asian Americans, all the other factors flowed from parental education and reading materials in the home. For the Asian Americans, the key factor was household wealth. All of these figures have been shown in the positive sense that parental education and its associated factors lead to achievement. As mathematical entities, these figures can be completely reversed, showing that low parental education, few reading materials in the home, and low parental interest lead to low achievement.

The comparisons also show that some social environments inhibit these possibilities. For Native Americans and Puerto Rican Americans in those days, the effects of parental education and encouragement were not sufficient to overcome other disadvantaging forces in the environment. As Rothstein (2004c) pointed out, the effects of low socioeconomic status can be comprehensively debilitating.

Fred Emery (1986) also made a comparison of educational achievement and quality of schooling. It showed that many of the resources provided to schools were wasted.

Further Studies Relevant to the Coleman Effect

Since the Coleman report appeared, there has been a continuing flow of major studies in the United States covering the same ground. A set of reports from the Wisconsin longitudinal study began in 1957 with a sample comparable to Coleman's White Northern 12th graders. Coleman's finding (1966) that the power of family socioeconomic status continued over the years of school was confirmed (Sewell & Shah, 1967). Until then, the prevailing view had been that the influence of family background declined once a student had overcome the hurdles to college. The Wisconsin studies also showed that the educational aspirations and plans of 12th graders were realistic with an 86% retention of 16- to 17-year-olds.

Other results followed. No gender differences were found (Sewell & Shah, 1968). The determinants of the educational process were practically identical for a large city, down to a small rural village. They were also identical for farm-reared males (Sewell, 1970). The last report, an 18-year follow-up of the original 1957 Wisconsin sample, again confirmed the basic findings (Sewell & Hauser, 1980). It showed that parents' education and occupation, the two critical dimensions of socioeconomic status, were the key not only to high school educational achievement and aspirations but also to achievement at college and first and current job status. This latter study found pronounced gender differences, arising not from the family but from school experiences. Boys can expect teacher support if there is evidence of parental ambitions; girls cannot expect this support until they demonstrate their ability in school performance or IQ tests. School performance, college achievement, and first-job status do not give a girl anywhere near the advantage that they give boys.

In another series of studies, Alexander's research team (Alexander & Eckland, 1975; Alexander & McDill, 1976) intended to recapture some of the ground for traditional educational policies. "Recognizing that such influences (school influences) are likely to be modest does not, however, mean that they must also be uninteresting or unimportant" (Alexander & Eckland, 1975; p. 402). However, both of these 1975 and 1976 reports showed that the type of school simply reflected parental wealth and did not contribute to educational attainment. Alwin and Otto (1977) also confirmed the negligible role of the school.

Heyns (1974) also was concerned to highlight the school's contribution to educational performance through such factors as counseling, encouragement, and selection on academic criteria. She selected over 30,000 of Coleman's sample to draw her conclusion that schools made a significant contribution. She used a form of analysis that involved making subjective judgments about the most probable arrangements. However, the nonsubjective causal path approach showed the "Coleman effect." Father's social class and a low number of children in the family lead to verbal ability and educational aspirations, which then lead to high school achievement and preparation for college (F. Emery, 1986).

In 1972 the National Center for Education Statistics launched a national longitudinal study of the high school class of 1972. It confirmed the Coleman effect (Richards & Gottfredson, 1983). It also confirmed that the causal paths for males and females were identical, except for the fact that prolonged schooling is more of a deterrent to marriage for young women than it is for men.

Rehberg and Schafer (1970) confirmed Coleman's finding and showed that the more education a person received, the more that education was valued not just as an instrument for a better career but also as a valuable end in itself. Children growing up in an educated household in the presence of books and other reading material are more likely to believe in the value of education for citizenship and democracy.

These many studies can only conclude, as did Coleman, that schools do little to close the achievement gap. Rothstein (2004c) provides a fitting summary of this section: "Since the Coleman report, refuting this conclusion has been an obsession of education research"; however, "no analyst has been able to attribute less than two-thirds of the variation in achievement among schools to the family characteristics of their students" (p. 14).

Yet, the myth continues. Americans believe that the achievement gap is the fault of "failing schools" because it makes no sense to believe otherwise; but this conclusion ignores the very powerful, if subtle, effects of social class (Rothstein, 2004c). Rothstein concluded that Americans are reluctant to confront their social stratification and that they therefore ignore the impact of lower and higher social classes. They cling to the myth that "teacher quality is the best single predictor of student success" (Grasmick, 2001, p. 78).

Some have made claims that shore up the myth that school can close the gap by its own efforts. Rothstein (2004c) has thoroughly debunked these claims. He has also accumulated a mass of evidence about the effect of social class. Its influence is so powerful that no amount of teacher training, internal school reform, or additional funding will enable schools to overcome it on their own. Rothstein has also debunked myths of a golden age of immigrant achievement in America that, if true, would reinforce the belief that it is only today that schools fail to close the gap. Similarly, he debunked the myth that America is alone in having "failing schools." As shown here, the relation of social class to achievement is highly stable and exists in almost every country in the world.

American Studies From 1986 to 2005

A selection of studies since Fred Emery's 1986 work shows that the Coleman effect is just as valid today as it was in 1966, but knowledge of it appears to have been lost in some quarters.

Steinberg, Brown, and Dornbush (1996) studied more than 20,000 students over a 3-year period in nine public high schools representative of middle America's ethnic and economic profiles. They concluded together with Olson (1996) that the most effective remedy for low student interest and achievement is found in students' lives outside school. Huang (1996) commented that this was quite different from the many other proposals to improve schools and classrooms.

Published data from the National Adult Literacy Survey have showed the Coleman effect. Parental education leads to literacy and educational attainment. This attainment then leads to income. Clearly, nothing changed the big picture in the United States from 1966 to 1998. "Equalizing access to years of schooling and even to educational credentials is not sufficient" (Raudenbush & Kasim, 1998, p. 65), and it is urgent to improve the quality of schooling and of nonschool educative environments, particularly for Hispanic and African American youth. Years of school reform have not improved student achievement (Steinberg et al., 1996). I discuss the question of improving "nonschool educative environments" in the following.

Studies continue to document the Coleman effect. The social capital of the family plays a more vital and greater role than do school and community capital in keeping students at school (Israel & Beaulieu, 2004). A large and longitudinal study showed that five-sixths of the differences in scores on tests of reading comprehension and mathematics could be attributed to differences between students. In particular, parents' education levels had significant effects on reading comprehension scores (Rothman & McMillan, 2003).

Comparable International Studies

International studies comparable to Coleman's studies (1966) are less detailed because they are less well funded. Kerckhoff (1974) in the United Kingdom showed the Coleman effect and concluded that despite the marked differences between the American and British school systems, they "differ little in the process of educational attainment. The degree of continuity of social level from father to son is almost identical in the two countries, and the relative importance of social origin and ability in affecting educational attainment is the same" (p. 797). Psacharopoulos (1977) and Halsey (1980) also confirmed the Coleman effect. Halsey recommended that to achieve equality, it was necessary to initially increase inequality. In other words, he could see the need for various types of affirmative action.

Australian researchers have also shown interest in educational processes (Anderson and Blakers, 1984), but only a few studies have adequately confronted the issues that Coleman (1966) raised. Broom and Lancaster-Jones (1976) showed that the father's occupation had a greater influence on a student's future job and income than did school. Bardsley (1976) and Williams (1985a, 1985b) confirmed the Coleman effect. The Australian Bureau of Statistics study in 1982 also showed the Coleman effect and emphasized the role of parental plans. If parents have made it clear that they want their children to complete Year 12, then in about 9 cases out of 10, the child will aim to do so. If parents show no interest in the educational achievement of their children, then two out of three of their children will drop out. If the parents have made it clear that they are happy to settle for less than completion of Year 12 (which means in effect that they accept a blue-collar future for their children), then only 1 in 20 of their children will set a higher goal for themselves.

More recent international studies have been conducted in many countries, including America—of mathematics and science achievement (41 countries) and of reading literacy (35 countries). Both the mathematics and science reports introduce their fourth chapters by writing "there is abundant evidence that student achievement is related to home background factors, and to students' activities and attitudes" (Martin et al., 2001, p. 115; Mullis et al., 2001, p. 113). Students from homes with large numbers of books, with a range of educational study aids, or with parents with higher education had higher achievements in both subjects. The study aids included such items as a dictionary, a desk, or a computer.

This international team reported in 2003 that they found a positive relationship between reading achievement at the fourth grade and students' experiencing literacy activities before starting school (e.g., reading books, telling stories, singing songs, playing with alphabet toys, and doing word games) in every country (Mullis, Martin, & Gonzalez, 2003). "Students with the highest reading achievement had parents who spent time reading" (p. 9) and had the most positive attitudes to school. This finding reinforces those from the earlier studies which showed that positive attitudes are influenced by the climate of the parental home: "Although formal instruction in reading is a school activity, there is little doubt that the foundation for future literacy is laid in the early years" (p. 93). Contrary to popular belief, efforts to increase student engagement are not likely to lead to improved literacy skills (Willms, 2003)

The Coleman effect holds regardless of the generation of children studied or the countries in which the research was taken place. It is among the most stable and predictable results of social research. At the time of the Coleman study (1966), knowledge of the results spread widely through professional circles such as the British Psychological Society (1986) and through American popular culture. The advantages of a rich home range from conversation and books to travel and a different sense of oneself. Poor children generally fall behind as long as they depend on school for their learning (Illich, 1971). Yet, Rothman and McMillan (2003) have asked

1. Is there a persistent link between socioeconomic status and school achievement?
2. Is achievement related to the number of educational resources in the home?

3. Or is it the opportunities that can be provided at home?
4. Can changes in the school environment alone influence student achievement?

The answer to the first three questions was yes in Coleman's study and in all studies thereafter. And despite the massive efforts that have been made in schools to close the gap, the answer to the fourth is still no. It is the home, not the school, that mainly determines achievement.

WHAT SCHOOLS CAN AND CANNOT DO TO CLOSE THE ACHIEVEMENT GAP

In this section, I examine some facets of the Coleman effect that schools may be able to change. Rothstein (2004c) has compiled and analyzed a comprehensive list of the effects of social class and race in *Class and Schools* and has suggested some solutions. I recommend Rothstein's book for anybody concerned about "the gap." However, I do not replicate those suggestions here. Rothstein has been criticized for many of his views (Schrag, 2005; Thernstrom, 2005) but appears to have answered these critics fully (Rothstein, 2005).

Schools Cannot Close the Income Gap

The cumulative effects of low income, poor-quality housing, poor maternal health, and the poor health of the child together with low rates of insurance detract from the time and effort that a child can put into schoolwork and homework. Poor children lose more than 30% of days from school than do middle-class children. "Good teaching can't do much for children who are not in school" (Rothstein, 2004c, p. 42).

The U.S. Department of Education was aware of the accumulated evidence of the Coleman effect but "remarkably" (Rothstein, 2004c, p. 21) guided a bill (No Child Left Behind Act) through Congress that demanded every school abolish the gap within 12 years. These changes were agreed by a bipartisan conference (Office of the Press Secretary, 2001). Rothstein believes that by putting the blame on schools, which are simply not in a position to change many of the factors that need changing, the legislation condemns excellent schools and teachers to attack. Current state and federal strategies that expect schools to remedy poor academic performance are simply flawed (Harvard Graduate School of Education, 2004).

It is even more unrealistic to expect schools to substantially reduce the income gap between the lower and middle classes at a time when it is in creasing (Center for Education Reform, n.d.). Today, lower-class and disad-vantaged minorities have less access to the Internet than does the general population (NFIE, 2000, p. 24), and the gap is increasing not only in eco-nomic terms but also in terms of segregation (*Economist*, 2004). Increasing segregation on its own is a powerful contributor to the achievement gap, as Black or lower-class children who sat next to White or middle-class children did better than those who sat next to their peers. As Senator Daniel P. Moyni-han and Professor Frederick Mosteller argued when the Coleman findings were first released, the implications of the report were radical, as they de-manded nothing less than economic and social policy initiatives to reduce the achievement gap. That conclusion remains valid today (Rothstein, 2004c).

Initiatives such as improving access to affirmative action programs and better health testing could reduce the gap if they were targeted to lower-class students. These initiatives would help more Blacks to use education as a step-ping stone to a higher socioeconomic level than that of their parents. But only a few of these changes are controlled by school districts, and they are simply not enough (Bali & Alvarez, 2003). America needs some national under-standings (Gardner, 1991), and these understandings should include a clear sense of what Americans want, as "teachers and schools . . . did not create the conditions that have made American education so difficult. They did not cre-ate an underclass" (Bruner, 1996, p. 118). If as a society, America chooses to continue with a large income gap between its lower and middle classes, then it has chosen a large achievement gap (Rothstein, 2004c).

Schools Cannot Directly Change the Complexities and Subtleties of Social Class

Most racial or minority differences in achievement are explained by family in-come, parental education, and occupational status, the three major dimen-sions of social class (Rothstein, 2004c). Social class, however, is not a simple entity but a complex phenomenon including occupational, psychological, at-titudinal, economic, and physical behaviors. These parts are not isolated but function as large systems. Many of the differences between social classes are subtle. A longitudinal survey by the federal government begun in 1998 has al-ready illustrated just how complex the relationships between social class and academic achievement really are (Rothstein, 2004c).

As shown, the crucial factors in a child's academic achievement are the parents' education and the presence of reading materials in the home. This matter is not one of simply putting reading material in every home. Both middle- and working-class parents read to their children, but middle-class parents read themselves, thus showing the enjoyment and importance of reading by their own behavior (Rothstein, 2004b). Middle-class children develop habits of thinking and behaving that encourage learning and achievement. These habits lead to a particular self-image.

For middle-class children who have been brought up in educationally oriented homes, learning is an accepted part of the environment. Middle-class parents do not urge their children to read or learn—it is taken for granted that they will. They have grown up with dictionaries, atlases, and encyclopedias. However, "too many children have little sense of why one should read, because they reside in environments where the adults do not read" (Gardner, 1991, p. 211). It is difficult for these children to evolve a concept of themselves as readers and writers. Approaches such as that of "whole language" have been designed to help with this problem. However, although children find these approaches exciting and stimulating, schools are limited in what they can achieve when the rest of a child's life bears no resemblance to that of the classroom.

Middle-class parents typically converse with their children as they read and ask the sort of questions that develop curiosity and creativity. Affluent parents give encouragement whereas welfare parents give little praise and more criticism. Being brought up with books is only part of a middle-class approach to life that includes parents' using a large vocabulary with their children. By age 3, middle-class children have not only twice the vocabulary size of lower-class children but also larger vocabularies than those of lower-class parents. Language, vocabulary, and ideas about learning are set in the first 3 years (Rothstein, 2004c).

Because patterns of behavior are so entrenched by age 3, it is difficult for schools to catch up with the differences between the classes. Students are typically in school for only 6 or 7 hours a day, and during the rest of the time, middle-class students are exposed to stimulating and sophisticated language, leisure pursuits, and other related experiences. Even when schools work to narrow the gap, this narrowing is more than nullified by the differing extracurricular experiences. Reading for pleasure is a key experience.

Studies have also shown "transfer effects" from the parents' job to their child-rearing practices. This finding is not surprising, as transfer effects from work to home have been documented for a long time (Elden, 1976; F. Emery, 1978b; Karasek, 1976; Karasek & Theorell, 1990; Sorensen, 1977). Parents with professional jobs that entail taking responsibility are more likely to expect their children to take responsibility for their own learning. When parents have to explore alternatives and negotiate compromises at work, they are more likely to expect their children to solve problems. When parents simply follow orders at work, they give orders at home. Again, international comparisons showed that child disciplinary practices varied with autonomy and creativity at work. Again, America was no different.

Almost every aspect of child-rearing behavior differs between social classes, and taken together, such aspects exert a powerful effect on children's readiness for school, their motivation and aspirations. The subtlety of these differences can never be approximated or neutralized by anything that a particular school can do or that a law can demand. Tougher discipline, higher standards, more basic education, and increased testing in schools are as unlikely to change these ingrained patterns of behavior as is simply pouring more money into schools (Rothstein, 2004a, 2004b).

These class differences include not only behaviors that have a direct influence on learning but also self-confidence, ability to work in teams, images of futures, familiarity with prestigious professions in society, self-discipline, and forms of self-expression. As schools predominantly reflect middle-class behaviors and expectations, lower-class children have to adjust to a new cultural environment. Middle-class children are in their element.

Some previous suggestions for school reform have focused on providing improved opportunities for the advancement of migrant children in particular. These suggestions include mentoring inexperienced teachers by teachers who have experience with migrant children and distinguishing carefully between learning difficulties and problems caused by a second language. Robust learning environments are fostered by building supportive relationships between all parties—children, parents, schools, and their wider communities (Suarez-Orozco, 2001)—and this suggestion is covered by the previous chapters of this book.

Other strategies have stressed respect, an emphasis on positive reinforcement, a democratic learning process, and a sensitivity to cultural differences and nuances. Gaps between the streets and the schools were bridged for some angry Chicano youth gangs from extremely disadvantaged homes with a lack of supportive networks and lack of self-esteem (Vigil, 1999). These intensive projects are, of course, expensive and beyond the reach of most schools.

Many critics still express sentiments and plan such well-intentioned strategies promoting improved schooling and specialized moves toward what is generally called social justice. These efforts continue while research continues to show that they have "generated no significant, enduring or widespread reductions in social inequality" (Sinclair, 2002, p. 86).

Schools Can Stop Tracking

Shortly after Coleman's study (1966) was published came another classical study, by Rist. It focused on one reason that the Coleman effect is maintained by schools. Not only are middle-class students at home in schools, but they are actually encouraged to learn whereas working-class students are discouraged. Fortunately, Rist's study was resurrected by the *Harvard Educational Review* in 2000 (Rist, 2000a, 2000b). What Rist found in 1970 was the following:

- Kindergarten teachers possessed a roughly constructed "ideal type" of the characteristics necessary for a student to succeed in school and therefore in society. Teachers are, or have become, middle class in their thinking.
- As soon as the children and teachers met, the teachers made subjective evaluations regarding whether or not the child possessed these characteristics. On the basis of these evaluations, the teacher divided the class into groups expected to succeed and those expected to fail. The teachers called those expected to succeed the "fast learners" whereas they called the others the "slow learners."
- The groups were treated differently. The fast learners got more teacher time, attention, and reward-directed behavior. In contrast, slow learners received more frequent control-oriented behavior.
- During the course of the school year, the interaction patterns between teachers and students became rigid, taking on castelike characteristics. As the year progressed, the gap between fast and slow learners in completing academic material widened.
- As the children progressed through the school years, teachers' subjective evaluations were replaced by a variety of other information, but the same processes continued. The same patterns were also observed, with the groups moving still further apart.

Rist (2000b) used the phrase "self-fulfilling prophecy" in the title of his research report, as that was clearly the process his team observed over the years. In addition to the main points of the prophecy, the team found that teachers actually tried to keep the two groups apart so that the fast learners would not be seduced by the attractiveness of the "street culture"; that is, they would not jeopardize their opportunities for middle-class status in society. Caste within the school translates into class in the world outside.

Middle-class students are more often located in the top levels of English and mathematics than lower-class students are (Lamb, Hogan, & Johnson, 2001). Classroom organization, such as the grouping and tracking of students, functions as a mechanism of social and gender segregation. These arrangements accounted for a third of the variation in American classrooms and a quarter of it in Australian schools (Lamb & Fullarton, 2002). The "public school system not only mirrors the configurations of the larger society, but also significantly contributes to maintaining them. Thus the system of public education in reality perpetuates what it is ideologically committed to eradicate—class barriers which result in inequality in the social and economic life of the citizenry" (Rist, 2000b, p. 300).

Schools continue to fail many young people, who resolve their difficulties by leaving as early as possible—this despite the fact that the more years of schooling that students undertake, the more successful they are (Jencks, 1979; Rothstein, 2004c). However, there is often a mismatch between what the schools offer and the lives the young people are living. These young people make rational decisions about what they want to learn and where and when they want to learn it. Their schools prove too inflexible and outdated to help them (Wyn, 2004). It will be difficult to convince lower-class youth to remain at school, particularly as the decision to drop out usually has parental support or acquiescence. Dropping out therefore prolongs the cycle of disadvantage. Yet Wyn's findings give hope that young people who want to learn but whose schools have failed them will find their way into adult education.

Margolis and Romero (1998) found exactly the same dynamics and outcomes as Rist (2000b) did, operating in a university department of sociology. They saw two forms of hidden curriculum operating to reproduce sociologists in the mould as the current staff. A "weak" form used the professionalization process essential to "becoming a sociologist" whereas a "strong" form acted directly to produce stratified and unequal social relations through such mechanisms as stereotyping and blaming the victim. It would seem that these patterns of maintaining the status quo in education are well entrenched and operate through all levels, from kindergarten to university.

"Tracking," the process of grouping students into distinct groups for "fast" and "slow" learners described by Rist (2000b), is well established and leads to segregation and discrimination (Welner & Oakes, 1996). Slow learners fall further and further behind and show increased levels of boredom and other signs of distress. Therefore, people have instituted a major movement toward "detracking," which includes moving disabled students into mainstream classrooms, where some improved outcomes have been found (Lipsky & Gartner, 1996).

However, efforts to detrack in racially mixed schools have met resistance not only from teachers and staff but also from parents. Elite parents sometimes engage in political practices to circumvent detracking. Legal attacks on tracking have had only limited success (Welner & Oakes, 1996). Resistance to detracking is based on class rather than color or race. During over 3 years of study, Wells and Serna (1996) documented the power and subtlety with which elite parents pursued their goal of maintaining the advantages that their children enjoyed through tracking. "It would not be misleading . . . to say that the more time passes, the more things stay the same" (Rist, 2000b, p. 258).

This unconscious bias of schools toward the middle class will be ame-
liorated somewhat by the democratization of staff (chapter 7) and will be significantly reduced as schools move toward group-based project work (chapter
8). If groups are mixtures of working- and lower-class students, they will learn
from each other, promoting the increased achievement of lower-class students
as shown by Coleman in 1966.

As seen in chapter 8, schools need to involve students in producing the
content of courses as well as better involve parents and communities in the
educational process (Mills & Gale, 2002). Democratizing the content by using ecological learning in projects can help all students see that their identities and experiences are relevant to their schooling. The more group projects
can be drawn from real examples in the lives of students, both lower and middle class, the faster that bias can be redressed. Lower-class students will shine
as their firsthand knowledge of project topics leads to successful project completion. Being natively good at something implies not only recognition but
also the ability to help others (Bruner, 1996, p. 82). It is a great equalizer.

Schools can certainly correct this bias toward middle-class students, but
schools should continue to be institutions that have as their primary goal the
production of students who become literate, numerate citizens with a sufficient level of general education to participate adequately in a modern democratic nation. Americans have shown that they want the achievement gap
closed and not by reducing education to the lowest common denominator.

Schools Can Encourage Working-Class Strategies for Achievement

Louie (2001) added further knowledge of how social class dynamics operate
in the United States when she studied Chinese Americans and found that all
had high educational expectations for their children. However, the socioeconomic status of the family was "a clear dividing line" (p. 455) for the strategies that parents developed to foster their children's education. Middle-class
families chose private schools if they could afford them and, failing that,
moved into what they considered to be the best public school districts. They
restricted television time, assigned additional homework, and offered help
through such means as hiring tutors or enrolling children in summer schools.
Parents took second jobs to pay for the extras.

Working-class families or families in low to middle ethnic communities
chose the best neighborhood parochial schools, even if they were of a different religion. These parents often did not know how to help their children.
They worked long hours and frequently did not have the language skills to
help with homework. Some did not realize that they had to ask how their
children were doing at school. Consequently, they formed networks to gauge

their children's performance and find better ways of helping. These networks were particularly useful.

In illustrating the networking strategies that working-class families used, Louie (2001) demonstrated the value that schools and communities offer when they provide more opportunities for networking. The more opportunities for networking, the more probable the rise in educational achievement. Networking offers new ways out for those trying to beat the barriers of lower social class. At the moment, our increasingly privatized societies (chapter 2) offer few such opportunities. The early chapters of this book show how to increase these opportunities for networking and therefore assist parents and children alike. As communities involve parents and citizens of all social classes, the size and utility of networks will multiply.

Schools Can Encourage Parents and Citizens Into Further Education

Many ways have been tried of making change in schools to reduce the gap in achievement between the students from working- and middle-class families. Many of the benefits are short-lived, if the changes are successful at all. Some middle-class parents resist change because they do not want to risk the future of their children as they see it. There appear to be few direct ways for schools to close the gap; however, there are more indirect ways to reduce the gap. In chapters 3 to 6, I show that schools can involve parents and citizens in the process of developing cohesive and adaptive networks and communities. And, as shown in chapter 7, schools can reorganize the structures of their staff and students into groups to reduce bias against working-class students.

There is one other way of reducing the gap that appears to have been overlooked by many. The Coleman effect is still alive and well, and the influence of the family's social class does not decline with increasing years of schooling: it extends beyond tertiary education and even the first job. Given that parental education continues to be the most powerful factor in student achievement, the most feasible way to raise the educational level of our democracies is to encourage parents to voluntarily return to the educational process via adult and continuing education. Some benefits will accrue to today's families and their children, and there will certainly be further benefits for generations to come. As school reform has had little effect on the gap, it is time to move beyond the conventional approaches to making change. It is time to encourage the further education of parents, enabling them and, therefore, their children to break out of the working-class trap.

The main determinants of social class are education, occupational status, and income, and there is a logical sequence to their acquisition through life. Education leads to occupational status, which then leads to income. Without good educational qualifications, it is difficult to get a high-status job, and without such a job, it is difficult to get a good income. The strategic element in the sequence is education, as it is the primary determinant of the other two. Education is therefore the logical starting point for addressing the needs of future generations. The continuing and reliable finding of the Coleman effect through years of research led Fred Emery (1986) to conclude that the most hopeful kind of direct intervention into this process would seem to be that which is directed to parents through adult and continuing education.

Mendel (2004) reinforced this conclusion when he reported on a series of studies over 30 years. These studies confirmed, often with brilliant results, that working with parents and children together overcomes the disadvantage suffered so early by lower-class children. Differences in parenting during the first 3 years had far more influence on a child's success in 3rd grade than did socioeconomic status directly. The most powerful programs were those that combined educational activities for the child with attention to parent–child interaction patterns and relationship building.

When working with parents, in addition to working with young children, it is important to move beyond simply asking parents to become involved in their children's learning or even suggesting major areas of activities, such as supervising homework, stressing the importance of school work, or reading to children. Such suggestions are not helpful to parents who are semiliterate, have few books at home, and are unfamiliar with schools and libraries. Many disadvantaged parents have neither the skills nor the confidence to support learning in these ways (Rothstein, 2000). The differences between the social classes are not mechanical but involve attitudes, motivations, and values.

In carefully designed programs with children and parents participating together, the parents who participated increased their own education and were far more likely to secure good jobs. Here we see the most important implication of the Coleman effect playing out through these programs. Only by operating on the education of parents can we hope to bridge the gap between children from lower and higher socioeconomic statuses. Mendel (2004) asked the question, when will policymakers start paying attention? Until policymakers do start paying attention and realize that helping adults gain further education is a cost-effective strategy for closing the achievement gap, school districts and their communities can encourage the continuing education of their citizens.

In a society exposed to rapid social, cultural, and technological changes where value shifts are often dramatic, a much wider range of the adult population has become more concerned with learning to update its knowledge (Ackoff, 1974). People are realizing that what they know is under challenge or even irrelevant. They need to update, and past educational achievement does not closely predict a return to education today (Elman & O'Rand, 2002). Professional recurrent education and vocational training meet some of this need whereas other forms are pursued for improving lifestyle. Intent does not matter.

Schools can encourage and help provide two qualitatively different forms of education. As discussed in chapter 3, the first form of continuing education is inherent in highly participative events such as search conferences. In them, participants learn how to learn and can create the settings for further learning (M. Emery, 1993c). That form of learning lays a foundation for any further education, as it encourages adults to identify for themselves what learning they need.

The Rover School in Tempe, Arizona, created the Center of Excellence, which has established "learning cells" within the larger community. It also has cooperative learning partnerships with Southwest Airlines and Desert Samaritan Hospital. This latter partnership involves training prospective parents to re-create the home as a learning environment so that children arrive at school "school-ready." Rover School's success flows from its original concept as a self-contained entity within "a larger web of connections" (Horne & McClelland, 2001, p. 244).

The second form is that which more people would recognize as education proper. It is an activity explicitly undertaken for learning. The most effective examples of this genre are based on the principle of "starting where people are at." Davies (1993b) showed over many years of work with many different examples that any course, workshop, or conference could be made genuinely participative and self-managing to meet the needs of its participants. People first identify what they want to do and then the learning that must be done to help them achieve their goals. For many disadvantaged people, the first requirement may simply be learning to read and write so that they can engage in the educational or political process.

Whether it is called adult, further, recurrent, or continuing education or the university for the third age, there are already extensive resources in all Western democracies dedicated to it. The United States has more than 10,000 schools that have community education programs (National Community Education Association, 2005). Schools can augment this effort further by thinking of new ways to make expanded or improved use of their facilities and resources to educate their surrounding communities. The North Central Regional Educational Laboratory (n.d.-c) concluded that parent education classes, childbirth classes, community services, and college classes offered at the school increase the sense that the school is a vital part of the community.

The school becomes a center for family services and helps build a community of learners. It is important that children see their parents experiencing learning as being positive and rewarding, not just a grind to get certification.

When adults enjoy their learning and find it exciting, these positive feelings motivate them to read at home and discuss their new learning with others or their children. This creates a home climate where children come to value reading, becoming immersed in new subjects, discussing them, and being surrounded by the physical materials that accompany learning. If all children went to school with these motivations and this familiarity, the battle of the gap would be just about won.

In chapter 2, I look at the example of the school for adults in Barcelona, the school "where dreams come true." Although this is a wonderful example of what is possible, improvements can be made by initiatives that are simpler and probably less expensive to set up in terms of community resources. For example, in Nelson Middle School in Renton, Washington, the facility was open to parents who learned from and taught their children on certain nights of the week. For any technology to be effective in a school, the school must be embedded in a supportive network of home and community links (NFIE, 2000).

These community networks arise through participative processes and are an essential component of moving toward the goal of increasing the education and learning of parents. Once the networks are formed, they can be mobilized for the second form of learning as and when adults realize they need it. If citizens are actively integrated into their school district communities they will not find their schools threatening or remote from their lives.

The Toyota Families for Learning Program (Young & Subban, 1997), which operates in 15 U.S. cities, specifically recognizes the Coleman effect, the link between the educational experiences of parents and the achievement of their children. In the New Orleans program, parents decided that literacy has a major role to play in improving their education and life chances and those of their children. The program has four parts:

1. Child and parent do separate academic work toward their goals.
2. Parent and child play and/or do joint learning together under the initiative of the child.
3. Parents discuss issues of relevance or participate in activities of interest.
4. Parents volunteer service to the school.

The program follows the principle of "starting where people are at." The educators start by asking participants to spell out their needs in order to jointly design precisely relevant activities. This program supports Mendel's conclusion (2004) that it is important to work with parents and children together.

If postschool education were to be addressed in a school district and its community, the accumulated results in terms of learning for present generations would have the potential to raise the level of learning for generations to come. It is not a question of closing the gap once and for all today; it is very much a question of creating the conditions today for the gap to be narrowed for future generations.

A BRIEF NOTE ON THE IMPORTANCE OF EDUCATION FOR WOMEN

A sample of 2,538 from the U.S. Department of Labor's National Longitudinal Survey of the Labor Market Experiences of Young Women showed that the educational process is related to early family formation. Interviews from 1968 to 1975 documented the Coleman effect—the importance of the home culture to educational goals and curricular choices, educational achievement, and the age of first marriage and the age at which the first child was born (Marini, 1984; Moore & Hofferth, 1980).

But women's education is of prime importance for other reasons as well. Since at least the middle of the 20th century, women's schooling has been found to influence the widespread trends toward low birth and child mortality rates (LeVine, LeVine, & Schnell, 2001). Educating women and girls is positively correlated with child survival and inversely related to fertility. Literacy and language skills learned in school affect later reproductive and health behavior, and the relevant skills learned in school are retained. However, if this learning is neglected during the early years, it is possible for women to catch up with it in later life to gain the advantages.

Here again we see the importance of opportunities for continuing education. Further education for women is required "to productively raise and nurture their children while challenging them to reach their own potential in the world" (Adair, 2001, p. 228). Extensive research shows that education is a necessary step in moving poor single mothers and their children out of poverty and into self-sufficiency.

That research continues. Education and income are directly related to emotional support and outweigh the influence of culture. Low socioeconomic status puts individuals at risk of conflict with family and friends, confounding the original disadvantage of having to confront stressful life events without significant networks of institutional support (Mickelson & Kubansky, 2003).

Single parents, of whom the majority are women, are less likely to participate in neighborhood networks that generate social control and cohesion (Duncan et al., 2003). Networking opportunities for women through participative education could do so much to reduce the costs associated with dysfunctional families and communities.

The learning produced by participative community events and networking and the more formal kinds of educational experience are more important for working-class women than for anybody else. Not only do they enable these women to become self-sufficient, but they also start their children on a road to high achievement and a desirable future.

NOTES

1. "North" included California, Alaska, and Hawaii. "South" included the Southwest—that is, Texas, Arizona, New Mexico, and Oklahoma.

2. The achievement group consisted of scores of the individual pupil on tests selected from a battery of tests widely used and standardized in the United States (e.g., SCAT—school and college ability tests).

Conclusion

$\mathcal{S}$chools are unique among institutions, and each is itself unique. At the same time, schools are instantly recognizable, not only across the United States, but also across the Western industrialized world. Classrooms, schools, and school districts share a design principle, a structure, and the same dynamics with the majority of organizations in the world. School districts, like hospitals and churches, are embedded in their communities.

When people plan and implement their futures and when students determine their own projects as vehicles for learning, they automatically build in the unique characteristics of their people, their ecological learning, and the nature of their circumstances. At all levels of activity, the personality of the individual, the organization, and the community is acknowledged and retained as a necessary continuity from past to future.

Because school districts share a DP1 structure with other organizations, school districts can learn from these organizations. As so many different organizations have been changed, a recognizable pattern of results has emerged that reflects the change of design principle; therefore, the results of changing the design principle in school districts become reasonably predictable.

Many who currently work with and in school systems are clear about what is required and what will work in school districts. This proposal brings many of those perceptions into being. From the first component of community involvement, using the search conference, the community and district develop "listening systems for emerging trends" and understand how to influence the external environment. Those who understand the social environment and respond to emerging trends are able to build a capacity for survival over time (Snyder, 2001). The community becomes mobilized around its ideals, creating a powerfully motivated, supportive, and dynamic context for the transformation of the school district.

The system now recognizes and supports continual learning, and staff are working proactively with students, community, and elected officials (Dale, 2001). The outcomes from community involvement produce the first new R—relationships (Roy & Piperato, 2001). These relationships are not in themselves end points, as they merely serve to produce a more important purpose. When the community feels more at home in its school district, members attend participative workshops initiated by the schools. In them, community members voluntarily work with staff on ways to meet their learning needs. The new relationships offer opportunities for adult (continuing) education, a factor shown to be most powerful in equalizing the achievements of working- and middle-class students.

From the second component of redesigning the district's structure with a legal change of design principle, every level of the district is provided with opportunities for honest, open conversations about goals, beliefs, and strategies. The struggle with the organization and personnel structures is over, as the new DP2 structures continue to evolve and improve over time. The redesigns have created the conditions in which information is shared, different perspectives are respected, risk taking is supported, feedback is used, and trust flourishes. The result is enhanced relationships between staff at all levels (Phillips, 2001).

Teacher compensation and employment practices have been renegotiated to a pay-for-skills system that is more competitive in the marketplace and more responsive to changing employee expectations (Dale, 2001). Teachers no longer have to accept administrative positions to get a pay rise. Self-managing groups of teachers are training and supporting each other on the job, and there is a significant increase in morale with a corresponding drop in sick days.

Significant cultural changes are seen (M. Emery, 1999), as the students are arranged into self-managing project groups composed of lower- and middle-class students working together. Outcomes from working on the second component illustrate the second new R—responsibility (Roy & Piperato, 2001), now located with those doing the work, the learning, and the planning.

The third central component of classroom practices (Anderson & Cascarino, 2001) now balances teaching and ecological learning. The self-managing groups of mixed lower- and middle-class students determine their projects so that they extract their learning from their experience of real-life cultural trends and practices. As the projects proceed, students learn how democracy works (Carter & Berreth, 2001). Student achievement increases all round, and the gap between the achievements of the lower- and middle-class students narrows. These changes are meeting the expectations that society has of its schools.

A bridge has been built from the schools to the lives of students. This bridge supports the suggestion "that the right to learn will be to the 21st century what the right to vote was to the 20th century." This bridge illustrates the third new R—relevance (Roy & Piperato, 2001). Relevance has powerful consequences: "As the common people regain confidence in their ability to know the world, and gain the opportunities for knowing that open up with participative forms of self government, we can expect a 'knowledge revolution' that will rather overshadow the information revolution of the microprocessor" (F. Emery, 1983, p. 133).

All the components of individual, organization, and community have been viewed as adaptive systems inherently designed to renew themselves. This synergy leads to better solutions and has shown its great potential to raise student achievement (Carter & Berreth, 2001). All three improvements have been incorporated into a fast-moving process in which they simultaneously evolve and influence each other. This set of mutual influences illustrates the connectivity inherent in an open systems approach, the "watchword for the new millenium" (Horne & McClelland, 2001, p. 253).

I may be confident that the processes described here will result in significant systemic change, but many have tried to improve the school system for a long time with meager success (Blick & Bradshaw, 2001; Elmore, 1996; F. Emery, 1980a; Rist, 2000a, 2000b; Rothstein, 2004c). Throughout the chapters I have presented evidence for alternative structures and practices that produce more satisfying work for teachers and other staff; higher achievement for students; and closer, more positive relationships with their communities. Yet few of these practices have been taken into the educational mainstream. From Ackoff (1974) to today, the belief has been growing that in an uncertain world, only a thoroughly systemic approach to change will prove effective. Yet even with a systemic approach, something has still been missing because most of the best thought-through and creative ideas have failed. The school system is in a state of inertia.

So what has been missing, and what makes me confident about the success of this proposal? When I look at systemic change from the perspective of education as an industry, I see that in most change projects, the conditions for sustainability are not built in. Unfortunately, most success stories do not pass the test of time. A short life is the most likely outcome of so much of what is being done in school districts because it is based on a wish and a prayer. Some of these short-lived outcomes have involved massive expenditures of time, energy, and money. That is a tragic waste that can be avoided. The major reason for the inertia in the education system is that none of the changes have touched the realities of industrial life, the formal and legal conditions that to a large extent govern the nature of human behavior. The design principles do not mix, and when they conflict, the legal one always wins.

So many projects talk about changes from bureaucratic to democratic structures but do not actually change the legalities that determine them. Therefore, these projects involve the mixing of the design principles. But the fundamental reality of the location of responsibility in DP1 structures gets in the road of the good intentions of many projects. Projects can put desirable reforms into conflict with the legal rights and responsibilities of staff. As seen with team teaching in chapter 7, it is tough trying to weld groups onto a hierarchy of dominance. Staff in DP1 structures are legally unequal. Fudging change by relabeling supervisors *team leaders* or *coaches* does not remove their legal responsibilities to control and coordinate the work of others, and everybody knows it. At the very least, this leads to bickering and bad feeling, and it can lead to apathy or growing cynicism about change (Blick & Bradshaw, 2001). Risking a promotion or a job by not observing a rule or by disobeying an order that conflicts with the implementation of an innovation is often a risk too great.

Teachers have individual responsibilities, and until these responsibilities and the rewards and punishments contingent on them are changed, they will continue to meet their responsibilities. Schools have muddled through to now only because of the dedication of teachers and other staff. They have achieved miracles despite the conditions that militate against them. Most staff enter the system with the highest ideals but end up enduring frustrations. Most attempt to cooperate and enjoy friendly, supportive relations with colleagues. They work hard for their students and will innovate as long as it does not intrude on their responsibilities.

This is the real bottom line, and until the responsibilities are legally changed, all reforms will be short lived. The paradox that Zuboff (1988) observed between the need for obedience and the desire to learn and create applies to staff as much as to students. Teachers are pressured into conformity of thought and action with a resultant waste of talent (Pence, 2001). No amount of well-intentioned work to improve staff relationships and school districts in general will work until that paradox is resolved. It will be resolved only when the design principle that requires obedience (DP1) is changed to that which requires shared learning and creative work (DP2).

This then is the challenge for school districts, the need to legally change their governing design principle. I am confident that this proposal will work better than many others because it sits on the solid foundation of a negotiated labor–management agreement. That agreement explicitly states that responsibility for coordination and control is located with the people doing the work, the learning, or the planning. It also includes new support systems of pay and conditions that are aligned with the second design principle. The success stories that endure in any field almost always involve genotypical change—that is, changes to the formal, legal structure that so strongly influence the behavior of those who work and learn within them.

For those school districts that bite the bullet and negotiate for a change in design principle, the effects are rewarding. In the short term, staff working in DP2 structures cooperate to meet their goals; they mutually support and respect each other as energy flows, creativity flourishes, ideals are revitalized, and students throw themselves into learning. These changes will not only be noted during the working day, as the emotions experienced at work are taken home. Families will notice that staff arrive home with sunnier dispositions and much more energy to engage with the family and its pursuits. Gone are the days when they arrived home deeply dispirited and tired, with barely enough energy to turn the television on.

In the longer term, the community also benefits from these indirect or flow-on changes. People who are being damaged by their experiences at work gradually lose their motivation, their sense of responsibility, and their zest for life. They no longer volunteer. But the damage done by dissociation is rarely irreversible. Damaged people can be restored to health, holism, and vitality by returning the environments in which they work to healthy, vital states. When people regain their purposefulness, they return to participating in and, indeed, initiating change in their communities.

As active, healthy communities energize school districts, so do active, healthy school districts energize communities. The whole system of relationships moves from dissociation to association. Not only is change possible, but it can also be exciting, joyful, and contagious. It can spread far and wide. Change that is fueled by positive feelings, and human energy can transform school districts and the people within them.

References

Ackoff, R. L. (1974). *Redesigning the future: A systems approach to societal problems.* New York: Wiley & Sons.

Ackoff, R. L., & Emery, F. E. (1972). *On purposeful systems.* London: Tavistock.

Adair, V. C. (2001). Poverty and the (broken) promise of higher education. *Harvard Educational Review, 71*(2), 217–239.

Aigner, S. M., Raymond, V. J., & Smidt, L. J. (2002). "Whole community organizing" for the 21st century [Abstract]. *Journal of Community Development Society, 33*(1), 86.

Aiken, W. (1942). *The story of the eight-year study.* New York: Harper.

Alexander, K., & Eckland, B. K. (1975). Contextual effects in the high school attainment process. *American Sociological Review, 40,* 402–416.

Alexander, K., & McDill, E. L. (1976). Selection and allocation within schools: Some causes and consequences of curriculum placement. *American Sociological Review, 41,* 963–980.

Alvarez, R., & Emery, M. (2000). From action research to system in environments: A method. *Systemic Practice and Action Research, 13,* 683–703.

Alwin, D. F., & Otto, L. B. (1977). High school context effects on aspiration. *Sociology of Education, 50,* 259–271.

Anderson, D. S., & Blakers, C. (1984). *Youth in transition: An annotated bibliography.* Canberra, Australia: Australian Government Publishing Service.

Anderson, J. L., & Cascarino, J. (2001). Toward the new American school district: Aligning improvement strategies for school systems and classroom practice. In F. M. Duffy & J. D. Dale (Eds.), *Creating successful school systems: Voices from the university, the field, and the community* (pp. 89–104). Norwood, MA: Christopher-Gordon.

Angyal, A. (1941). *Foundations for a science of personality.* Cambridge, MA: Harvard University Press.

Angyal, A. (1965). *Neurosis and treatment: A holistic theory.* New York: Wiley & Sons.

Aranda Primary School Board. (1975). *An approach to community involvement in schooling.* Unpublished manuscript.

Aroca, M. S. (1999). La Verneda—Sant Marti: A school where people dare to dream. *Harvard Educational Review, 69*(3), 320–335.

Asch, S. E. (1952). *Social psychology*. New York: Prentice Hall.

Association for Supervision and Curriculum Development. (2003). Mathematics instruction in the United States. *Research Brief, 22*(1). Retrieved October 28, 2003, from http://www.ascd.org/publications/researchbrief/index.html

Aughton, P. (1997, May 13–16). *The participative design workshop at Southcorp Wines Pty. Ltd., Australia.* Paper presented at the Fifth Ecology of Work Conference, Dublin, Ireland.

Australian Bureau of Statistics. (1982). *Reasons for completion or non-completion of secondary education, Australia* (Catalogue No. 4214.0). Canberra, Australia: Author.

Australian Council for Educational Research. (2003). Impact of school libraries on student achievement. *Research Developments, 10*, 4–5.

Baburoglu, O. N., & Garr, A. M. (1992). Search conference methodology for practitioners. In M. R. Weisbord (Ed.), *Discovering common ground* (pp. 73–81). San Francisco: Berrett-Koehler.

Bachmann, R., & van Witteloostuijn, A. (2003). Preface: Networks, social capital, and trust: A multidisciplinary perspective on interorganizational relations (part I). *International Studies of Management and Organizations, 33*(2), 3–6.

Baillie, L., Broughton, S., Bassett-Smith, J., Aasen, W., Oostindie, M., Marino, B. A., et al. (2004). Community health, community involvement, and community empowerment: Too much to expect? *Journal of Community Psychology, 32*, 217–228.

Bain, L., Crawfor, L., & Mortimer, D. (1996). Negotiation in practice: Context and exercises. In D. Mortimer, P. Leece, & R. Morris (Eds.), *Workplace reform and enterprise bargaining* (pp. 359–401). Sydney, Australia: Harcourt, Brace.

Baird, M., & Grey, I. (1996). Negotiating change: A practical guide. In D. Mortimer, P. Leece, & R. Morris (Eds.), *Workplace reform and enterprise bargaining* (pp. 347–358). Sydney, Australia: Harcourt, Brace.

Baldwin, A. L. (1981). *Theories of child development* (2nd ed.). New York: Wiley & Sons.

Bali, V. A., & Alvarez, R. M. (2003). Schools and educational outcomes: What causes the "race gap" in student test scores? *Social Science Quarterly, 84*(3), 485–507.

Banathy, B. (1987). The characteristics and acquisition of evolutionary competence. *World Futures, 23*, 123–144.

Barber, S. (1998). Navigating the emerging decision-making paradigm. In N. Hamson (Ed.), *After Atlantis: Working, managing and leading in turbulent times* (pp. 174–185). Boston: Butterworth-Heinemann.

Bardsley, W. W. (1976). *Student alienation and commitment to school: A multivariate analysis of home and school environments.* Unpublished doctoral dissertation, Australian National University, Canberra, Australia.

Bartel, S., & Emery, M. (1999). *Resistance to open systems theory and practice: A research note.* Unpublished manuscript.

Baum, F., Modra, C., Bush, R., Cox, E., Cooke, R., & Potter, R. (1999). Volunteering and social capital: An Adelaide study [Abstract]. *Australian Journal on Volunteering, 4*(1), 13.

Beavers, H., & DeTurck, D. (2000, April 25). Team teaching and the harmony of collaboration. *Almanac, 46*, 30. Retrieved November 21, 2004, from http://www.upenn.edu/almanac/v46/n30/tatBeavers-DeTurck.html

Becker, H. J. (2000). *Findings from the teaching, learning and computing survey: Is Larry Cuban right?* Paper written for the January 2000 School Technology Leadership Conference of the Council of Chief State School Officers, Washington, DC. Retrieved December 1, 2004, from http://www.crito.uci.edu/tlc/findings/ccsso.pdf

Beer, S. (1972). *The brain of the firm.* London: Professional Library.

Bennett Pelz, E. (1947). Some factors in "group decision." In E. E. Maccoby, T. M. Newcomb, & E. L. Hartley (Eds.), *Readings in social psychology* (pp. 212–219). London: Methuen.

Berkowitz, B. (1996). Personal and community sustainability. *American Journal of Community Psychology, 24*(4), 441–459.

Berry, D. S. (1991). Child and adult sensitivity to gender information in patterns of facial motion. *Ecological Psychology, 3*(4), 349–366.

Bhattacharyya, J. (2004). Theorizing community development [Abstract]. *Journal of Community Development Society, 34*(2).

Bion, W. R. (1952). Group dynamics: A review. *International Journal of Psychoanalysis, 33*, 235–247.

Bion, W. R. (1961). *Experiences in groups.* London: Tavistock.

Bishop, P. (1999). School-based trust in Victoria: Some telling lessons. *Australian Journal of Education, 43*(3), 273–284.

Blank, M. J., & Cady, D. (2004). System change through community schools. *School Administrator Web Edition.* Retrieved November 24, 2004, from http://www.aasa.org/publications/sa/2004_01/Blank.htm

Blick, C. (1998). Students, parents and community members as partners in strategic school-community planning. *Classroom Leadership, 2*(2). Retrieved November 24, 2004, from http://www.ascd.org/publications/class_lead/199810/blick_2.html

Blick, C., & Bradshaw, C. (2001). Whole-system change: New paths to innovation, "response-ability," and commitment. In F. M. Duffy, & J. D. Dale (Eds.), *Creating successful school systems: Voices from the university, the field, and the community* (pp. 173–197). Norwood, MA: Christopher-Gordon.

Bluestone, I. (1983). Labor's stake in improving the quality of working life. In H. Kolodny & H. van Beinum (Eds.), *The quality of working life and the 1980s* (pp. 33–41). New York: Praeger.

Blum, R. E. (2003). Preface: Principals in the spotlight. *Association for Supervision and Curriculum Development (ASCD).* Retrieved October 28, 2003, from http://www.ascd.org/publications/books/103309/preface.html

Boorman, S. A. (1971). *The protracted game.* Oxford: Oxford University Press.

Bopape, M. (n.d.). *The South African new mathematics curriculum: People's mathematics for people's power.* Retrieved February 12, 2005, from http://www.nottingham.ac.uk/csme/meas/papers/bopape.html

Borsch, F., Jurgen-Lohmann, J., & Giesen, H. (2001) *Achievement gains through cooperative learning: Jigsaw in German elementary schools.* Poster presented at the Seventh European Congress of Psychology, London.

British Psychological Society. (1986). Achievement in the primary school: Evidence to the Education, Science and Arts Committee of the House of Commons. *Bulletin of the British Psychological Society, 39*, 121–125.

Brokhaug, I. (1992). Informing participants of what to expect. In M. R. Weisbord (Ed.), *Discovering common ground* (pp. 95–100). San Francisco: Berrett-Koehler.

Broom, L., & Lancaster-Jones, F. (1976). *Opportunity and attainment in Australia.* Canberra, Australia: Australian National University Press.

Brothers, D. (2003). Parent involvement in the learning community. *Sunrise School Division.* Retrieved November 30, 2004, from http://www.sunrisesd.ca/index.asp? sec=1&too=30&eve=1&ppa=1146

Brown, M. J. (1996). What can community organizers teach us? *Journal for Quality and Participation, 19*(5), 78–84.

Bruner, J. (1996). *The culture of education.* Cambridge, MA: Harvard University Press.

Brunner, E., & Marmot, M. (1996). Social organization, stress and health. In M. Marmot & R. G. Wilkinson (Eds.), *Social determinants of health* (pp. 16–43). Oxford: Oxford University Press.

Buchanan, M. (2004, November 20). A billion brains are better than one. *New Scientist,* 34–37.

Buckminster Fuller, R. (1970). *Operating manual for spaceship Earth.* New York: Pocket Books.

Bundy, J. C., & McAbee, J. J. (1996). A community transforming itself from the inside out. *Journal for Quality and Participation, 19*(5), 20–24.

Butterfield, J., Dale, G., Ninham, P., & Travis, J. (1976). *Gerden Gardens.* Unpublished manuscript.

Carmin, J. (2003). Local action in a transitional state: Community responses to proposed development in the Czech Republic, 1992–1996. *Social Science Quarterly, 84*(1), 191–209.

Carter, G. R., & Berreth, D. G. (2001). Redesigning leadership for the third millenium. In F. M. Duffy & J. D. Dale (Eds.), *Creating successful school systems: Voices from the university, the field, and the community* (pp. 21–34). Norwood, MA: Christopher-Gordon.

Carter, M., & Francis, R. (2000). *Mentoring and beginning teachers' workplace learning.* Paper presented to Australian Association for Research in Education Conference, Sydney, Australia. Retrieved November 11, 2004, from http://www.aare.edu.au/ 00pap/car00232.htm

Caudwell, C. (1937). *Illusion and reality. A study of the sources of poetry.* London: Lawrence & Wishart.

Center for Education Reform. (n.d.). *Education manifesto: A nation still at risk.* Retrieved December 16, 2005, from http://www.edreform.com/index.cfm?fuseAction =siteSearch

Chatfield, D. L. (1999). Expectations of civic infrastructure in an age-restricted retirement community: Implications for community development. *Dissertation Abstracts International* (Humanities and Social Sciences).

Chavis, D. M., & Wandersman, A. (1990). Sense of community in the urban environment: A catalyst for participation and community development. *American Journal of Community Psychology, 18*(1), 55–81.

Chein, I. (1972). *The science of behaviour and the image of man.* New York: Basic Books.

Chugach School District. (2004). *Voyage to excellence: Chugach School District.* Retrieved November 11, 2004, from http://www.chugachschools.com

Coch, L., & French, J. R. P. (1947). Overcoming resistance to change. In E. E. Maccoby, T. M. Newcomb, & E. L. Hartley (Eds.), *Readings in social psychology* (pp. 233–250). London: Methuen.

Coleman, J. S. (1966). *Equality of educational opportunity.* Washington, DC: U.S. Government Printing Office.

Cox, P. J., Leder, G. C., & Forgazz, H. J. (2004). Victorian certificate of education: Maths, science and gender. *Australian Journal of Education, 48*(1), 27–46.

Cromwell, S. (2002). Team teaching: Teaming teachers offer tips. *Education World.* Retrieved November 21, 2004, from http://www.educationworld.com/a_admin/admin/admin290.shtml

Crowder, K., & South, S. J. (2003). Neighborhood distress and school dropout: The variable significance of community context. *Social Science Research, 32,* 659–698.

Cuban, L. (1986). *Teachers and machines: The classroom use of technology since 1920.* New York: Teachers College Press.

Cuban, L. (1993). *How teachers taught: Constancy and change in American classrooms, 1890–1990* (2nd ed.). New York: Teachers College Press.

Dale, J. D. (2001). Professional educators for our future: Restructuring the teacher workforce. In F. M. Duffy & J. D. Dale (Eds.), *Creating successful school systems: Voices from the university, the field, and the community* (pp. 125–138). Norwood, MA: Christopher-Gordon

Danovitch, J. H., & Keil, F. C. (2004). Should you ask a fisherman or a biologist? Developmental shifts in ways of clustering knowledge. *Child Development, 75*(3), 918–929.

Davies, A. (1981). *A strategy for planning a public service union* (Paper No. 63D). QWL and the '80s Conference, Toronto, Ontario.

Davies, A. (1983). Participative tools and their application. In T. Aspengren & K. Selvig (Eds.), *Teori I praksis: Festskrift til Einar Thorsrud* (pp. 172–217). Oslo, Norway: Tanum-Norli.

Davies, A. (1992). Setting national and local priorities: Australian Consumer Forum for the Aged. In M. R. Weisbord (Ed.), *Discovering common ground* (pp. 265–281). San Francisco: Berrett-Koehler.

Davies, A. (1993a). An alternative general studies curriculum: A description, results and evaluation. In M. Emery (Ed.), *Participative design for participative democracy* (pp. 258–270). Canberra: Centre for Continuing Education, Australian National University.

Davies, A. (1993b). Participation and self management in course, workshop and conference design: Principles and methods. In M. Emery (Ed.), *Participative design for participative democracy* (pp. 271–313). Canberra: Centre for Continuing Education, Australian National University.

Davis, L. (1971). The coming crisis for production management. *International Journal of Production Research, 9,* 65–82. In E. Trist & H. Murray (Eds.), *The social engagement of social science: A Tavistock anthology: Vol. 2* (1993; pp. 303–313). Philadelphia: University of Pennsylvania Press.

Davis, L., & Sullivan, S. (1993). A new type of labor–management contract involving the quality of working life. In E. Trist & H. Murray (Eds.), *The social engagement of social science: A Tavistock anthology: Vol. 2* (pp. 532–553). Philadelphia: University of Pennsylvania Press.

Dawson, C. (2000). Selling snake oil: Must science educators continue to promise what they can't deliver? In R. Cross & P. J. Fensham (Eds.), *Science and the citizen: For educators and the public* (pp. 121–132). Melbourne, Australia: Arena.

De, N. R. (1983). Meta-ideals-based futures design. In T. Aspengren & K. Selvig (Eds.), *Teori I praksis: Festskrift til Einar Thorsrud* (pp. 236–248). Oslo, Norway: Tanum-Norli.

De, N. R. (1984). *Alternative designs of human organizations.* New Delhi, India: Sage.

De, N. (1991). *Organisational scanning.* New Delhi, India: Prentice-Hall of India.

De, N., Goyal, T. C., Talbgar, A. S., & Paramjit, S. J. (1986). Modified Search Conference with the police in Delhi: A brief report. *Quality of Work Life, 3*(3–4), 189–203.

De Bono, E. (1976). *Teaching thinking.* Harmondsworth, England: Penguin.

De Bono, E. (1979). *Learning to think.* Harmondsworth, England: Penguin.

de Guerre, D. W. (2000). The codetermination of cultural change over time. *Systemic Practice and Action Research, 13*(5), 645–663.

de Guerre, D. W. (2005). Review essay: Democratic social engagement. *Innovation Journal, 10*(1). Retrieved from http://www.innovation.cc/The%20Innovation%20Journal/book-reviews/guerre-essay.pdf

de Guerre, D. W., & Hornstein, H. (2004). Active adaptation of municipal governance: An action research report. *Innovation Journal, 9*(1). Retrieved from http://www.innovation.cc/peer-reviewed/deguerre-hornstein-emp.pdf

de Guerre, D., & Noon, M. (1998). Redesign throughout Syncrude has achieved results. In Amerin Consulting Group, *A Canadian success story using Australian know-how* (overhead 5). Melbourne, Australia: Amerin Consulting Group.

Delbanco, A. (2005). The endangered university. *New York Review of Books, 52*(5), 19–22.

Dellagnelo, L. V. (2000). Participation in schools: What do mothers get out of it? *Dissertation Abstracts International* (Humanities and Social Sciences).

DeMiranda, M. A. (2004). The grounding of a discipline: Cognition and instruction in technology education [Abstract]. *International Journal of Technology and Design Education, 14*(1), 61.

DeMiranda, M. A., & Folkestad, J. E. (n.d.). Linking cognitive science theory and technology education practice: A powerful connection not fully realized. *Journal of Industrial Teacher Education, 37*(4). Retrieved February 27, 2005, from http://scholar.lib.vt.edu/ejournals?JITE/v37n4/demiranda.html

Department of Transport and Regional Services. (2001). *Success factors: Managing change in regional and rural Australia.* Canberra, Australia: Regional and Rural Women's Unit.

Dewey, J. (1922). *Democracy and education.* New York: Macmillan.

Dillon, B. (2001). Redesigning an entire school system for the 21st century. In F. M. Duffy & J. D. Dale (Eds.), *Creating successful school systems: Voices from the university, the field, and the community* (pp. 55–67). Norwood, MA: Christopher-Gordon

Down, B. (2001). Educational science, mental testing, and the ideology of intelligence. *Melbourne Studies in Education, 42*(1), 1–23.

Drago, R., Caplan, R., Markowitz, A., Spiros, R., & Riggs, T. L. (1996). Is participatory decision making family friendly? *Journal of Quality and Participation, 19*, 90–93.

Dreyfus, H. L., & Dreyfus, S. E. (1986). *Mind over matter: The power of human intuition and expertise in the era of the computer.* Oxford: Basil Blackwell.

Drucker, P. F. (1982). *The changing world of the executive.* New York: Times Books.

Drucker, P. F. (1985). *Innovation and entrepreneurship: Practice and principles.* New York: Harper & Row.

Dubos, Rene. (1976). *A god within.* London: Abacus.

Duenas, G. (2000). Universities as creators of social capital. In O. N. Baburoglu & M. Emery (Eds.), *Educational futures: Shifting paradigm of universities and education* (pp. 73–82). Istanbul, Turkey: Sabanci University.

Duffy, F. M. (1997). Keeping our past before us like a beacon and calling it the future: Why traditional supervision can't improve knowledge organizations [Abstract]. *Central Business Review, 16*(1). Retrieved November 24, 2004, from http://www.busn.ucok.edu/cbreview/97win/

Duffy, F. M. (2001). Redesigning school systems for the 3rd millenium: A systems approach to improvement. In F. M. Duffy & J. D. Dale (Eds.), *Creating successful school systems: Voices from the university, the field, and the community* (pp. 141–171). Norwood, MA: Christopher-Gordon.

Duffy, F. M. (2004). Navigating whole-district change: Eight principles for moving an organization upward in times of unpredictability. *School Administrator Web Edition.* Retrieved November 24, 2004, from http://www.aasa.org/publications/sa/2004_01/Duffy.htm

Duffy, F. M., & Dale, J. D. (2001a). Conclusion. In F. M. Duffy & J. D. Dale (Eds.), *Creating successful school systems: Voices from the university, the field, and the community* (pp. 275–279). Norwood, MA: Christopher-Gordon.

Duffy, F. M., & Dale, J. D. (Eds.). (2001b). *Creating successful school systems: Voices from the university, the field, and the community.* Norwood, MA: Christopher-Gordon.

Duffy, F. M., Rogerson, L. G., & Blick, C. (2000). *Redesigning America's schools: A systems approach to improvement.* Norwood, MA: Christopher-Gordon.

Duffy, S. (2001). Epilogue: Last call for voices. In F. M. Duffy & J. D. Dale (Eds.), *Creating successful school systems: Voices from the university, the field, and the community* (pp. 274–275). Norwood, MA: Christopher-Gordon.

Duncan, T. E., Duncan, S. C., Okut, H., Strycker, L. A., & Hix-Small, H. (2003). A multilevel contextual model of neighborhood collective efficacy. *American Journal of Community Psychology, 32*(3/4), 245–252.

Economist. (1994, April 9). New work order. P. 80.

Economist. (2003, October 25). Think before you meet. Tough at the top: A survey of corporate leadership. P. 13.

Economist. (2004, May 22). Brown v. Board of Education: *Change gotta come.* Pp. 12–13.

Edwards, R. W. (2004). *Measuring social capital: An Australian framework and indicators* (Information Paper 1378.0). Canberra, Australia: Australian Bureau of Statistics.

Eisler, R. (1995). *The chalice and the blade.* San Francisco: HarperCollins.

Elden, J. M. (1976). *Democracy at work for a more participatory politics.* Unpublished doctoral dissertation, University of California, Los Angeles.

Elden, M. (1983). Social science for policy-making as a learning process. In T. Aspengren & K. Selvig (Eds.), *Teori I praksis: Festskrift til Einar Thorsrud* (pp. 218–235). Oslo, Norway: Tanum-Norli.

Elman, C., & O'Rand, A. M. (2002). Perceived job insecurity and entry into work-related education and training among adult workers. *Social Science Research, 31*(1), 49–76.

Elmore, R. F. (1996). Getting to scale with good educational practice. *Harvard Educational Review, 66*(1), 1–26.

Else, L. (2004, November 27). The passionate life. *New Scientist*, 44–47.

Emery, F. E. (1966). *The rationalisation of conflict: A case study* (TIHR Document No. T821). London: Tavistock.

Emery, F. (1967a). The next thirty years. *Human Relations, 20,* 199–237. Reprinted with postscript in *Human Relations* (1997), *50*(8), 885–935.

Emery, F. E. (1967b). The nine-step model. In E. Trist & H. Murray (Eds.), *The social engagement of social science: A Tavistock anthology: Vol. 2* (1993; pp. 569–79). Philadelphia: University of Pennsylvania Press.

Emery, F. (1975). Continuing education under a gumtree. *Australian Journal of Adult Education, 15*(1), 17–19.

Emery, F. (1976a). Adaptive systems for our future governance. In M. Emery (Ed.), *Participative design for participative democracy* (pp. 185–199). Canberra: Centre for Continuing Education, Australian National University.

Emery, F. (1976b). The jury system and participative democracy. In M. Emery (Ed.), *Participative design for participative democracy* (pp. 207–211). Canberra: Centre for Continuing Education, Australian National University.

Emery, F. (1977). *Futures we are in.* Leiden, Netherlands: Martinus Nijhoff.

Emery, F. E. (1978a). Characteristics of socio-technical systems. In F. Emery, *The emergence of a new paradigm of work* (pp. 38–86). Canberra, Australia: Centre for Continuing Education, Australian National University,

Emery, F. (1978b). Epilogue: Reflections on the quality of work life. In F. Emery, *The emergence of a new paradigm of work* (pp. 149–151). Canberra: Centre for Continuing Education, Australian National University.

Emery, F. (1978c). Youth—Vanguard, victims, or the new vandals? In F. Emery (Ed.), *Limits to choice.* Melbourne, Australia: Fred Emery Institute.

Emery, F. (1980a). Educational paradigms: An epistemological revolution. In M. Emery (Ed.), *Participative design for participative democracy* (pp. 40–85). Canberra: Centre for Continuing Education, Australian National University.

Emery, F. (1980b). Designing socio-technical systems for "greenfield" sites. *Journal of Occupational Behaviour, 1,* 19–27.

Emery, F. (1983). Sociotechnical foundations for a new social order. In H. Kolodny & H. van Beinum (Eds.), *The quality of working life and the 1980s* (pp. 109–137). New York: Praeger.

Emery, F. (1984). Foreword. In R. De Nitish, *Alternative designs of human organizations* (pp. 9–16). New Delhi, India: Sage.

Emery, F. E. (1986). *Directions in secondary education.* Unpublished manuscript.

Emery, F. (1988). Laissez-faire vs. democratic groups. In M. Emery (Ed.), *Participative design for participative democracy* (pp. 172–175). Canberra: Centre for Continuing Education, Australian National University.

Emery, F. (1989a). The light on the hill, 1988: "Skill formation" or "the democratization of work." In M. Emery (Ed.), *Participative design for participative democracy* (pp. 89–99). Canberra: Centre for Continuing Education, Australian National University.

Emery, F. (1989b). The management of self-managing groups. In M. Emery (Ed.), *Participative design for participative democracy* (pp. 156–161). Canberra: Centre for Continuing Education, Australian National University.

Emery, F. (1993). The second design principle: Participation and the democratization of work. In E. Trist & H. Murray (Eds.), *The social engagement of social science: A Tavistock anthology: Vol. 2* (pp. 214–232). Philadelphia: University of Pennsylvania Press.

Emery, F. (1996). Some observations on workplace reform: The Australian experience. In D. Mortimer, P. Leece, & R. Morris (Eds.), *Workplace reform and enterprise bargaining* (pp. 25–35). Sydney, Australia: Harcourt, Brace.

Emery, F. (1998). *Toward real democracy.* Melbourne, Australia: Fred Emery Institute.

Emery, F. (1999). The perceptual logic of creativity. In R. E. Purser & A. Montuori (Eds.), *Social creativity: Vol. 2* (pp. 91–124). Cresskill, NJ: Hampton Press.

Emery, F., & Emery, M. (1974). Participative design: Work and community life. In M. Emery (Ed.), *Participative design for participative democracy* (pp. 100–122). Canberra: Centre for Continuing Education, Australian National University.

Emery, F., & Emery, M. (1976). *A choice of futures.* Leiden, Netherlands: Martinus Nijhoff.

Emery, F., & Emery, M. (1979). Project Australia: Its chances. In E. Trist & H. Murray (Eds.), *The social engagement of social science: A Tavistock anthology: Vol. 3* (1997; pp. 336–353). Philadelphia: University of Pennsylvania Press.

Emery, F. E., & Phillips, C. (1976). *Living at work.* Canberra: Australian Government Publishing Service.

Emery, F., & Thorsrud, E. (1969). *Form and content in industrial democracy.* London: Tavistock.

Emery, F., & Thorsrud, E. (1976). *Democracy at work.* Leiden, Netherlands: Martinus Nijhoff.

Emery, F. E., & Trist, E. L. (1965). The causal texture of organisational environments. *Human Relations, 18,* 21–32.

Emery, M. (Ed.). (1974). *Planning our town: Gungahlin.* Canberra: Centre for Continuing Education, Australian National University

Emery, M. (1976). Draft policy proposal for a primary school. Unpublished manuscript.

Emery, M. (1978). Getting to grips with the great "small group" conspiracy. In M. Emery (Ed.), *Participative design for participative democracy* (pp. 176–179). Canberra: Centre for Continuing Education, Australian National University.

Emery, M. (1986). Toward an heuristic theory of diffusion. *Human Relations, 39*(5), 411–432.

Emery, M. (1988). The hidden contribution of adult/continuing education to productivity. In J. E. Collins & W. Moore (Eds.), *Adult and continuing education: Its contribution to the Australian economy* (pp. 45–64). Newcastle: Australian Association of Adult Education.

Emery, M. (1989). Introduction. In M. Emery (Ed.), *Participative design for participative democracy* (pp. 7–27). Canberra: Centre for Continuing Education, Australian National University.

Emery, M. (1990). Postscript to "Battle of design principles." In F. Frei & I. Udris (Eds.), *Das Bild der Arbeit* (pp. 267–268). Bern, Switzerland: Verlag Hans Huber.

Emery, M. (1992a). Workplace Australia: Lessons for the planning and design of multisearches. *Journal of Applied Behavioural Science, 28*(4), 520–533.

Emery, M. (1992b). The concept of TLC—Trainer, leader, coach. In M. Emery (Ed.), *Participative design for participative democracy* (pp. 148–152). Canberra: Centre for Continuing Education, Australian National University.

Emery, M. (Ed.). (1993a). *Participative design for participative democracy.* Canberra: Centre for Continuing Education, Australian National University.

Emery, M. (Ed.). (1993b). Further learnings about participative design. In M. Emery (Ed.), *Participative design for participative democracy* (pp. 123–140). Canberra: Centre for Continuing Education, Australian National University.

Emery, M. (1993c). Introduction to part III: Democracy throughout the system. In M. Emery (Ed.), *Participative design for participative democracy* (pp. 180–181). Canberra: Centre for Continuing Education, Australian National University.

Emery, M. (1993d). Introduction to the 1993 edition. In M. Emery (Ed.), *Participative design for participative democracy* (pp. 1–6). Canberra: Centre for Continuing Education, Australian National University.

Emery, M. (1995). The power of community searches. *Journal of Quality and Participation, 18*(7), 70–79.

Emery, M. (1997). *Open systems is alive and well.* Presented to the symposium on sociotechnical systems at the U.S. Academy of Management Conference, Boston.

Emery, M. (1999). *Searching: The theory and practice of making cultural change.* Philadelphia: John Benjamins.

Emery, M. (2000a). The six criteria for intrinsic motivation in education systems: Partial democratization of a university experience, partial success. In O. N. Baburoglu & M. Emery (Eds.), *Educational futures: Shifting paradigm of universities and education* (pp. 309–334). Istanbul, Turkey: Sabanci University.

Emery, M. (2000b). The current version of Emery's open systems theory. *Systemic Practice and Action Research, 13*(5), 623–643.

Emery, M. (2000c). The evolution of open systems to the 2 stage model. In M. M. Beyerlein (Ed.), *Work teams: Past, present and future* (pp. 85–103). Norwell, MA: Kluwer Academic.

Emery, M., & Bartel, S. (2000). Affects, personality and the motivation to diffuse. Unpublished manuscript.

Evans, J. (2004, February 13). Trainers: Understaffed, overworked. *Washington Post.* Retrieved May 4, 2005, from http://www.washingtonpost.com/wp-dyn/articles/A37686-2004Feb12.html

Falk, I., & Kilpatrick, S. (2000). What is social capital? A study of interaction in a rural community. *Sociologia Ruralis, 40*(1), 87–110.

Farb, P. (1973). *Word play: What happens when people talk.* New York: Bantam Books.

Farrell, S. J., Aubry, T., & Coulombe, D. (2004). Neighborhoods and neighbors: Do they contribute to personal well-being? *Journal of Community Psychology, 32,* 9–25.

Feldman, S. (2002, January). A boost for good teaching. In American Federation of Teachers, *Where we stand.* Retrieved May 4, 2005, from http://www.aft.org/stand/previous/2002/0102.html

Fells, R. (1996). Negotiating workplace change: An overview of research into negotiation behaviour. In D. Mortimer, P. Leece, & R. Morris (Eds.), *Workplace reform and enterprise bargaining* (pp. 327–345). Sydney: Harcourt, Brace.

Fiorelli, J. (1988). Power in work groups: Team member's perspectives. *Human Relations, 41,* 1–12.

Flora, J. L. (1998). Social capital and communities of place [Abstract]. *Rural Sociology, 63*(4), 481.

Flores, M. A. (2003). Teacher learning in the workplace: Processes and influencing factors. Retrieved November 29, 2004, from http://www.hiceducation.org/Edu_Proceedings/Maria%2520A.%2520Flores.pdf+Teacher+Learning+in+the+Workplace&hl=en

Florin, P., & Wandersman, A. (1990). An introduction to citizen participation, voluntary organizations, and community development: Insights for empowerment through research. *American Journal of Community Psychology, 18*(1), 41–45.

Foreman, P. J., Gresham, R. L., & James, D. (1997). Bringing family, school and community together with the help of trained volunteers [Abstract]. *Journal of Family Studies, 3*(1), 109.

Forster, M. (2004). Higher order thinking skills. *Research Developments, 11,* 10–15.

Freire, P. (1972). *The pedagogy of the oppressed.* Harmondsworth, England: Penguin.

Friedrich, O. (1983, August 15). What do babies know? More than many realize and much earlier, according to new research. *Time,* pp. 52–59.

Fromm, E. (1963). *The sane society.* London: Routledge & Kegan Paul.

Fukuyama, F. (1995). *Trust: The social virtues and the creation of prosperity.* New York: Free Press.

Gambill, K., Pfaff, S., & Yates, R. (1995a). Summary of research on benefits of multiage classrooms. *Chimacum Intermediate Multiage Program.* Retrieved November 21, 2004, from http://www.chimacum.wednet.edu/elementary/imap/multiage research.html

Gambill, K., Pfaff, S., & Yates, R. (1995b). Team teaching. *Chimacum Intermediate Multiage Program*. Retrieved November 21, 2004, from http://www.chimacum .wednet.edu/elementary/imap/teaming.html

Gardell, B. (1977). Autonomy and participation at work. *Human Relations, 30*(6), 515–533.

Gardell, B., & Gustavsen, B. (1980). Work environment research and social change. *Journal of Occupational Behaviour, 1*(1), 3–17.

Gardner, H. (1991). *The unschooled mind*. London: Fontana Press.

Gardner, J. W. (1994). There is more than a ray of hope for America's future . . . Rebuilding America's sense of community. *Journal of Quality and Participation*. Retrieved November 23, 2004, from http://www.worldtrans.org/qual/american community.html

Garforth, F. W. (1980). *Educative democracy: John Stuart Mill on education in society*. Oxford: Oxford University Press.

Garson, B. (1988). *The electronic sweatshop: How computers are transforming the office of the future into the factory of the past*. New York: Simon & Schuster.

Gibson, E., & Levin, H. (1975). *The psychology of reading*. Cambridge, MA: MIT Press.

Gibson, J. J. (1966). *The senses considered as perceptual systems*. Boston: Houghton Mifflin.

Gibson, J. J. (1967). New reasons for realism. *Synthese, 17*, 162–172.

Gibson, K., Cameron, J., & Veno, A. (1999). *Negotiating restructuring: A study of regional communities experiencing rapid social and economic change* (AHURI Working Paper No. 11). Melbourne: Australian Housing and Urban Research Institute, Department of Geography and Environmental Science and School of Humanities and Public Policy, Monash University.

Gibson, L. (2005, March 6). Technology relieves the boredom at school. *Canberra Sunday Times*, p. 17.

Glaser, S., & Halliday, M. (1999). Ideology in organisations—A comparison of East and West. *Learning Organization, 6*(3), 101–106.

Glencoe Online. (2004). Contributing to a successful teaching team: Teaching tips of the week. *Teaching Today*. Retrieved November 21, 2004, from http://www.glencoe .com/sec/teachingtoday/weekly tips.phtml/156

Gorney, R. (1968). *The human agenda*. New York: Bantam Books.

Grasmick, N. S. (2001). Maryland 10 years later: Reform for a new century. In F. M. Duffy & J. D. Dale (Eds.), *Creating successful school systems: Voices from the university, the field, and the community* (pp. 71–88). Norwood, MA: Christopher-Gordon.

GreatSchools.net. (2005). Commerce City schools—District elementary, middle, and high school information. Retrieved March 14, 2005, from http://www.greatschools .net/cgi-bin/ga/district_profile/45/

Haith, M. M. (1980). *Rules that babies look by: The organization of newborn visual activity*. Hillsdale, NJ: Erlbaum.

Hall, E. T. (1976). *Beyond culture*. New York: Anchor Press/Doubleday.

Halsey, A. H. (1980). *Origins and destinations: Family, class and destination in modern Britain*. Oxford: Clarendon Press.

Hamson, N. (1998). Working, managing and leading in turbulent times. In N. Hamson (Ed.), *After Atlantis: Working, managing and leading in turbulent times* (pp. 3–25). Boston: Butterworth-Heinemann.

Hanushek, E. A. (1996). *The productivity collapse in schools.* National Center for Education Statistics, U.S. Department of Education. Retrieved March 20, 2005, from http://nces.ed.gov/pubs97/97535/97535k.asp#top

Hari, J. (2004, January 16). Cults in a puzzle of American violence. *Canberra Times,* p. 15.

Harris, L. (2004). Virtual online environments creating an external social presence—MOO. *Melbourne Studies in Education, 45*(1), 1–22.

Hart, L. (1943). *Thoughts on war.* London: Faber and Faber.

Hart, L. (1946). *The strategy of the indirect approach.* London: Faber and Faber.

Harvard Graduate School of Education. (2004). Tinkering towards Utopia: A century of public school reform. Excerpts from a conversation at the Askwith Education Forum. *HGSE News.* Retrieved November 29, 2004, from http://www.gse.harvard.edu/news/features/utopia03012004.html

Haskell, J., & Prichard, J. (2004). Creating productive meetings. *Journal of Extension, 42*(2). Retrieved from http://www.joe.org/joe/2004april/iw3.shtml

Haugen, R. (1992). Adapting to rapid change using search conferences. In M. R. Weisbord (Ed.), *Discovering common ground* (pp. 83–94). San Francisco: Berrett-Koehler.

Hauser, S. M. (2000). Education, ability and civic engagement in the contemporary United States. *Social Science Research, 29,* 556–582.

Havelock, E. A. (1978). *The Greek concept of justice.* Cambridge, MA: Harvard University Press.

Heckman, F. (1995). A new method for achieving community excellence. *Journal for Quality and Participation, 18*(7), 80–89.

Heckman, F. (1998). Designing organizations for flow and adaptability. In N. Hamson (Ed.), *After Atlantis: Working, managing and leading in turbulent times* (pp. 27–64). Boston: Butterworth-Heinemann.

Hegarty, S. (2003, April 3). Teachers not buying state's performance bonus program. *St. Petersburg Times.* Retrieved April 30, 2004, from http://www.sptimes.com/2003/04/03/news_pf/State/Teachers_not_buying_s.shtml

Heider, F. (1946). Attitudes and cognitive organization. *Journal of Psychology, 21,* 107–112.

Henry, M., & Thompson, P. (Eds.) (1980). *Future directions: 1980 conference report.* Melbourne: Australian Frontier.

Herbst, D. P. (1976). *Alternatives to hierarchies.* Leiden, Netherlands: Martinus Nijhoff.

Herbst, D. P. (1990). The battle of design principles—A conceptual-strategical note on a Human Futures Conference. In F. Frei & I. Udris (Eds.), *Das Bild der Arbeit* (pp. 258–268). Bern, Switzerland: Verlag Hans Huber.

Herbst, D. P. (1993). A learning organization in practice: M/S Balao. In E. Trist & H. Murray (Eds.), *The social engagement of social science: A Tavistock anthology: Vol. 2* (pp. 408–416). Philadelphia: University of Pennsylvania Press.

Herzberg, F. (1987). One more time: How do you motivate employees? *Harvard Business Review, 65*(5), 109–120.

Heyns, B. (1974). Social selection and stratification within schools. *American Journal of Sociology, 79*, 1434–1451.

Hill, J. (2003). The new Grange. *National Grange*. Retrieved May 4, 2005, from http://www.nationalgrange.org/news-events/GrangeToday/NG_arch_may_jun03.htm

Hiller, J. (2002). Schools to keep transfer policy. *Honolulu Advertiser*. Retrieved May 4, 2005, from http://the.honoluluadvertiser.com/article/2002.Dec/12/In/In46a education.html

Hitchcock, D. (1994). Creating a high-performance society: Your community wants you. *Journal of Quality and Participation*. Retrieved November 23, 2004, from http://www.worldtrans.org/qual/communitywantsyou.html

Hodkinson, P., & Hodkinson, H. (2003, June). Expanding learning environments for secondary school teachers. In *Teaching and Learning*. Leeds, England: Lifelong Learning Institute, Continuing Education, University of Leeds.

Holman, J. (1986, February 13). School science meets the real world. *New Scientist*, pp. 45–47.

Horne, J. F., & McClelland, S. (2001). Leveraging change within a school district. In F. M. Duffy & J. D. Dale (Eds.), *Creating successful school systems: Voices from the university, the field, and the community* (pp. 237–254). Norwood, MA: Christopher-Gordon.

Huang, S. T. (1996). Review of Steiner et al., *Beyond the classroom, Library Journal*. Retrieved November 29, 2004, from http://www.amazon.com/exec/obidos/tg/detail/-/0684835754/102-7317942-3499334?v

Huntingdon Area School District. (2005). [Home page]. Retrieved March 14, 2005, from http://hasd.tiu.k12.pa.us/

Illich, I. D. (1971). *Deschooling society*. London: Calder & Boyars.

Illich, I. D. (1973). *Tools for conviviality*. London: Calder & Boyars.

Ingersoll, R. M. (1999). The problem of underqualified teachers in American secondary schools. *Educational Researcher, 28*(2), 26–37.

Institut fur Padagogische Psychologie. (n.d.). *Cooperative theory and learning at schools and universities*. Frankfurt, Germany: Johann Wolfgang Goethe University. Retrieved February 27, 2005, from http://216.239.37.104/translate_c?hl=en&sl=de&u=http://web.uni-frankfurt.de/fb05/ifpp

Ireland, D. (1971). *The unknown industrial prisoner*. Sydney, Australia: Angus and Robertson.

Israel, G. D., & Beaulieu, L. J. (2004). Investing in communities: Social capital's role in keeping youth in school [Abstract]. *Journal of Community Development Society, 34*(2), 35.

Jencks, C. (1979). *Who gets ahead?* New York: Basic Books.

Jimenez, J., & Aguirre-Vazquez, J. (2000). The role of the search conference as a catalyst for long-range change and adaptation in higher education. In O. N. Baburoglu

& M. Emery (Eds.), *Educational futures: Shifting paradigm of universities and education* (pp. 285–297). Istanbul, Turkey: Sabanci University.

Jordan, N. (1973). Some thinking about "system." In S. L. Optener (Ed.), *Systems analysis* (pp. 53–67). New York: Penguin.

Joyner, F. (1996). Quality and participation in community settings. *Journal for Quality and Participation, 19*(5), 12–18.

Karasek, R. (1976). *The impact of the work environment on life outside the job: A longitudinal study of the Swedish labour force 1968–1974.* Unpublished doctoral dissertation, MIT, Cambridge, MA.

Karasek, R., & Theorell, T. (1990). *Healthy work: Stress, productivity and the reconstruction of working life.* New York: Basic Books.

Karmel, P. (1985). *Quality of education in Australia.* Canberra: Australian Government Publishing Service.

Kemmis, D. (1990). *Community and the politics of place.* Norman: University of Oklahoma Press.

Kemmis, D. (1995). *The good city and the good life: Renewing the sense of community.* Boston: Houghton Mifflin.

Kenyon, P., & Black, A. (Eds.). (2001). *Small town renewal: A report for the Rural Industries Research and Development Corporation.* Canberra, Australia: Rural Industries Research and Development Corporation.

Kerckhoff, A. C. (1974). Stratification processes and outcomes in England and the U.S.A. *American Sociological Review, 39,* 789–801.

Kloth, C. (1992). Ohio childhood development conference. In M. R. Weisbord (Ed.), *Discovering common ground* (pp. 381–386). San Francisco: Berrett-Koehler.

Knight, T. (2000). Inclusive education and educational theory. *Melbourne Studies in Education, 41*(1), 17–43.

Knight, T. (2002). Equity in Victorian education and "deficit" thinking. *Melbourne Studies in Education, 43*(1), 83–105.

Knudtson, P., & Suzuki, D. (1992). *The wisdom of the elders.* Toronto: Stoddart.

Kolodny, H., & van Beinum, H. (Eds.). (1983). Preface. In *The quality of working life and the 1980s* (pp. vii–x). New York: Praeger.

La Lopa, J. M., & Holecek, D. F. (1996). A community-based service quality training program. *Journal for Quality and Participation, 19*(5), 48–52.

Lamb, S., & Fullarton, S. (2002). Classroom and school factors affecting mathematics achievement: A comparative study of Australia and the United States using TIMSS. *Australian Journal of Education, 46*(2), 154–171.

Lamb, S., Hogan, D., & Johnson, T. (2001). The stratification of learning opportunities and achievement in Tasmanian secondary schools. *Australian Journal of Education, 45*(2), 153–167.

Lansbury, R., Bamber, G., & Davis, E. (1996). The Australian auto industry in transition: Changing patterns of industrial relations and human resources. In D. Mortimer, P. Leece, & R. Morris (Eds.), *Workplace reform and enterprise bargaining* (pp. 89–113). Sydney, Australia: Harcourt, Brace.

Leuenberger, J. (1994). Schools of quality: An experiment in cooperation. *Journal of Quality and Participation.* Retrieved November 23, 2004, from http://www .worldtrans.org/qual/schoolquality.html

Leverich, J. (n.d.). *The economy, social programs and education.* Wisconsin Education Association Council. Retrieved March 20, 2005, from http://www.weac.org/ Resource/Talkpts.htm

LeVine, R. A., LeVine, S. E., & Schnell, B. (2001). "Improve the women": Mass schooling, female literacy and worldwide social change. *Harvard Educational Review, 71*(1), 1–50.

Levine, J. M., & Moreland, R. L. (2004). Collaboration: The social context of theory development. *Personality and Social Psychology Review, 8*(2), 164–172.

Lewin, K. (1947). Group decision and social change. In T. M. Newcomb & E. L. Hartley (Eds.), *Readings in social psychology* (pp. 330–344). New York: Henry Holt.

Limerick, D., & Cunningham, B. (1993). *Managing the new organization: A blueprint for networks and strategic alliances.* Chatswood, New South Wales: Business & Professional Publishing.

Lingard, B., & Mills, M. (2003). Teachers and school reforms: Working with productive pedagogies and productive assessment. *Melbourne Studies in Education, 44*(2), 1–18.

Linhart, R. (1981). *The assembly line* (M. Crosland, Trans.). London: John Calder.

Linn, M. C., Slotta, J. D., & Baumgartner, E. (2000). *Teaching high school science in the information age: A review of courses and technology for inquiry-based learning.* Santa Monica, CA: Milken Family Foundation.

Lippitt, R. (1940). An experimental study of the effect of democratic and authoritarian group atmospheres. *University of Iowa Studies in Child Welfare, 16*(3), 43–195.

Lippitt, R., & White, R. K. (1943). The "social climate" of children's groups. In R. G. Barker, J. S. Kounin, & H. F. Wright (Eds.), *Child behavior and development* (pp. 485–508). Norwood, NJ: Ablex.

Lippitt, R., & White, R. (1947). An experimental study of leadership and group life. In T. M. Newcomb & E. L. Hartley (Eds.), *Readings in social psychology* (pp. 315–330). New York: Henry Holt.

Lipsky, D. K., & Gartner, A. (1996). Inclusion: School restructuring and the remaking of American society. *Harvard Educational Review, 66*(3), 762–796.

Ljungberg van Beinum, I. (2000). *Using the lamp instead of looking into the mirror.* Amsterdam, Netherlands: John Benjamins.

Llewellyn, H. (1996). *Obstacles to change in a middle sized manufacturer* (Monograph No. 1). Sydney, Australia: Centre for Employment Relations, University of Western Sydney.

Lockwood, A. T. (n.d.). *Making schools productive.* Retrieved March 20, 2005, from http://www.ncrel.org/cscd/pubs/lead31/31making.htm

Lopez, G. R. (2001). The value of hard work: Lessons on parent involvement from an (im)migrant household. *Harvard Educational Review, 71*(3), 416–437.

Louie, V. (2001). Parents' aspirations and investment: The role of social class in the educational experiences of 1.5- and second-generation Chinese Americans. *Harvard Educational Review, 71*(3), 438–474.

Loveland, K. A. (1991). Social affordances and interaction II: Autism and the affordances of the human environment. *Ecological Psychology, 3*(2), 99–119.

Lovett, R. (2004, March 20). Running on empty. *New Scientist,* pp. 42–45.

Lyons, T. (1998). Shared learning. In N. Hamson (Ed.), *After Atlantis: Working, managing and leading in turbulent times* (pp. 66–93). Boston: Butterworth-Heinemann.

Maccoby, M. (1976). *The gamesman: The new corporate leaders.* New York: Simon & Schuster.

Macintosh, M. (1996). Compliance or enlightened management in occupational health and safety? A manufacturing case. In D. Mortimer, P. Leece, & R. Morris (Eds.), *Workplace reform and enterprise bargaining* (pp. 217–231). Sydney: Harcourt, Brace.

Madrick, J. (2005). The producers. *New York Review of Books, 52*(4), 26–29.

Margolis, E., & Romera, M. (1998). "The department is very male, very white, very old and very conservative": The functioning of the hidden curriculum in graduate sociology departments. *Harvard Educational Review, 68*(1), 1–32.

Marini, M. M. (1984). Women's educational attainment and the timing of entry into parenthood. *American Sociological Review, 49,* 491–510.

Marmot, M. (1999). Introduction. In M. Marmot & R. G. Wilkinson (Eds.), *Social determinants of health* (pp. 1–16). Oxford: Oxford University Press.

Marmot, M., Siegrist, J., Theorell T., & Feeney, A. (1999). Health and the psychosocial environment at work. In M. Marmot & R. G. Wilkinson (Eds.), *Social determinants of health* (pp. 105–131). Oxford: Oxford University Press.

Marsden, D. (1991). What is community participation? In R. C. Crook & A. M. Jerve (Eds.), *Government and participation: Institutional development, decentralization and democracy in the third world.* Bergen, Norway: Chr Michelsen Institute, Department of Social Science and Development.

Martin, M. O., Mullis, I. V. S., Gonzalez, E. J., Gregory, K. D., Smith, T. A., Chrostowski, S. J., et al. (2001). *TIMSS 1999: International science report.* Chestnut Hill, MA: International Study Center, Boston College, Lynch School of Education.

Mathews, J. (1989). *Tools of change: New technology and the democratisation of work.* Sydney, Australia: Pluto Press.

Maton, K. I., & Salem, D. A. (1995). Organizational characteristics of empowering community settings: A multiple case study approach. *American Journal of Community Psychology, 23*(5), 631–656.

McInerney, P. (2003). Renegotiating schooling for social justice in a age of marketisation. *Australian Journal of Education, 47*(3), 251–264.

McKnight, J. (1995). *The careless society: Community and its counterfeits.* New York: Basic Books.

Megill, K. A. (1970). *The new democratic theory.* New York: Free Press.

Mendel, D. (2004, November 1). Leave no parent behind. *American Prospect Online.* Retrieved December 16, 2005, from http://www.prospect.org/web/page.ww?name =View+Author&section=root&id=1162

Merrow, J. (2004, February 2). Educational foresight: The quality of schools will affect the quality of your life. *Mercury News.* Retrieved May 4, 2005, from http://www.pbs.org/merrow/news/mercury_news.html

Michaels, C. F., & Carello, C. (1981). *Direct perception*. New York: Prentice Hall.

Mickelson, K. D., & Kubansky, L. D. (2003). Social distribution of social support: The mediating role of life events. *American Journal of Community Psychology, 32*(3/4), 265–281.

Milken, L. (1999). *A matter of quality: A strategy for assuring the high caliber of America's teachers*. Santa Monica, CA: Milken Family Foundation. Retrieved December 5, 2004, from http://www.mff.org/about/lmilken.taf?page=speech_quality

Miller, E. J. (1993). The Ahmedabad experiment revisited: Work organization in an Indian weaving shed, 1953–1970. In E. Trist & H. Murray (Eds.), *The social engagement of social science: A Tavistock anthology: Vol. 2* (pp. 130–156). Philadelphia: University of Pennsylvania Press.

Mills, C., & Gale, T. (2002). Schooling and the production of social inequalities: What can and should we be doing? *Melbourne Studies in Education, 43*(1), 107–128.

Minuchin, P. (1969). *The psychological impact of the school experience: A comparison study of nine-year-old children in contrasting schools*. New York: Basic Books.

Montuori, A., & Conti, I. (1993). *From power to partnership: Creating the future of love, work, and community*. San Francisco: Harper.

Montuori, A., & Purser, R. E. (1996). Ecological futures: Systems theory, postmodernism and participative learning in an age of uncertainty. In D. M. Boje, R. P. Gephart, & T. J. Thatchenkery (Eds.), *Postmodern management and organization theory* (pp. 181–201). Thousand Oaks, CA: Sage.

Moore, A. B. (2002). Community development practice: Theory in action [Abstract]. *Journal of Community Development Society, 33*(1), 20.

Moore, K. A., & Hofferth, S. L. (1980). Factors affecting early family formation model. *Population and Environment, 3,* 73–98.

Morley, D., & Trist, E. (1992). Planning, designing and managing large-scale searches. In M. R. Weisbord (Ed.), *Discovering common ground* (pp. 187–213). San Francisco: Berrett-Koehler.

Morris, R. (1996). The age of workplace reform in Australia. In D. Mortimer, P. Leece, & R. Morris (Eds.), *Workplace reform and enterprise bargaining* (pp. 11–23). Sydney, Australia: Harcourt, Brace.

Mullis, I. V. S., Martin, M. O., & Gonzalez, E. J. (2003). *PIRLS 2001 international report: IEA study of reading literacy achievement in primary schools*. Chestnut Hill, MA: International Study Center, Boston College, Lynch School of Education.

Mullis, I. V. S., Martin, M. O., Gonzalez, E. J., Gregory, K. D., Garden, R. A., O'Connor, K. M., et al. (2001). *TIMSS 1999: International mathematics report*. Chestnut Hill, MA: International Study Center, Boston College, Lynch School of Education.

Murata, R. (2002). *What does team teaching mean? A case study of interdisciplinary teaming*. Retrieved November 21, 2004, from http://www.questia.com/PM.qst?action=getPage&docId=5001940805&keywords=&We

Napier, W., & Hasler-Waters, L. (2003). Building team collaboration in the virtual classroom. *Educational Perspectives, 35*(2), 13–20.

National Center for Education Statistics. (2002). *Characteristics of the 100 largest public elementary and secondary districts in the United States of America 2000–2001*. Retrieved September 29, 2003, from http://nces.ed.gov/pubs2002/100_largest/table_06_1.asp

National Community Education Association. (2005). [Home page]. Retrieved February 12, 2005, from http://www.ncea.com

National Foundation for the Improvement of Education (NFIE). (2000). *Connecting the bits: A reference for using technology in teaching and learning in K–12 schools.* Washington, DC: Author.

National Middle School Association. (1999). *Research summary #6: Heterogeneous grouping.* Retrieved February 27, 2005, from http://www.ncmsa.net/ressum6.htm

Nelson, A. L., & Schwirian, K. P. (1998). Social and economic distress in large cities, 1970–1990: A test of the urban crisis thesis. *Social Science Research, 27,* 410–431.

Newcomb, T. M. (1953). An approach to the study of communicative acts. *Psychological Review, 60,* 283–304.

Newman, F. M., King, M. B., & Rigdon, M. (1997). Accountability and school: Implications from restructuring schools. *Harvard Educational Review, 67*(1), 41–74.

North Carolina Department of Public Instruction. (1996). *NC technology competencies for educators.* Retrieved November 20, 2004, from http://www.dpi.state.nc.us/tap/techcomp performance.htm

North Central Regional Educational Laboratory. (n.d.-a). *New leaders for tomorrow's schools: Strategies for educational productivity.* Retrieved March 20, 2005, from http://www.ncrel.org/cscd/pubs/lead31/31strate.htm

North Central Regional Educational Laboratory. (n.d.-b). Preliminary characteristics of productive schools. Retrieved March 20, 2005, from http://www.ncrel.org/cscd/pubs/lead31/31prdist.htm

North Central Regional Educational Laboratory. (n.d.-c). *Sense of community.* Retrieved November 23, 2004, from http://www.ncrel.org/sdrs/areas/issues/students/earlycld/ea1lk2.htm

Oeser, O. A. (Ed.). (1955). *Teacher, pupil and task: Elements of social psychology applied to education.* London: Tavistock.

Office of the Press Secretary. (2001, December 11). *President pleased with education agreement* [Press release]. Retrieved April 30, 2004, from http://www.whitehouse.gov/news/releases/2001/12/print/20011212.html

Olson, R. (1996). Review of Steiner et al., *Beyond the classroom,* 1996. *Booklist.* Retrieved November 29, 2004, from http://www.amazon.com/gp/product/product-description/0684835754/102-7317942-349

Ong, W. J. (1967). *The presence of the word.* New Haven, CT: Yale University Press.

Onyx, J., & Bullen, P. (2000). Measuring social capital in five communities. *Journal of Applied Behavioral Science, 36*(1), 23–42.

Opie, I., & Opie, P. (1959). *The lore and language of schoolchildren.* Oxford: Oxford University Press.

Pajak, E. F., & Hairston, J. A. (2001). School systems for the near future. In F. M. Duffy & J. D. Dale (Eds.), *Creating successful school systems: Voices from the university, the field, and the community* (pp. 219–235). Norwood, MA: Christopher-Gordon.

Palmer, I., & McGraw, P. (1996). A new era for joint consultation? Human resources managers perceptions of JCCs and enterprise bargaining. In D. Mortimer, P. Leece, & R. Morris (Eds.), *Workplace reform and enterprise bargaining* (pp. 173–185). Sydney, Australia: Harcourt, Brace.

Papert, S. (1980). *Mindstorms: Children, computers and powerful ideas.* Brighton, England: Harvester Press.

Parsons, J. (1996a). Sharing productivity gains. *CFO Magazine.* Retrieved November 14, 2004, from http://www.cfoweb.com.au/stories/19960801/6623.asp

Parsons, J. (1996b). Sharing productivity gains. *CFO Magazine.* Retrieved November 14, 2004, from http://www.cfoweb.com.au/stories/19960801/6624.asp

Parsons, J. (1996c). Sharing productivity gains. *CFO Magazine.* Retrieved November 14, 2004, from http://www.cfoweb.com.au/stories/19960801/6625.asp

Passmore, W. A., Francis, C., Shani, A., & Halderman, J. (1982). Sociotechnical systems: A North American reflection on empirical studies of the seventies. *Human Relations, 32,* 1179–1204.

Pateman, C. (1970). *Participation and democratic theory.* Cambridge: Cambridge University Press.

Paton, J., & Emery, M. (1996). Community planning in the Torres Strait. *Journal of Quality and Participation, 19*(5), 26–35.

Pavett, C. M. (1986). High stress professions, satisfaction, stress and well-being of spouses of professionals. *Human Relations, 39*(12), 1141–1154.

Pawley, M. (1973). *The private future.* London: Thames and Hudson.

Pence, K. K. (2001). Epilogue: Last call for voices. In F. M. Duffy & J. D. Dale (Eds.), *Creating successful school systems: Voices from the university, the field, and the community* (pp. 273–74). Norwood, MA: Christopher-Gordon.

Pepitone, E. A. (1990). Social comparison, relative deprivation, and pupil interaction: Homogenous and heterogeneous classrooms. In S. A. Wheelan, E. A. Pepitone, & V. Abt (Eds.), *Advances in field theory* (pp. 165–176). Newbury Park, CA: Sage.

Phillips, V. L. (2001). Finishing the race: A district perspective of standards-based reform. In F. M. Duffy & J. D. Dale (Eds.), *Creating successful school systems: Voices from the university, the field, and the community* (pp. 105–123). Norwood, MA: Christopher-Gordon.

Pinchot, G., & Pinchot, E. (1993). *The end of bureaucracy and the rise of the intelligent organization.* San Francisco: Berrett-Koehler.

Polanyi, M. (1958). *Personal knowledge.* London: Routledge and Kegan Paul.

Polanyi, M. (1969). *Knowing and being* (M. Grene, Ed.). London: Routledge and Kegan Paul.

Presser, H. A., Boyd, G. W. D., & Lea, R. C. G. (1955). The social conditions for successful learning. In O. A. Oeser (Ed.), *Teacher, pupil and task: Elements of social psychology applied to education* (pp. 30–49). London: Tavistock.

Prestby, J. E., Wandersman, A., Florin, P., Rich, R., & Chavis, D. (1990). Benefits, costs, incentive management and participation in voluntary organizations: A means to understanding and promoting empowerment. *American Journal of Community Psychology, 18*(1), 117–149.

Pringle, J. K., & Collins, S. (1998). Women leading which ways? [Abstract] *International Review of Women and Leadership, 4*(1), 1–12.

Psacharopoulos, G. (1977). Family background, education and achievement: A path model of earnings determinants in the U.K. and some alternatives. *British Journal of Sociology, 28,* 321–335.

Purser, R. E., & Cabana, S. (1998). *The self managing organization: How leading companies are transforming the work of teams for real impact.* New York: Free Press.

Putnam, R. (2000). *Bowling alone: The collapse and revival of American community.* New York: Simon & Schuster.

Rado, D. (2001, May 3). Budget plan offers bonus for teachers. *St. Petersburg Times.* Retrieved November 14, 2004, from http://www.sptimes.com/News/050301/news _pf/State/Budget_plan_offers_bo.shtml

Randerson, J. (2004, July 31). It's the brain not the body that hits the wall. *New Scientist,* p. 11.

Raudenbush, S. W., & Kasim, R. M. (1998). Cognitive skill and economic inequality: Findings from the National Adult Literacy Survey. *Harvard Educational Review, 68*(1), 33–79.

Reed, E., & Jones, R. (1982). *Reasons for realism: Selected essays of James J. Gibson.* Hillsdale, NJ: Erlbaum.

Rehberg, R. A., & Schafer, W. E. (1970). Toward a temporal sequence of adolescent achievement variables. *American Sociological Review, 35,* 34–47.

Rehm, B., Schweitz, R., & Granata, E. (1992). Water quality in the upper Colorado river basin. In M. R. Weisbord (Ed.), *Discovering common ground* (pp. 215–227). San Francisco: Berrett-Koehler.

ResearchWorks. (2002). *Team teaching.* College of Education and Human Development, University of Minnesota. Retrieved November 21, 2004, from http://education .umn.edu/research/ResearchWorks/team.html

Rice, A. K. (1993). Productivity and social organization: An Indian automated weaving shed. In E. Trist & H. Murray (Eds.), *The social engagement of social science: A Tavistock anthology: Vol. 2* (pp. 106–129). Philadelphia: University of Pennsylvania Press.

Richards, J. M., & Gottfredson, D. C. (1983). Education, work and family formation in early adulthood. *Population and Environment, 6,* 241–254.

Riger, S. (1993). What's wrong with empowerment? *American Journal of Community Psychology, 21*(3), 279–292.

Riger, S. (1994). Challenges of success: Stages of growth in feminist organizations. *Feminist Studies, 20*(2), 273–300.

Rist, R. C. (2000a). Author's introduction: The enduring dilemmas of class and color in American education. *Harvard Educational Review, 70*(3), 257–265.

Rist, R. C. (2000b). Student social class and teacher expectations: The self-fulfilling prophecy in ghetto education. *Harvard Educational Review, 70*(3), 266–301.

Robinson, R. V., & Jackson, E. F. (2001). Is trust in others declining in America? An age-period-cohort analysis. *Social Science Research, 30,* 117–145.

Rothman, S., & McMillan, J. (2003). *Longitudinal surveys of Australian youth: Influences on achievement in literacy and numeracy* (Research Report No. 36). Australian Council for Educational Research. Retrieved November 14, 2004, from http:// www.acer.edu.au

Rothman, S., & McMillan, J. (2004). Positive school climate helps students achieve positive results. *Research Developments, 11,* 16–17.

Rothstein, R. (1999, December 6). Blaming teachers. *American Prospect, 11*(2). Retrieved November 20, 2004, from http://www.prospect.org/print//V11/7/ rothstein-r.html

Rothstein, R. (2000, February 14). The parent panacea. *American Prospect, 11*(7). Retrieved November 20, 2004, from http://www.prospect.org/web/print-friendly-view.ww?id=8772

Rothstein, R. (2004a, November 1). Too young to test. *American Prospect Online*. Retrieved December 16, 2005, from http://www.prospect.org/web/page.ww?name=View+Author&section=root&id=93&pageNumber=1

Rothstein, R. (2004b). Must schools fail? *New York Review of Books, 51*(19), 29–37.

Rothstein, R. (2004c). *Class and schools: Using social, economic and educational reform to close the Black-White achievement gap.* Washington, DC: Economic Policy Institute.

Rothstein, R. (2005). Must schools fail? An exchange. *New York Review of Books, 52*(3), 49–50.

Roy, J., & Piperato, D. (2001). Transforming school culture for the 3rd millennium. In F. M. Duffy & J. D. Dale (Eds.), *Creating successful school systems: Voices from the university, the field, and the community* (pp. 201–217). Norwood, MA: Christopher-Gordon.

Russell, G., & Russell, N. (2001). Virtualization and the late age of schools. *Melbourne Studies in Education, 45*(1), 25–44.

Sacks, O. (1984). *A leg to stand on.* London: Picador, Pan Books.

Salamon, S., Farnsworth, R. L., & Rendziak, J. A. (1998). Is locally led conservation planning working? A farm town case study [Abstract]. *Rural Sociology, 63*(2), 214.

Saskatoon Public School Division. (2004). What is indirect instruction? *Instructional Strategies Online.* Retrieved February 27, 2005, from http://olc.spsd.sk.ca/DE/PD/instr/indirect.html

Sawyer, W. W. (1971). Foreword. In C. Stern & M. B. Stern, *Children discover arithmetic: An introduction to structural arithmetic* (pp. vii–xii). New York: Harper & Row.

Schafft, K. A., & Greenwood, D. J. (2003). Promises and dilemmas of participation: Action research, search conference methodology, and community development [Abstract]. *Journal of Community Development Society, 34*(1), 18.

Schmacher, E. F. (1973). *Small is beautiful.* London: Abacus.

Schmuck, R., & Schmuck, P. (1992). *Small districts, big problems: Making school everybody's house.* Newbury Park, CA: Corwin.

Schoenheimer, H. (1972, August 5). Wanted: A new model school. Progress report: Concluding a special series on education. *The Australian.*

Schon, D. A. (1971). *Beyond the stable state.* London: Temple Smith,

Schrag, P. (2005). Must schools fail? An exchange. *New York Review of Books, 52*(3), 49–50.

Schroy, J. O. (2004). *Productivity flim-flam.* Retrieved December 16, 2005, from http://www.capital-flow-analysis.com/essays/productivity.htm

Schulman, M. D., & Anderson, C. (1999). The dark side of the force: A case study of restructuring and social capital [Abstract]. *Rural Sociology, 64,* 351.

Schweitz, R. (1996). Searching for a quality environment. *Journal for Quality and Participation, 19*(5), 36–40.

Schwinn, C., & Schwinn, D. (1996). Lessons for organizational transformation. *Journal for Quality and Participation, 19*(5), 6–10.

Sewell, W. H. (1970). The educational and early occupational attainment process. *American Sociological Review, 47*, 82–98.

Sewell, W. H., & Hauser, R. M. (1980). Sex, schooling and occupational status. *American Journal of Sociology, 86*, 551–582.

Sewell, W. H., & Shah, U. P. (1967). Socioeconomic status, intelligence and the attainment of higher education. *Sociology of Education, 40*, 1–17.

Sewell, W. H., & Shah, U. P. (1968). Parents' education and children's educational aspirations and achievements. *American Sociological Review, 33*, 191–208.

Shafer, I. (2001). Team teaching: Education for the future. *University of Science and Arts of Oklahoma.* Retrieved November 21, 2004, from http://www.usao.edu/-facshaferi/teamteaching.htm

Shand, A. I. (1926). *The foundation of character.* New York: MacMillan.

Shattuck, R. (2005). The shame of the schools. *New York Review of Books, 52*(6), 66–69.

Shaw, M. E. (1947). A comparison of individuals and small groups in the rational solution of complex problems. In T. M. Newcomb & E. L. Hartley (Eds.), *Readings in social psychology* (pp. 304–314). New York: Henry Holt.

Shelby, J. M., & Musgrove, K. A. (2001). Redesigning the Franklin Special School District. In F. M. Duffy & J. D. Dale (Eds.), *Creating successful school systems: Voices from the university, the field, and the community* (pp. 255–268). Norwood, MA: Christopher-Gordon.

Sinclair, M. (2002). Social justice in education in Australia circa 1983–1996: The becoming of a market. *History of Education Review, 31*(2), 74–86.

Slee, R. (2000). Professional partnerships for inclusive education. *Melbourne Studies in Education, 41*(1), 1–15.

Smith, E. C. (2004). Have you checked your social capital lately? The Keystone Project. *Community Education Journal, 27*(3/4). Retrieved February 14, 2005, from http://www.ncea.com/pubs_products/Keystonearticle2-ncea1.pdf

Snyder, I. (1999). Packaging literacy, new technologies and "enhanced" learning. *Australian Journal of Education, 43*(3), 285–299.

Snyder, K. J. (2001). Preparing school districts for the great transitions of our times. In F. M. Duffy & J. D. Dale (Eds.), *Creating successful school systems: Voices from the university, the field, and the community* (pp. 35–54). Norwood, MA: Christopher-Gordon.

Soler-Gallart, M. (2000). Editor's review. *Harvard Educational Review, 70*(1), 109–117.

Sorensen, B. A. (1977). *The making of an industrial community.* Oslo, Norway: Work Research Institute.

Stansfeld, S. (1999). Social support and social cohesion. In M. Marmot & R. G. Wilkinson (Eds.), *Social determinants of health* (pp. 155–178). Oxford: Oxford University Press.

Starkey, P., Spelke, E. S., & Gelman, R. (1983). Detection of intermodal numerical correspondence by human infants. *Science, 222*(4620), 179–181.

Starnes, D. M. (2004). Community psychologists—Get in the arena!! *American Journal of Community Psychology, 33*(1/2), 3–6.

Steffens, R. (n.d.). *Jigsaw or group puzzle—A cooperative sample of learning.* Retrieved February 27, 2005, from http://216.239.104/translate_c?hl=en&sl+de&u=http://www.mued.de/html/aufsatz/ex

Steinberg, L., Brown, B. B., & Dornbush, S. M. (1996). *Beyond the classroom: Why school reform has failed.* New York: Simon & Schuster.

Stern, C., & Stern, M. B. (1971). *Children discover arithmetic: An introduction to structural arithmetic.* New York: Harper & Row.

Still, L., & Mortimer, D. (1996). The effectiveness of award restructuring and the training levy in providing a more educated workforce: A comparative study. In D. Mortimer, P. Leece, & R. Morris (Eds.), *Workplace reform and enterprise bargaining* (pp. 37–54). Sydney, Australia: Harcourt, Brace.

St. Julien, J. (2000). Changing conceptions of human intelligence and reasoning: Implications for the classroom. *Australian Journal of Education, 44*(3), 254–271.

Suarez-Orozco, C. (2001). Afterword: Understanding and serving the children of immigrants. *Harvard Educational Review, 71*(3), 579–589.

Sun, Y. (1999). The contextual effects of community social capital on academic performance. *Social Science Research, 28,* 403–426.

Sun Tzu. (1943). The art of war. In T. R. Phillips (Ed.), *Roots of strategy* (pp. 9–34). London: John Lane.

Sutton, R. E., & Wheatley, K. F. (2003). Teachers' emotions and teaching: A review of the literature and directions for future research [Abstract]. *Educational Psychology Review.* 15(4), 327.

Svendsen, G. L. H., & Svendsen, G. T. (2000). Measuring social capital: The Danish co-operative dairy movement. *Sociologia Ruralis, 40*(1), 72–86.

Tan, B. C. (2002). How best to conduct team teaching. *CTDLink, 6*(2), 7. Singapore: Centre for Development of Teaching and Learning.

Thatcher, R. W., & John, E. R. (1977). *Foundations of cognitive processes.* Hillsdale, NJ: Erlbaum.

Thernstrom, S. (2005). Must schools fail? An exchange. *New York Review of Books, 52*(3), 49–50.

Thomas, G. (1985). What psychology had to offer education—then. *Bulletin of the British Psychological Society, 38,* 322–326.

Thomas, J. (2000). Using controversies in the classroom: Opportunities and concerns. In R. Cross & P. J. Fensham (Eds.), *Science and the citizen: For educators and the public* (pp. 133–144). Mebourne, Australia: Arena.

Thompson, R. A. (2004, November 1). Shaping the brains of tomorrow. *American Prospect Online.* Retrieved December 16, 2005, from http://www.prospect.org/web/page.ww?name=View+Author&section=root&id=1164

Thomson, P., & Nash, K. (Eds.). (1991). *Designing the future: Workplace reform in Australia.* Melboune: Workplace Australia.

Thorsrud, E. (1977). Democracy at work: Norwegian experiences with nonbureaucratic forms of organization. *Journal of Applied Behavior Science, 13*(3), 410–421.

Thorsrud, E. (1983). International perspectives on QWL. In H. Kolodny & H. van Beinum (Eds.), *The quality of working life and the 1980s* (pp. 97–107). New York: Praeger.

Tomkins, S. S. (1962). *Affect, imagery, consciousness*. New York: Springer.

Trist, E. (1977). Collaboration in work settings: A personal perspective. *Journal of Applied Behavior Science, 13*(3), 268–278.

Trist, E. L., & Bamforth, K. W. (1951). Social and psychological consequences of the longwall method of coal-getting. *Human Relations, 4*(1), 3–38.

Trist, E., & Dwyer, C. (1993). The limits of laissez-faire as a socio-technical change strategy. In E. Trist & H. Murray (Eds.), *The social engagement of social science: A Tavistock anthology: Vol. 2* (pp. 449–473). Philadelphia: University of Pennsylvania Press.

Trist, E. L., & Emery, F. E. (1960, July 10–16). *Report on the Barford conference for Bristol/Siddeley, aero-engine corporation* (TIHR Document No. 598). London: Tavistock.

Trist, E., Emery F., & Murray, H. (Eds.). (1997). *The social engagement of social science: A Tavistock anthology: Vol. 3*. Philadelphia: University of Pennsylvania Press.

Trist, E., & Murray, H. (1990a). Historical overview: The foundation and development of the Tavistock Institute. In E. Trist & H. Murray (Eds.), *The social engagement of social science: A Tavistock anthology: Vol. 1* (pp. 1–34). Philadelphia: University of Pennsylvania Press.

Trist, E., & Murray, H. (1990b). Introduction to volume I. In E. Trist & H. Murray (Eds.), *The social engagement of social science: A Tavistock anthology: Vol. 1* (pp. 37–38). Philadelphia: University of Pennsylvania Press.

Trist, E., & Murray, H. (Eds.). (1993). *The social engagement of social science: A Tavistock anthology: Vol. 2*. Philadelphia: University of Pennsylvania Press.

Tuckman, B. W. (1965). Developmental sequence in small groups. *Psychological Bulletin, 63*, 384–99.

Tucson Unified School District. (2005). [Home page]. Retrieved March 14, 2005, from http://www.tusd.k12.az.us

Tyler, W. (1977). *The sociology of educational inequality*. London: Methuen.

Valenti, S. S., & Good, J. M. M. (1991). Social affordances and interaction I: Introduction. *Ecological Psychology, 3*(2), 77–98.

van Acker, R., & Valenti, S. S. (1989). Perception of social affordances by children with mild handicapping conditions: Implications for social skills research and training. *Ecological Psychology, 1*(4), 383–405.

van Eijnatten, F. M. (1993). *The paradigm that changed the work place*. Assen, Netherlands: Gorcum.

Vaughan, G. (2003) Participative design: An overview. *OD Practitioner, 35*(2), 12–17.

Vigil, J. D. (1999). Streets and schools: How educators can help Chicano marginalized gang youth. *Harvard Educational Review, 69*(3), 270–287.

Walker-Andrews, A. S., Bahrick, L. E., & Raglioni, S. S. (1991). Infants' bimodal perception of gender. *Ecological Psychology, 3*(2), 55–75.

Ward, A. P., & Murphy, L. J. (1955). Problems and effects of changing the social structure of the classroom. In O. A. Oeser (Ed.), *Teacher, pupil and task: Elements of social psychology applied to education* (pp. 87–104). London: Tavistock

Washington, V. (2004, November 1). Where do we go from here? *American Prospect Online*. Retrieved November 20, 2004, from http://www.proposect.org/web/printfriendly-view.ww?id=8779

Weisbord, M. R. (1987). *Productive workplaces: Organizing and managing for dignity, meaning, and community.* San Francisco: Jossey-Bass.

Weisbord, M. R. (Ed.). (1992). *Discovering common ground.* San Francisco: Berrett-Koehler.

Weiser, M. (1991, September). The computer for the 21st century. *Scientific American,* pp. 66–75.

Wells, A. S., & Serna, I. (1996). The politics of culture: Understanding local political resistance to detracking in racially mixed schools. *Harvard Educational Review, 66*(1), 93–118.

Welner, K. G., & Oakes, J. (1996). (Li)Ability grouping: The new susceptibility of school tracking systems to legal challenges. *Harvard Educational Review, 66*(4), 451–470.

Wheatley, M. J. (2001). Bringing schools back to life: Schools as living systems. In F. M. Duffy & J. D. Dale (Eds.), *Creating successful school systems: Voices from the university, the field, and the community* (pp. 3–19). Norwood, MA: Christopher-Gordon.

White, R. (1990). Democracy in the research team. In S. A. Wheelan, E. A. Pepitone, & V. Abt (Eds.), *Advances in field theory* (pp. 19–22). Newbury Park, CA: Sage.

White, R., & Wyn, J. (1998). Youth agency and social context [Abstract]. *Journal of Sociology, 34*(3), 314–327.

Wilkinson, R. G. (1996). *Unhealthy societies: The afflictions of inequality.* London: Routledge.

Williams, T. A. (1975). *Democracy in learning.* Canberra: Centre for Continuing Education, Australian National University.

Williams, T. A. (1982). *Learning to manage our futures.* New York: Wiley & Sons.

Williams, T. (1985a). *Post-compulsory education: Participation and equity* (Working Paper No. 85/5). Melbourne: Australian Council for Educational Research.

Williams, T. (1985b). *Post-secondary education: Participation and equity* (Working Paper No. 85/2). Melbourne: Australian Council for Educational Research.

Williams, T. A. (1988). *Computers, work and health: A socio-technical approach.* London: Taylor & Francis.

Williams, T. A. (1993). Visual display technology, worker disablement and work organization. In E. Trist & H. Murray (Eds.), *The social engagement of social science: A Tavistock anthology: Vol. 2* (pp. 508–531). Philadelphia: University of Pennsylvania Press.

Williams, T. A., & Watkins, G. G. (1974). *Participative playground design.* Unpublished manuscript.

Willie, C. V. (2000). The evolution of community education: Content and mission. *Harvard Educational Review, 70*(2), 191–210.

Willms, J. D. (2003). *Student engagement at school: A sense of belonging and participation.* Paris: Organisation for Economic Co-operation and Development.

Wilson, S. (2002). Student participation and school culture: A secondary school case study. *Australian Journal of Education, 46*(1), 79–102.

Winby, S. (1998). Foreword. In R. E. Purser & S. Cabana, *The self managing organization: How leading companies are transforming the work of teams for real impact.* New York: Free Press.

Wiske, S. (2000). A new culture of teaching for the 21st century. In D. T. Gordon (Ed.), *The digital classroom: How technology is changing the way we teach and learn* (pp. 69–77). Cambridge, MA: Harvard Educational Letter.

Wright, S., & Morley, D. (1989). *Learning works: Searching for organizational futures.* Toronto, Ontario: York University, Faculty of Environmental Studies.

Wyn, J. (2004). [Review of *Dropping out, drifting off, being excluded: Becoming somebody without school.*] *Melbourne Studies in Education, 45*(1), 121–122.

Young, A. H., & Subban, J. E. (1997). Strengthening community development through literacy. In *H-Urban Seminar on the History of Community Organizing and Community-Based Development.* Retrieved February 12, 2005, from comm-org.utoledo.edu/papers97/young.htm

Yuen, A. H. K. (2000). Teaching computer programming: A connectionist view of pedagogical change. *Australian Journal of Education, 44*(3), 240–253.

Zeldin, S. (2004). Preventing youth violence through the promotion of community engagement and membership. *Journal of Community Psychology, 32,* 623–641.

Zimbardo, P. G. (2004). Does psychology make a significant difference in our lives? *American Psychologist, 59*(5), 339–351.

Zimmerman, M. A., & Rappaport, J. (1988). Citizen participation, perceived control and psychological empowerment. *American Journal of Community Psychology, 16*(5), 725–750.

Zimmerman, M. A., Israel, B. A., Schulz, A., & Checkoway, B. (1992). Further explorations in empowerment theory: An empirical analysis of psychological empowerment. *American Journal of Community Psychology, 20*(6), 707–727.

Zuboff, S. (1988). *In the age of the smart machine: The future of work and power.* New York: Basic Books.

Index

237

About the Author

Merrelyn Emery has spent most of her life in the education system, learning, teaching, and researching. She obtained her bachelor of arts in psychology from the University of New England in 1964 and her doctorate in marketing from the University of New South Wales in 1986. Between 1970 and 1997, she worked with Fred Emery on the development of the theory and practice of open systems theory. She continues that work and teaches intensive workshops around the world on the history and state of the art of open systems. She has worked with many organizations and communities around the world, including several in the United States.

She has published several books and many articles. Her best-known books are *Participative Design for Participative Democracy* (1993) and *Searching: The Theory and Practice of Making Cultural Change* (1999). She is currently an adjunct professor in the Department of Applied Human Sciences at Concordia University, a visitor at the Centre for Continuing Education at the Australian National University, and a founding director of the Fred Emery Institute. She lives in Australia.